Everything I Need t

I Learned on JERRY SPRINGER

JAVITS 2008

To Arlene,
I'll never forget
those two days in Gdansk!
Cheers!
John McPherson

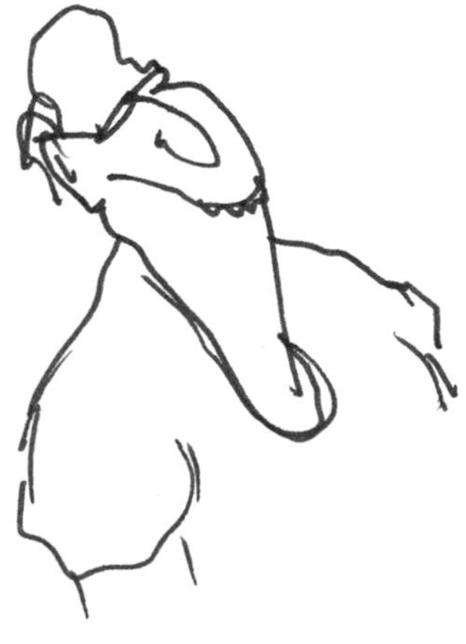

Everything I Need to Know I Learned on JERRY SPRINGER

A *Close to Home* Collection by John McPherson

Close to Home is distributed internationally by Universal Press Syndicate.

Everything I Need to Know I Learned on _Jerry Springer_ © 2007 by John McPherson. All rights reserved. Printed in China. No part of this book may be used or reproduced in any manner whatsoever without written permission except in the case of reprints in the context of reviews. For information, write Andrews McMeel Publishing, LLC, an Andrews McMeel Universal company, 4520 Main Street, Kansas City, Missouri 64111.

07 08 09 10 11 SDB 10 9 8 7 6 5 4 3 2 1

ISBN-13: 978-0-7407-6846-0
ISBN-10: 0-7407-6846-8

Library of Congress Control Number: 2007925391

Close to Home may be viewed on the Internet at www.GoComics.com.

Visit the _Close to Home_ Web store at www.closetohome.com.

E-mail John at closetohome@mac.com.

www.andrewsmcmeel.com

──────── **ATTENTION: SCHOOLS AND BUSINESSES** ────────

Andrews McMeel books are available at quantity discounts with bulk purchase for educational, business, or sales promotional use. For information, please write to: Special Sales Department, Andrews McMeel Publishing, LLC, 4520 Main Street, Kansas City, Missouri 64111.

Other *Close to Home* Books
by John McPherson

Close to Home
One Step Closer to Home
Dangerously Close to Home
Home: The Final Frontier
The Honeymoon Is Over
The Silence of the Lamberts
Striking Close to Home
The Close to Home Survival Guide
Close to Home Uncut
The Scourge of the Vinyl Car Seats
Close to Home Exposed
Ferociously Close to Home
When Bad Things Happen to Stupid People
A Million Little Pieces of Close to Home

Treasury Collections
Close to Home Revisited
Close to Home Unplugged

Also from John McPherson
High School Isn't Pretty
Close to Home: A Book of Postcards
The Barber of Bingo
The Get Well Book
Give Mommy the Superglue and Other Tips on Surviving Parenthood
Get Well, Doctor's Orders! A Close to Home Get Well Box

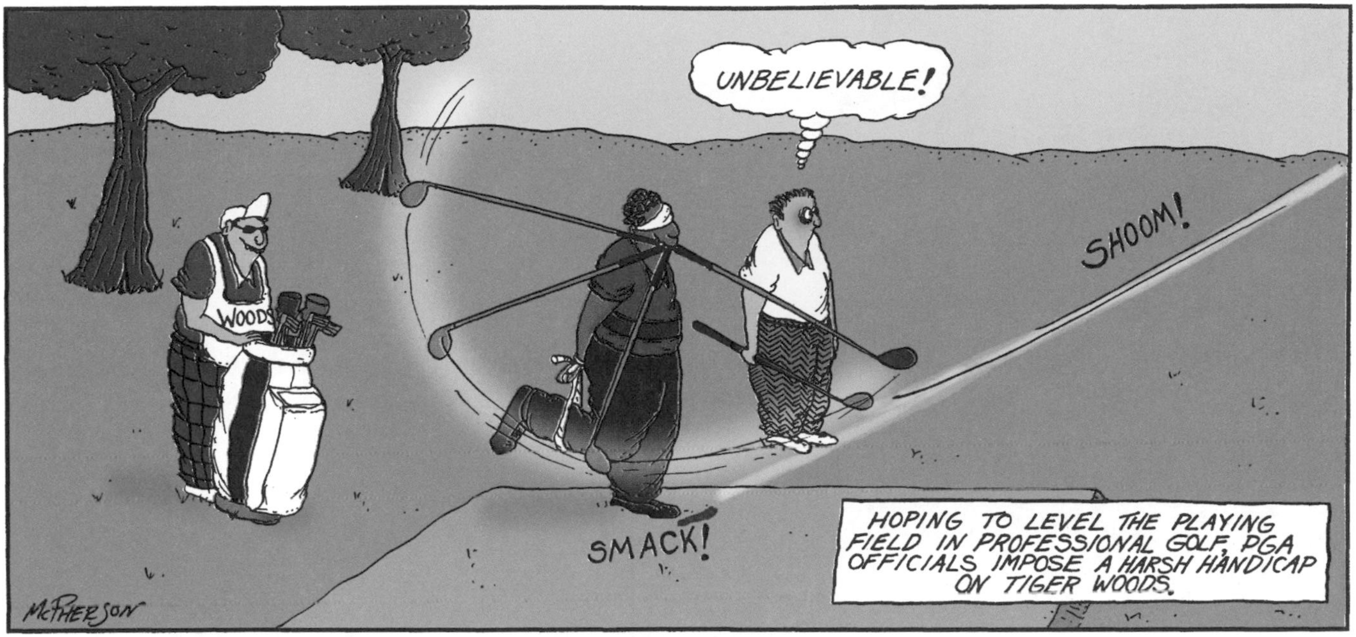
UNBELIEVABLE!
SHOOM!
WOODS
SMACK!
HOPING TO LEVEL THE PLAYING FIELD IN PROFESSIONAL GOLF, PGA OFFICIALS IMPOSE A HARSH HANDICAP ON TIGER WOODS.
McPHERSON

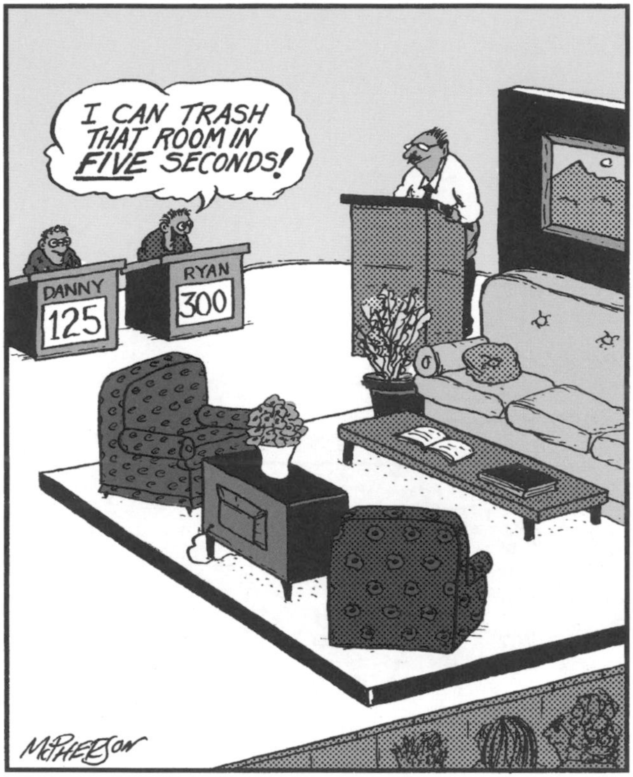
I CAN TRASH THAT ROOM IN FIVE SECONDS!
DANNY
125
RYAN
300
McPHERSON

Toddler game shows

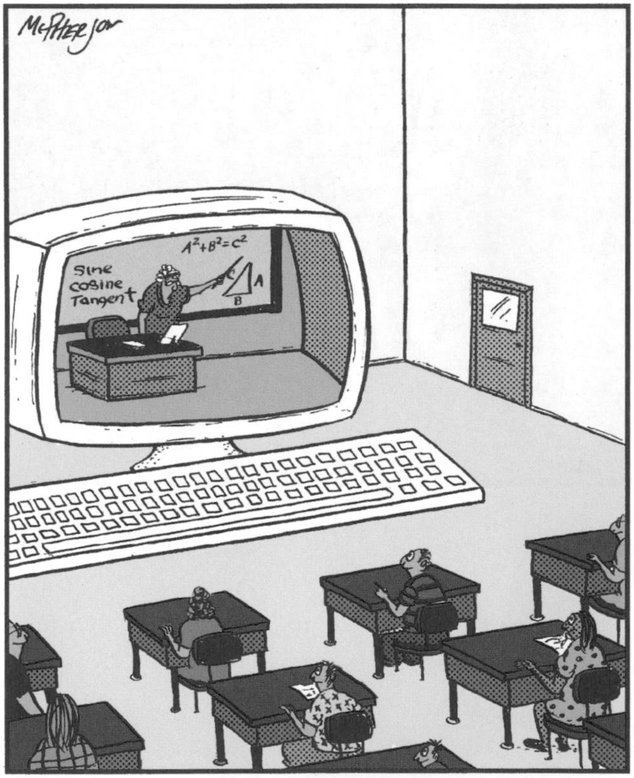
McPHERSON
$A^2+B^2=C^2$
Sine
cosine
Tangent
A
B

The faculty at Rosemont Junior High devises a brilliant method for holding students' attention.

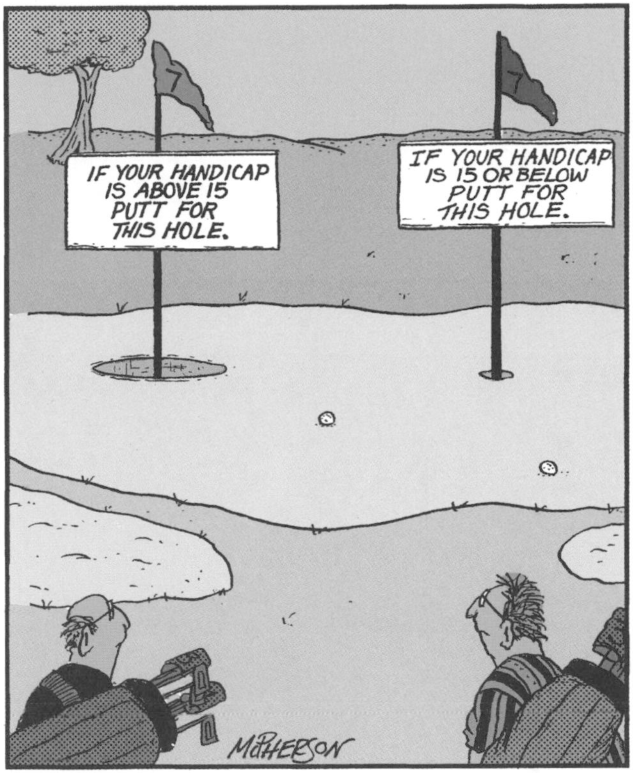
7
7
IF YOUR HANDICAP IS ABOVE 15 PUTT FOR THIS HOLE.
IF YOUR HANDICAP IS 15 OR BELOW PUTT FOR THIS HOLE.
McPHERSON

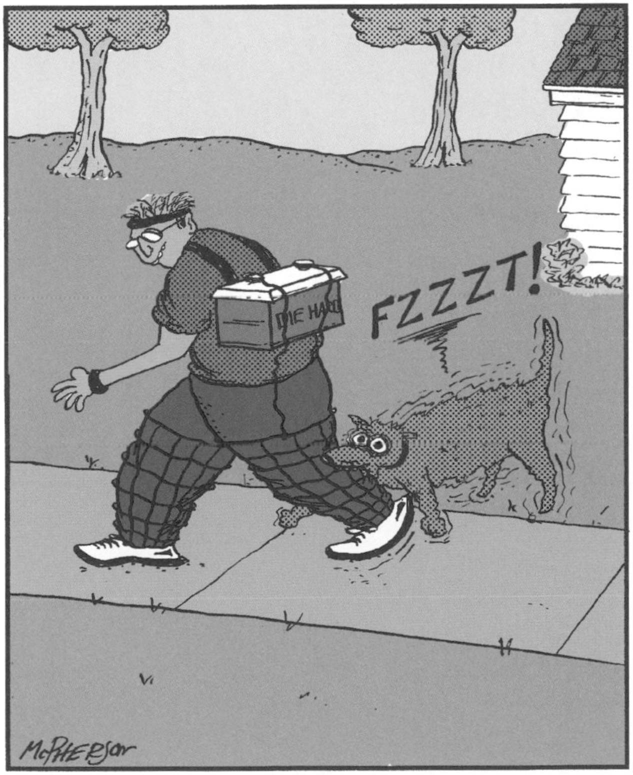
DIE HARD
FZZZT!
McPHERSON

Knowing that the Hurlmans' Doberman was unleashed, Karl wisely wore his electrified jogging pants.

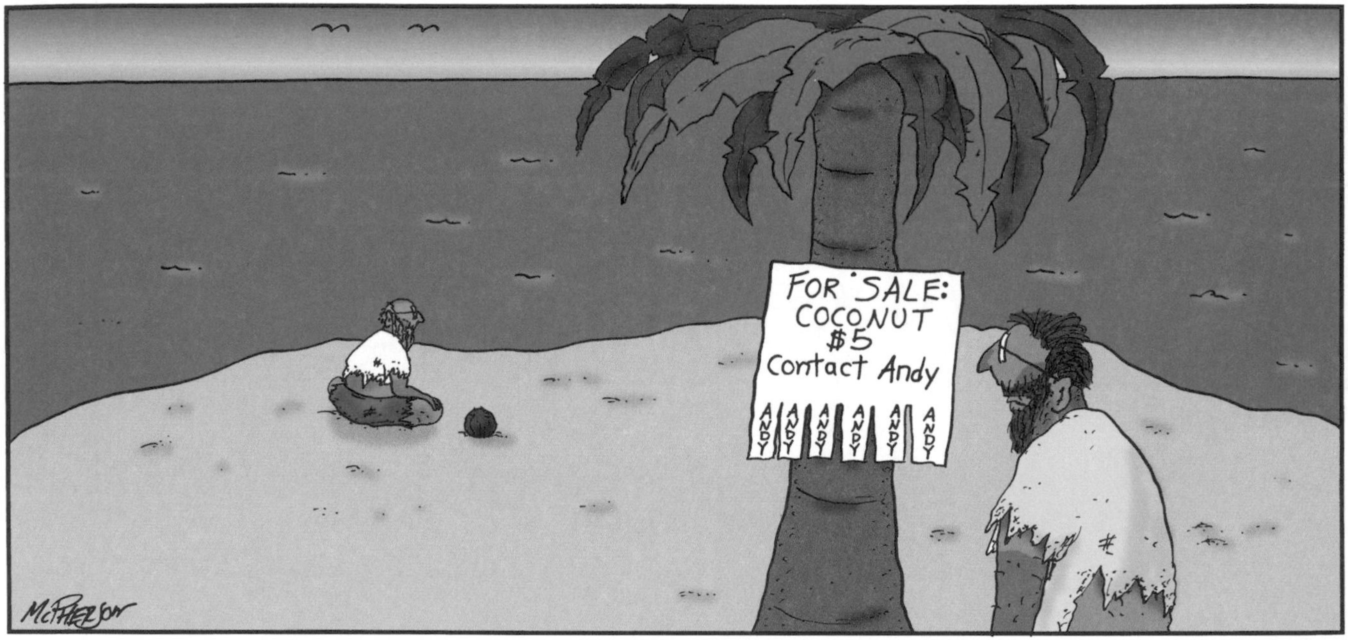
FOR SALE:
COCONUT
$5
Contact Andy
ANDY
ANDY
ANDY
ANDY
ANDY
ANDY
McPHERSON

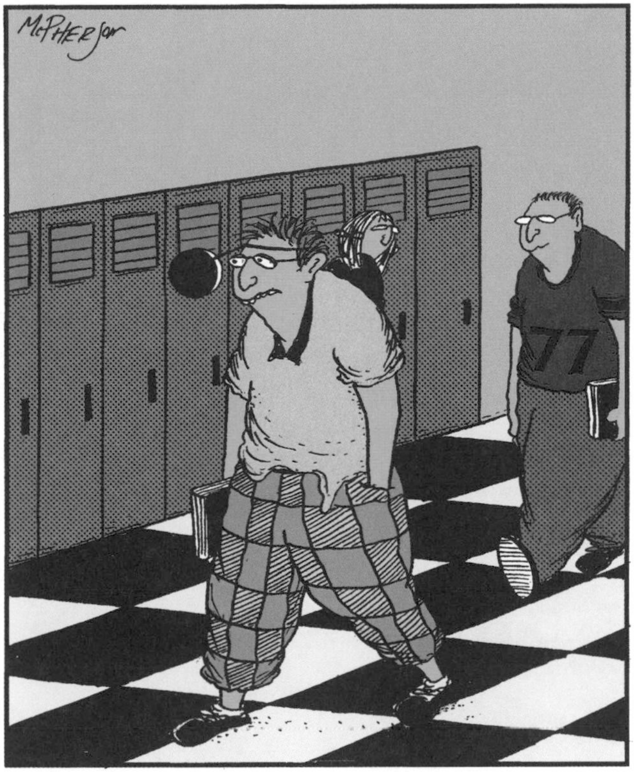
McPHERSON

Thanks to his rearview mirror, Rodney was able to avoid the trauma of a surprise wedgie.

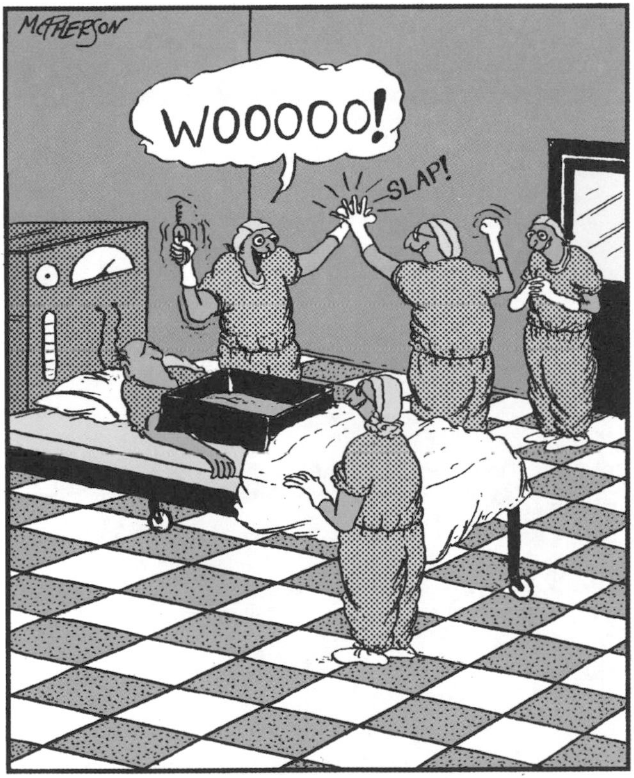
McPHERSON
WOOOOO!
SLAP!

Acting on a dare from another surgeon, Dr. Kromski successfully completed the entire quadruple bypass using only a Swiss Army Knife.

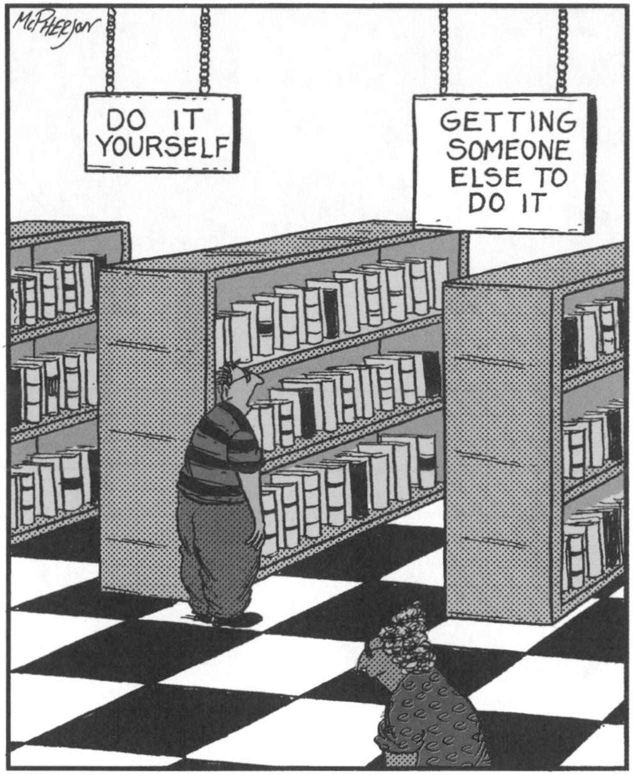
McPHERSON
DO IT YOURSELF
GETTING SOMEONE ELSE TO DO IT

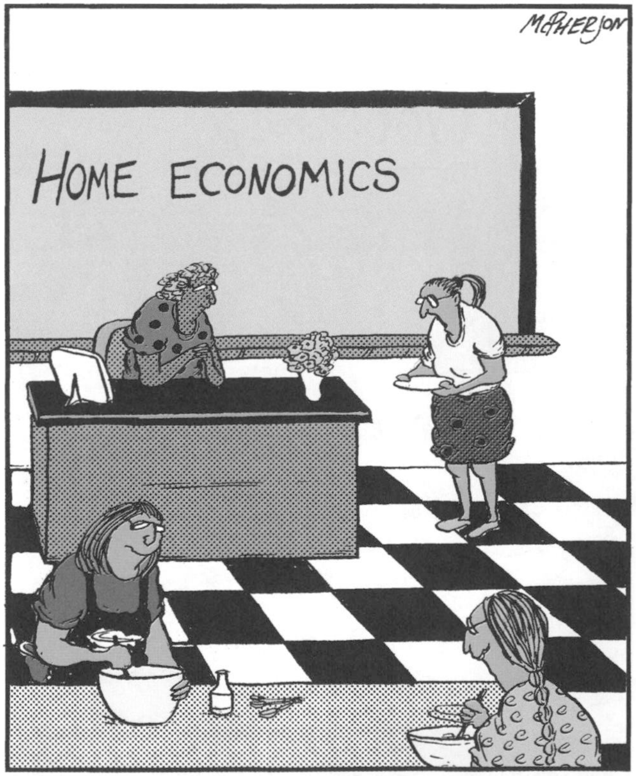
McPHERSON
HOME ECONOMICS

"My dog ate my homework."

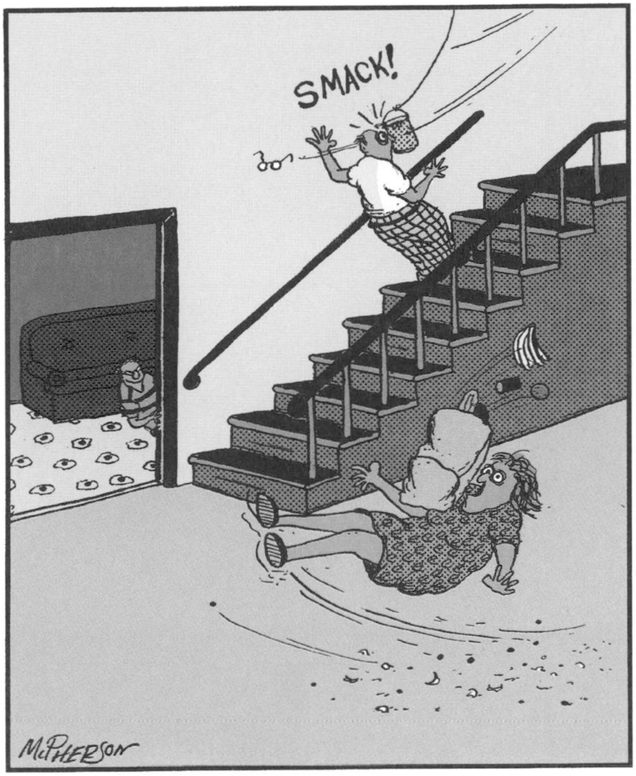
SMACK!
McPHERSON

The Wurtleys quickly regretted renting *Home Alone* for Bradley.

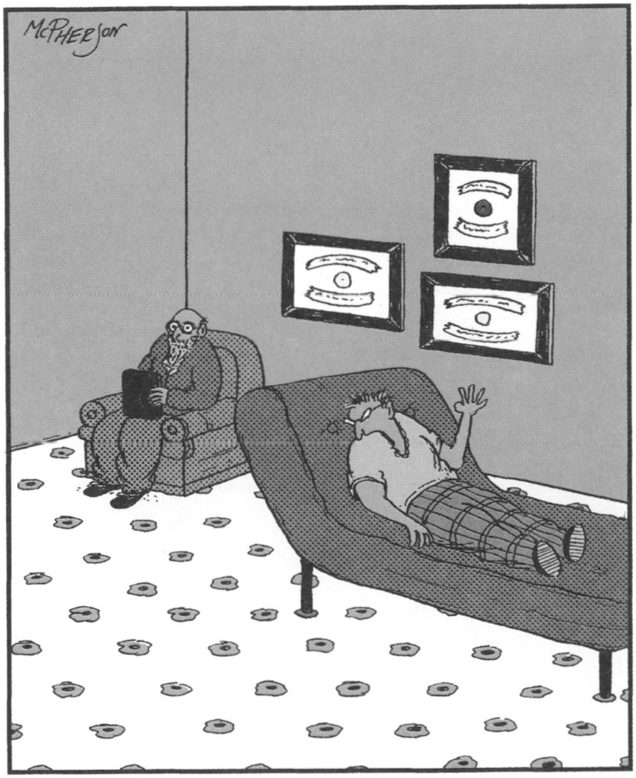
McPHERSON

"I *said*, 'I have trouble developing close relationships with people!' For cryin' out loud, clean out your ears, fathead!"

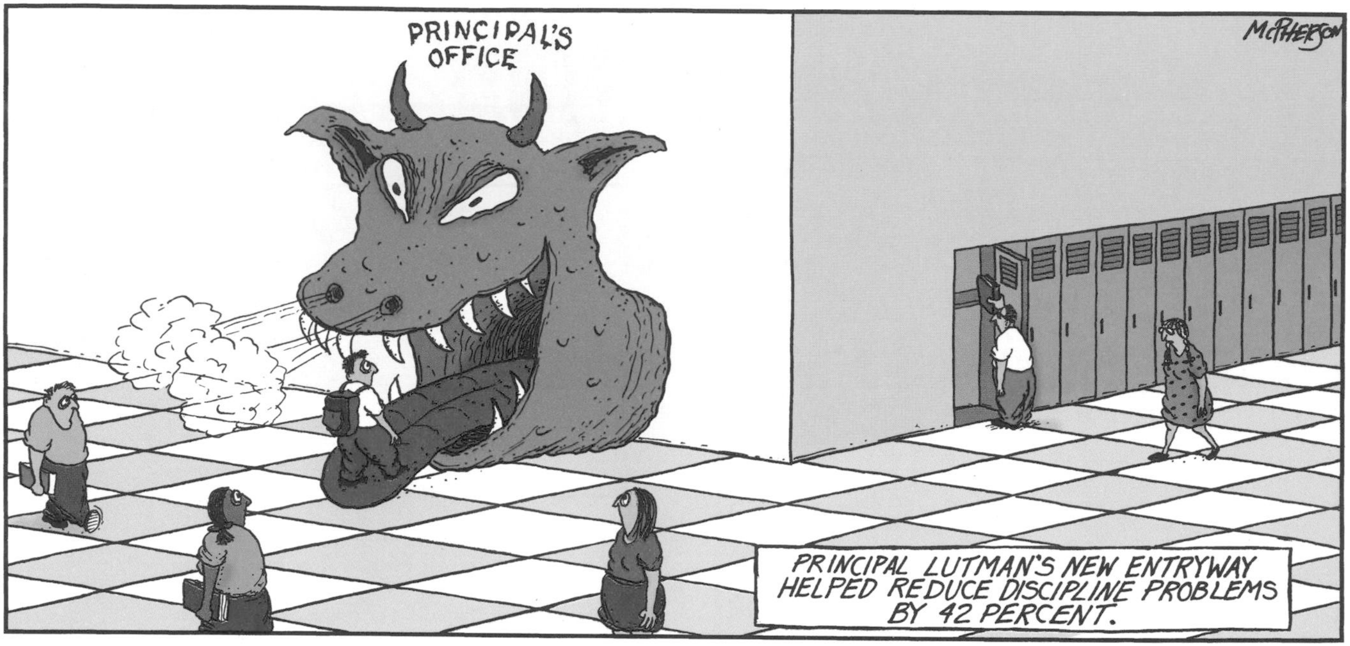
PRINCIPAL'S OFFICE
McPHERSON
PRINCIPAL LUTMAN'S NEW ENTRYWAY HELPED REDUCE DISCIPLINE PROBLEMS BY 42 PERCENT.

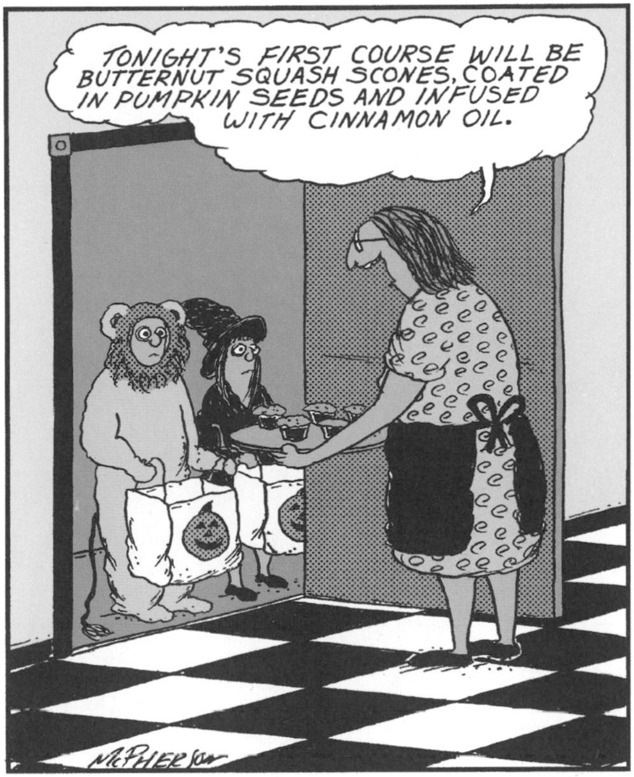
TONIGHT'S FIRST COURSE WILL BE BUTTERNUT SQUASH SCONES, COATED IN PUMPKIN SEEDS AND INFUSED WITH CINNAMON OIL.
MCPHERSON

Trick-or-treating at Martha Stewart's house

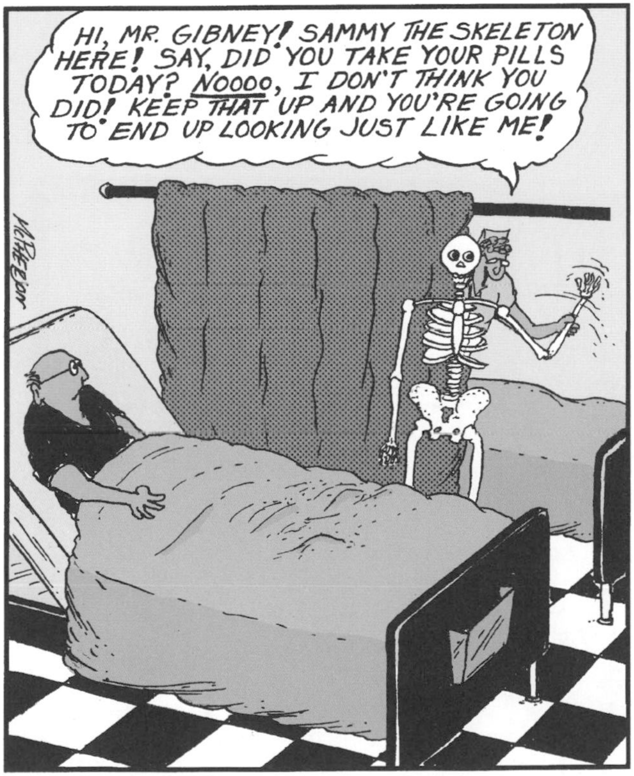
HI, MR. GIBNEY! SAMMY THE SKELETON HERE! SAY, DID YOU TAKE YOUR PILLS TODAY? NOOOO, I DON'T THINK YOU DID! KEEP THAT UP AND YOU'RE GOING TO END UP LOOKING JUST LIKE ME!
MCPHERSON

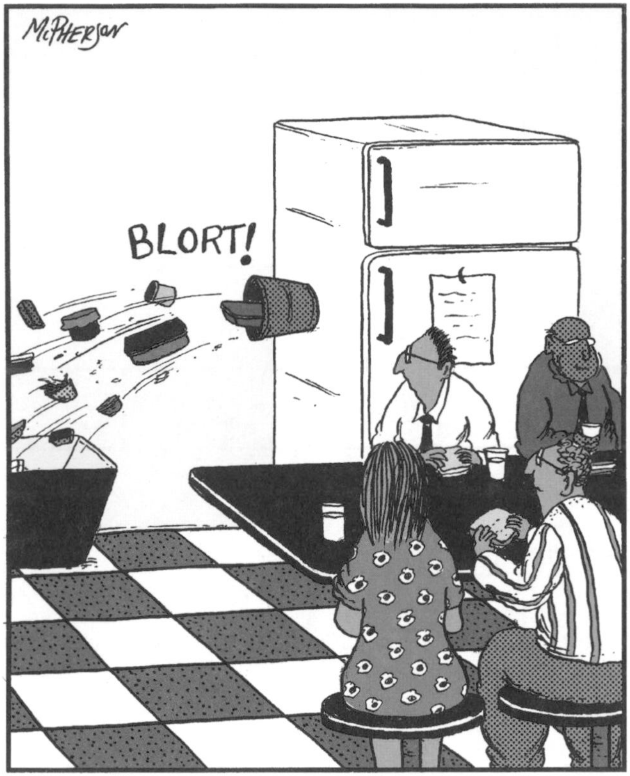
McPHERSON
BLORT!

To eliminate the buildup of noxious leftovers, the office refrigerator was equipped with an automatic purge valve.

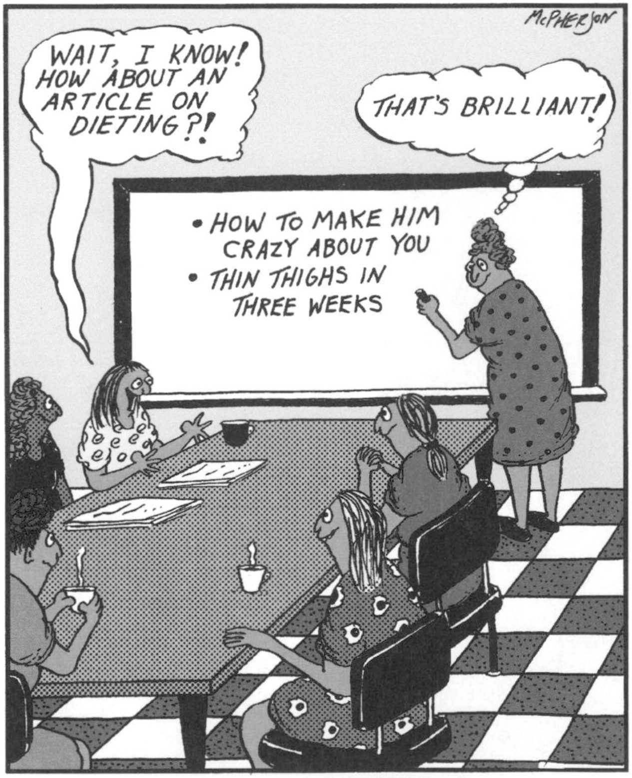
McPHERSON
WAIT, I KNOW! HOW ABOUT AN ARTICLE ON DIETING?!
THAT'S BRILLIANT!
• HOW TO MAKE HIM CRAZY ABOUT YOU
• THIN THIGHS IN THREE WEEKS

Another monthly brainstorming session at a leading women's magazine

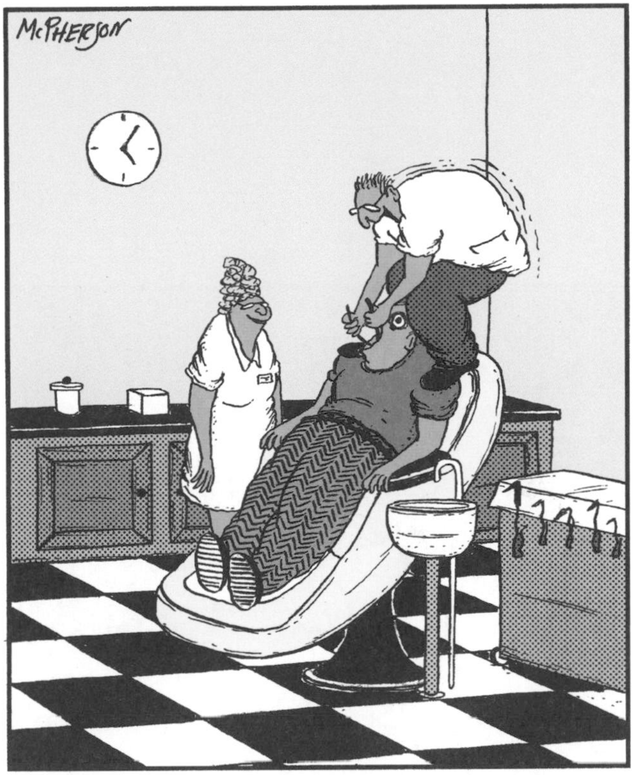
McPHERSON

"OK, Mr. Dagner, let me just get a little better leverage here . . . ready? On three."

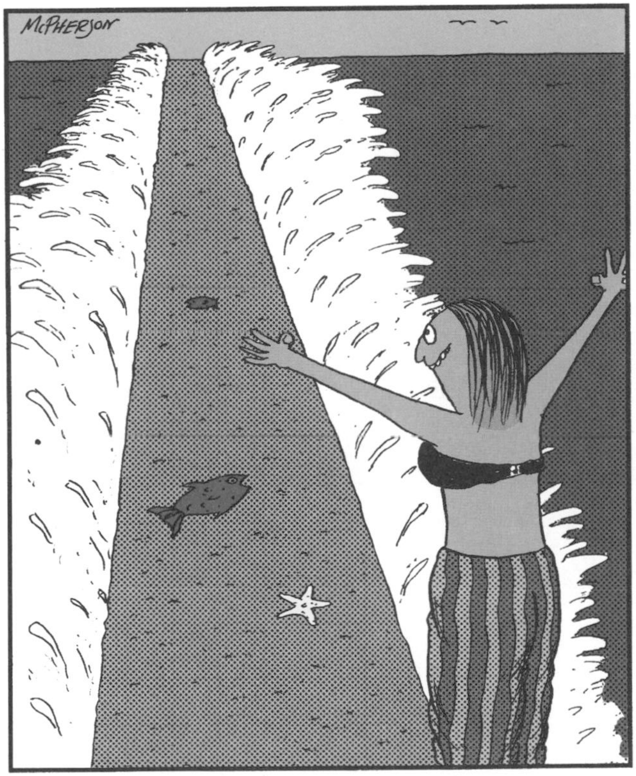
McPHERSON

Linda tried out her Miracle Bra.

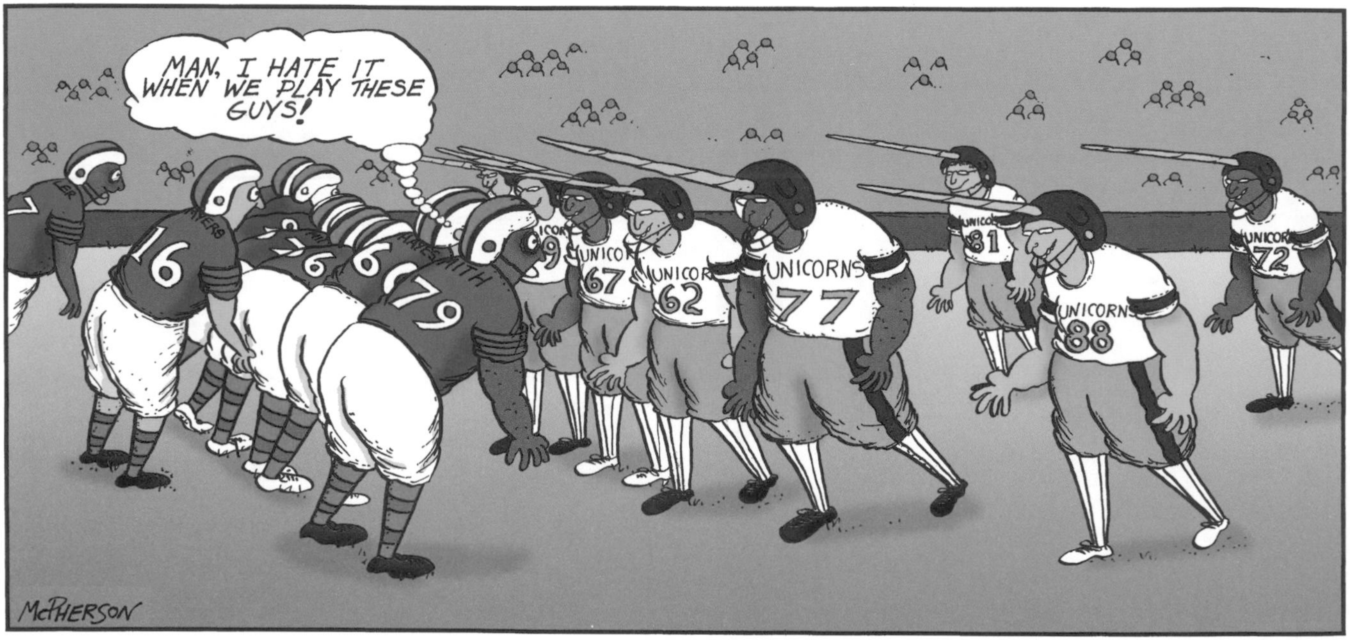
MAN, I HATE IT WHEN WE PLAY THESE GUYS!
UNICORNS
McPHERSON

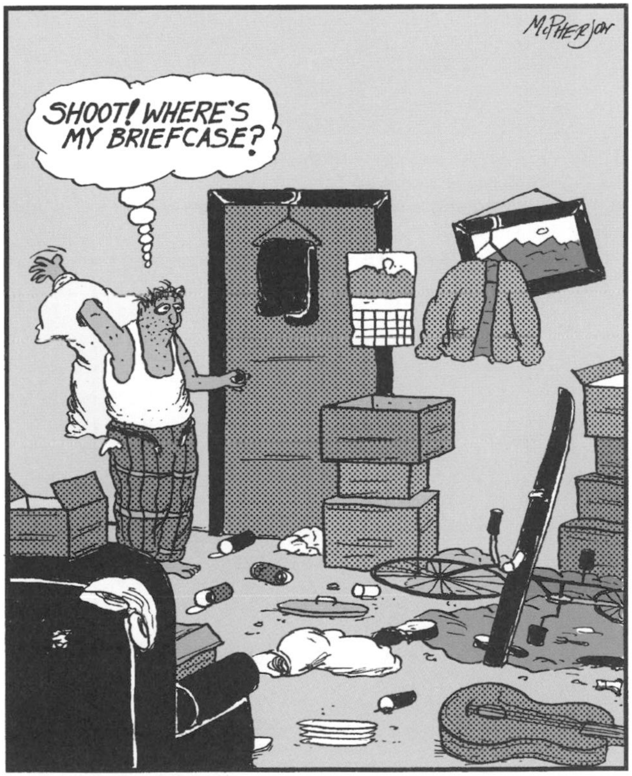
McPHERSON
SHOOT! WHERE'S MY BRIEFCASE?

The inventor of the Day Planner at home

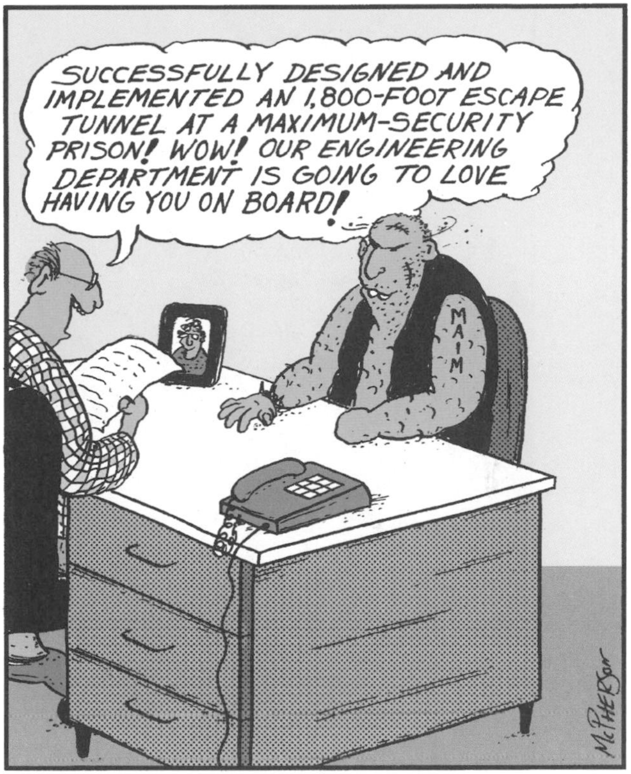
SUCCESSFULLY DESIGNED AND IMPLEMENTED AN 1,800-FOOT ESCAPE TUNNEL AT A MAXIMUM-SECURITY PRISON! WOW! OUR ENGINEERING DEPARTMENT IS GOING TO LOVE HAVING YOU ON BOARD!
MAIM
McPHERSON

With good technical people in short supply, many employers have loosened their hiring standards.

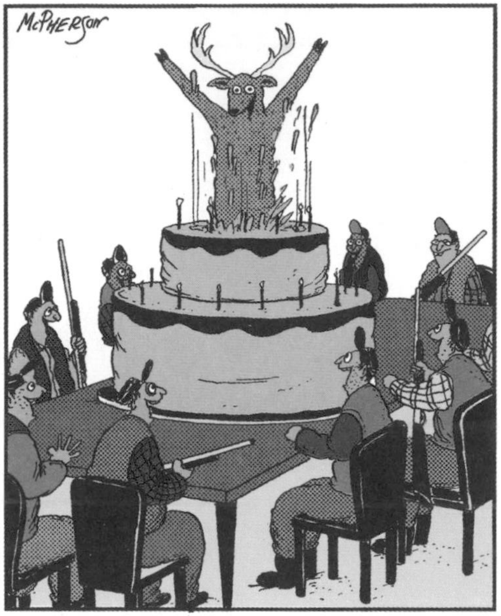
McPHERSON

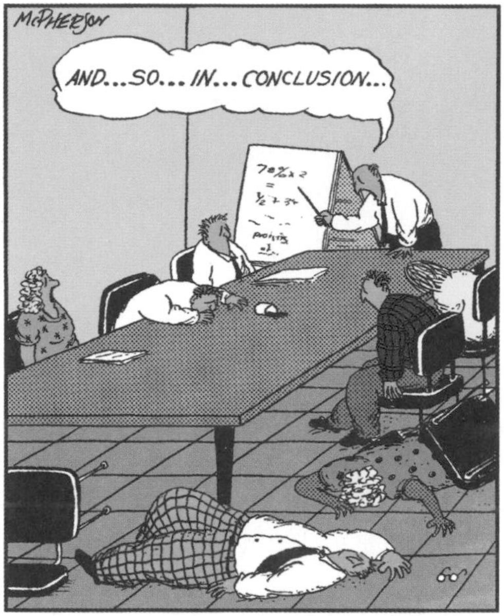
McPHERSON
AND...SO...IN...CONCLUSION...

To keep meetings from running indefinitely, conference rooms at Zartech Industries were allotted only a forty-five-minute supply of air.

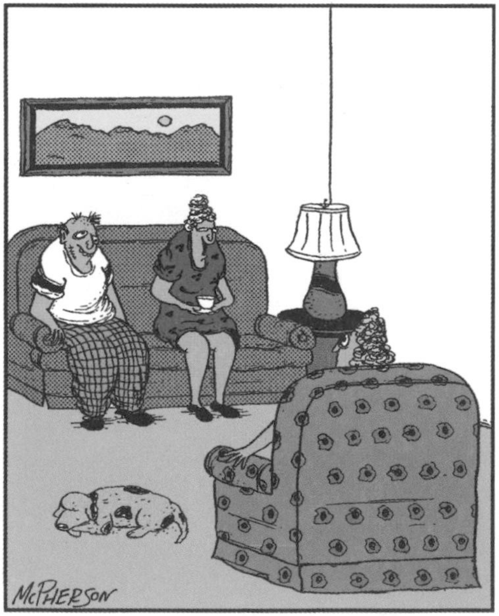
McPHERSON

"Jerry's heart stopped while he was taking a bath last year. I threw the toaster in the tub and saved his life."

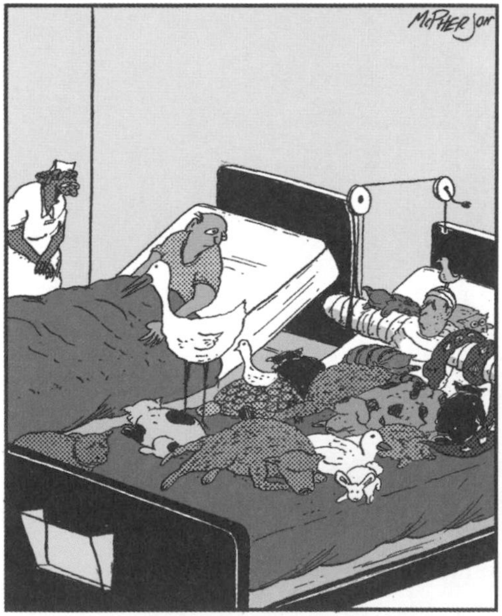
McPHERSON

"How about you, Mr. Clark? Would you also like to be a part of our pet therapy program?"

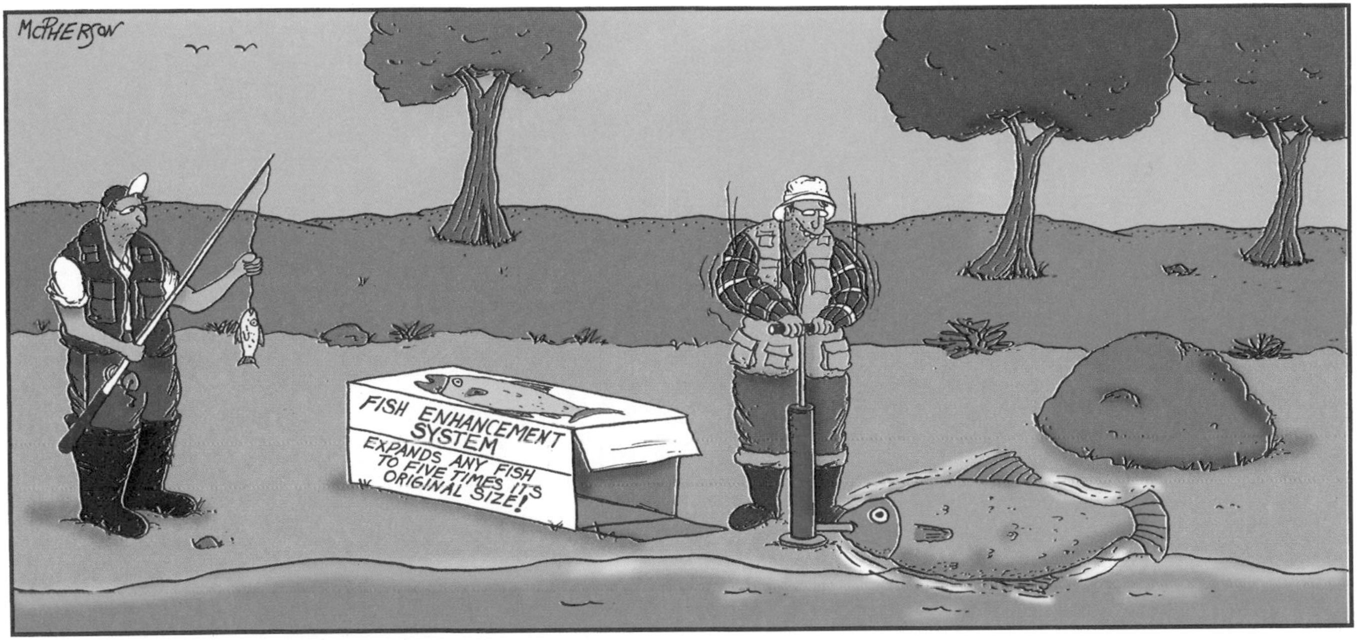
MCPHERSON
FISH ENHANCEMENT SYSTEM
EXPANDS ANY FISH TO FIVE TIMES IT'S ORIGINAL SIZE!

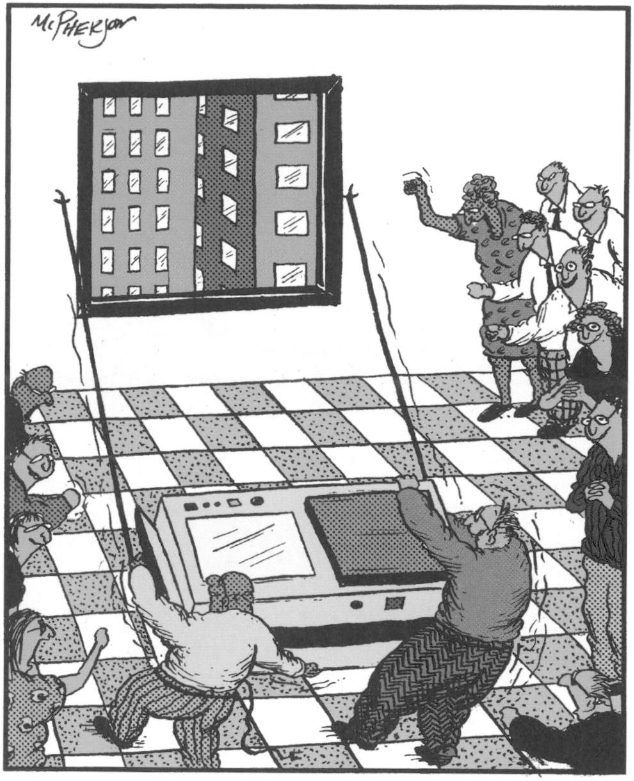

Morale in the office soared thanks to the new industrial-strength broken-copier slingshot.

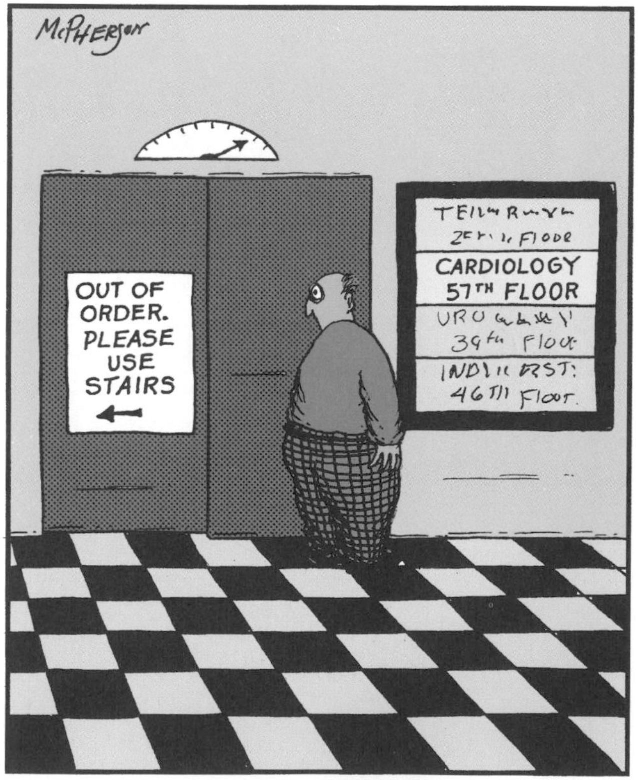
OUT OF ORDER. PLEASE USE STAIRS
CARDIOLOGY 57TH FLOOR

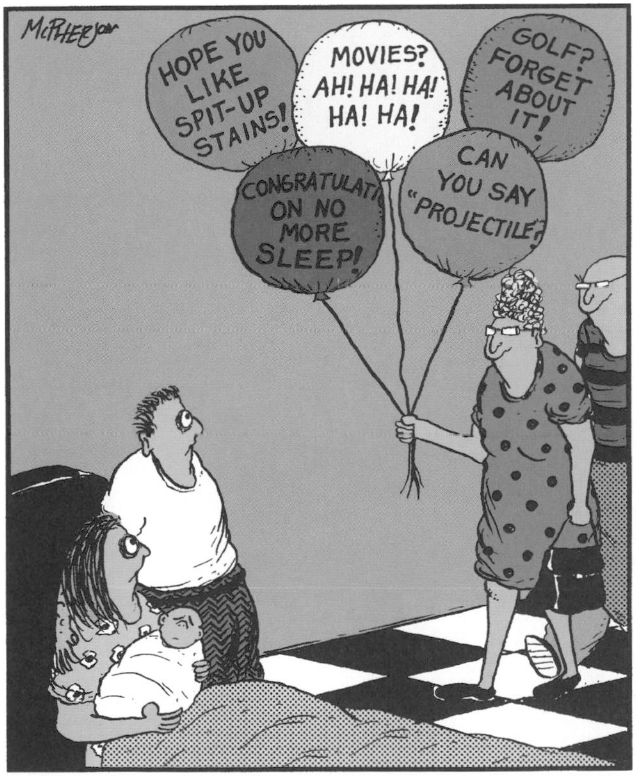
McPHERSON
HOPE YOU LIKE SPIT-UP STAINS!
MOVIES? AH! HA! HA! HA! HA!
GOLF? FORGET ABOUT IT!
CONGRATULATI ON NO MORE SLEEP!
CAN YOU SAY "PROJECTILE?

At last, gift balloons that reflect the reality of parenting

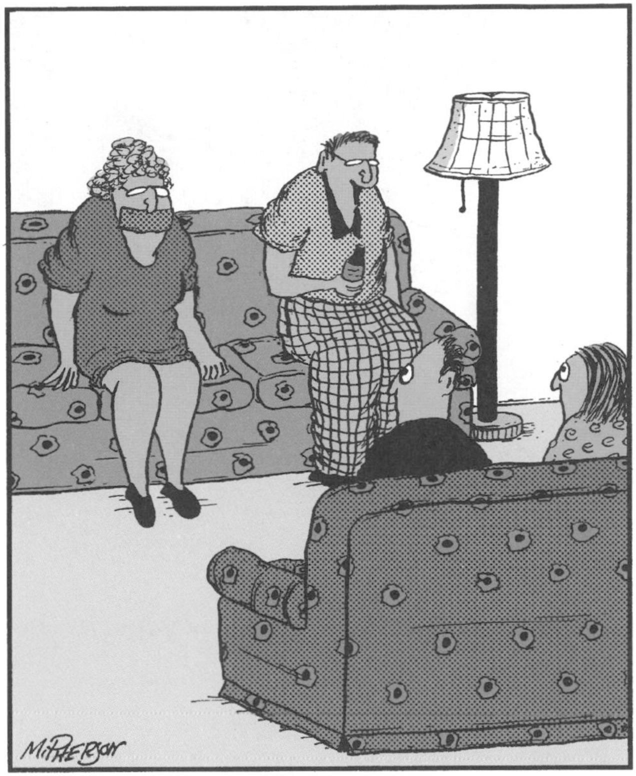
McPHERSON

"Louise is trying that new Duct Tape Diet."

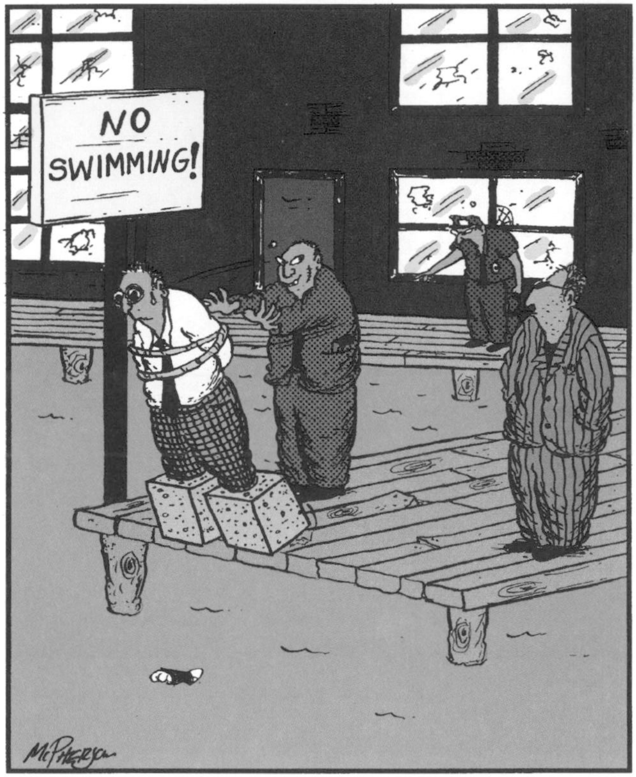
NO
SWIMMING!
McPHERSON

"Hey, you three! Can't you read?"

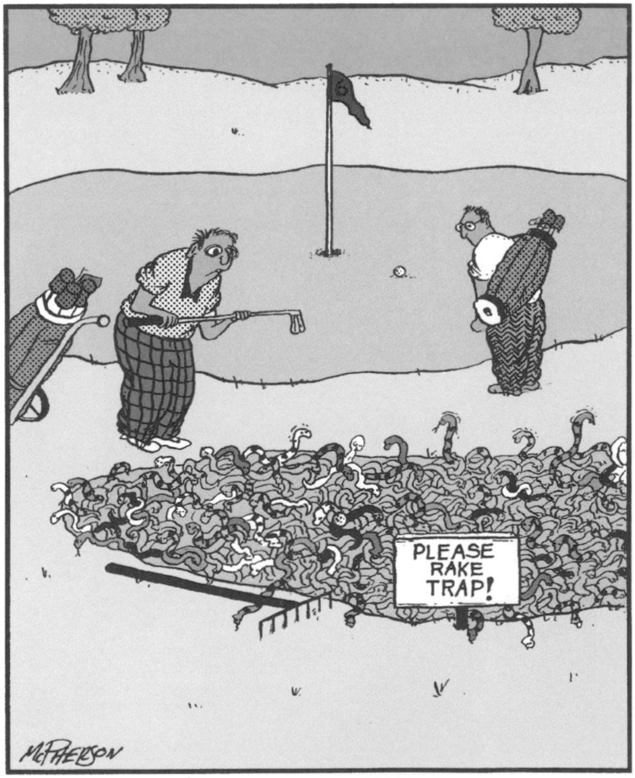
PLEASE
RAKE
TRAP!
McPHERSON

Jerry lands in one of Pinehurst Country Club's infamous snake traps.

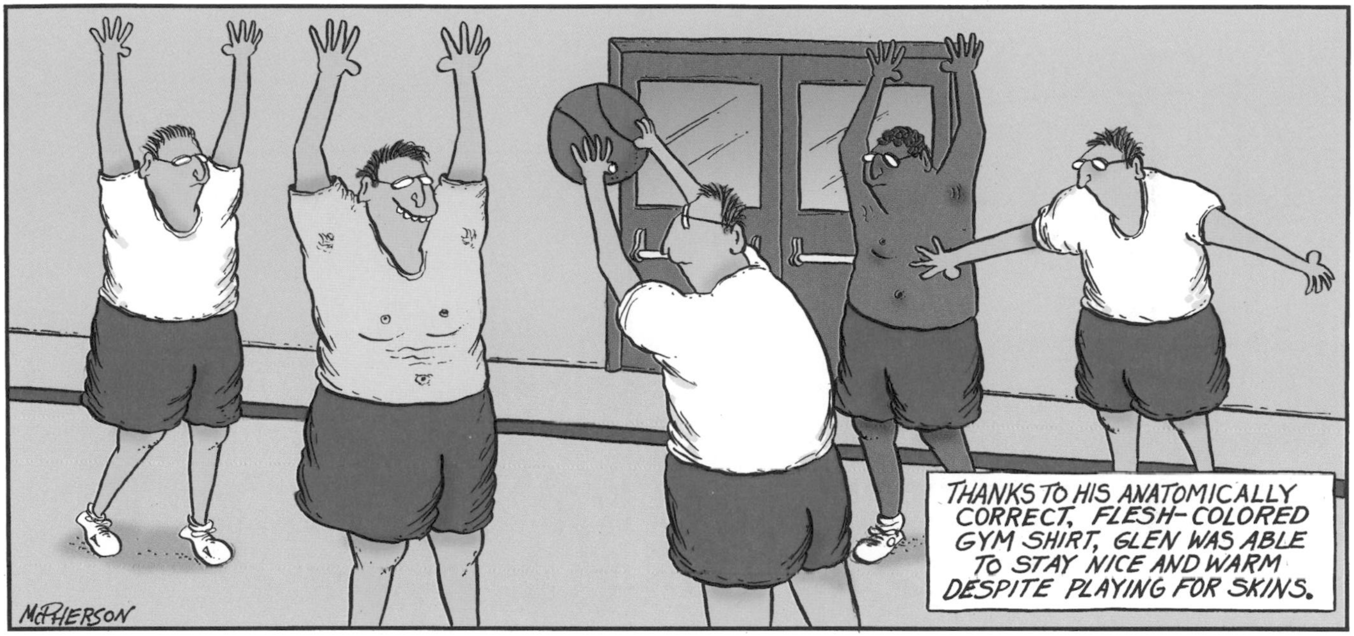
THANKS TO HIS ANATOMICALLY CORRECT, FLESH-COLORED GYM SHIRT, GLEN WAS ABLE TO STAY NICE AND WARM DESPITE PLAYING FOR SKINS.
McPHERSON

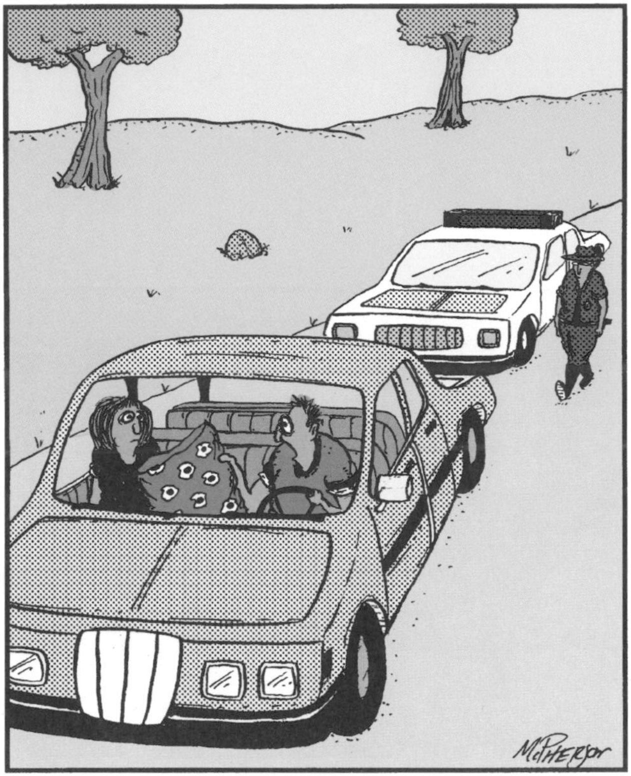

"Here he comes. Stick this pillow under your shirt, tell him your contractions are one minute apart, and moan like crazy!"

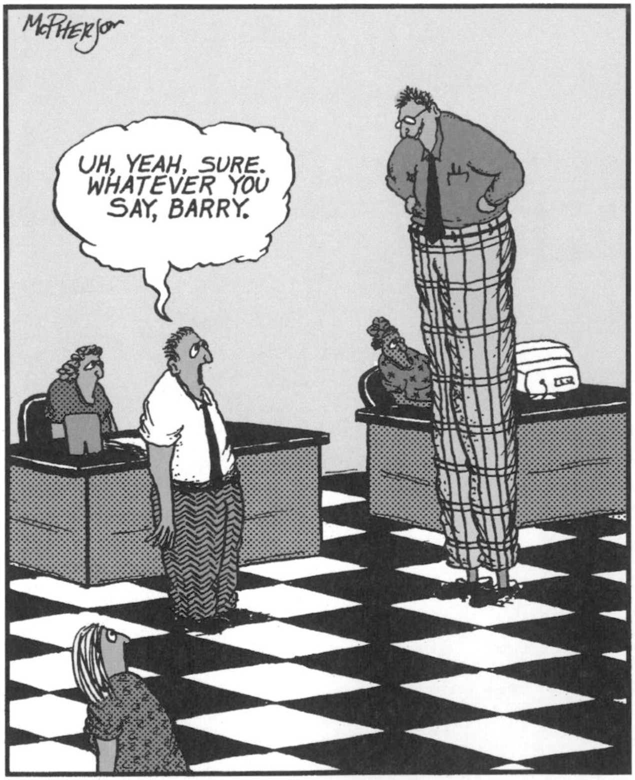
UH, YEAH, SURE. WHATEVER YOU SAY, BARRY.

Barry's new Executive Power Stilts™ gave him an air of superiority over coworkers who once intimidated him.

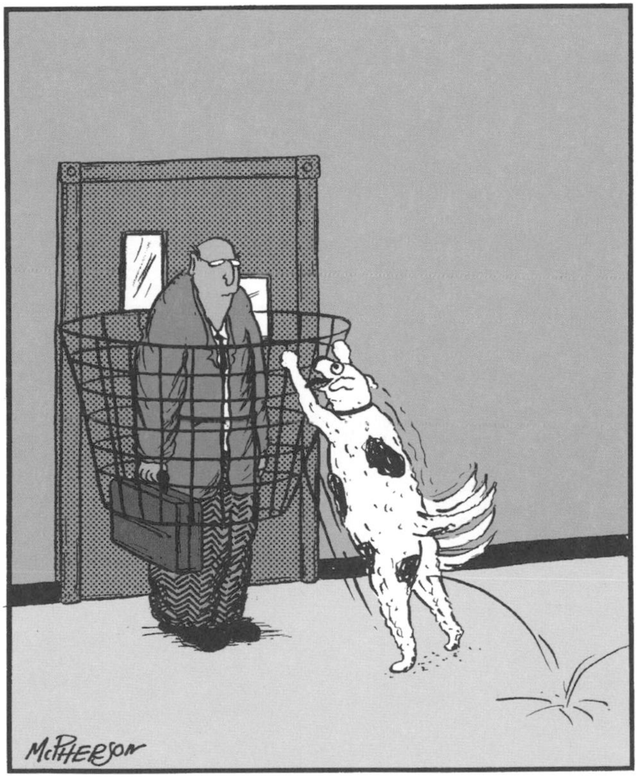

Before returning from work each day, Karl was careful to put on his leaping pooch guard.

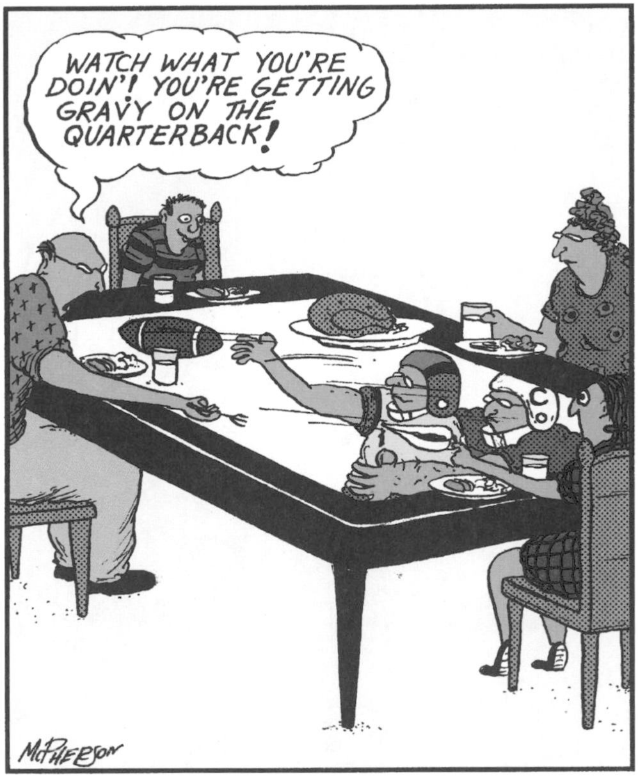
WATCH WHAT YOU'RE DOIN'! YOU'RE GETTING GRAVY ON THE QUARTERBACK!

The Gundersons' combination big-screen TV and dinner table was the perfect compromise for Thanksgiving Day.

McPHERSON
ACUPUNCTURE

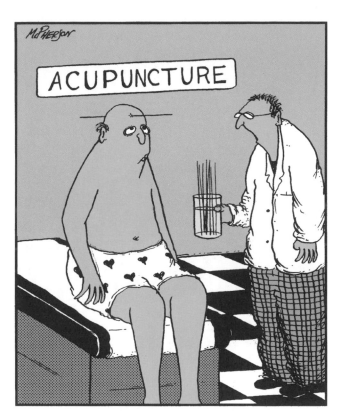

"Next time, warn me when you're going to sneeze."

McPHERSON

A pair of mountain climbers make a startling new zoological discovery: the Himalayan Mountain Bike Goat.

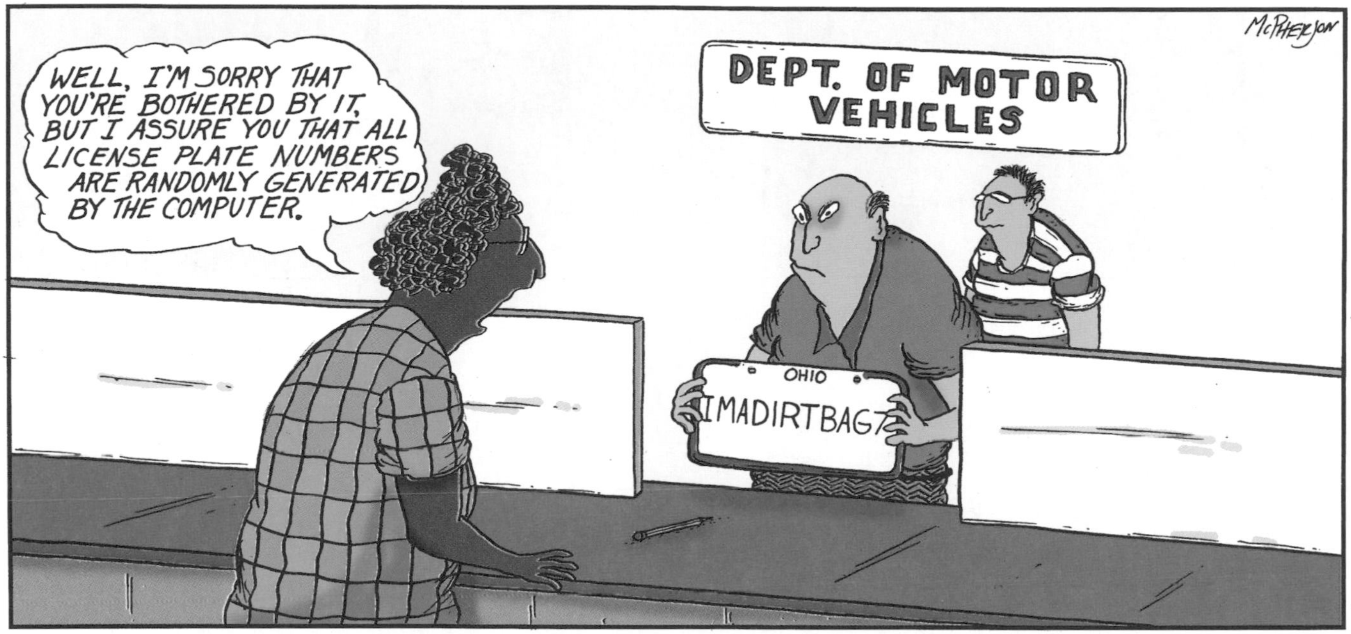
McPHERSON
WELL, I'M SORRY THAT YOU'RE BOTHERED BY IT, BUT I ASSURE YOU THAT ALL LICENSE PLATE NUMBERS ARE RANDOMLY GENERATED BY THE COMPUTER.
DEPT. OF MOTOR VEHICLES
OHIO
IMADIRTBAG7

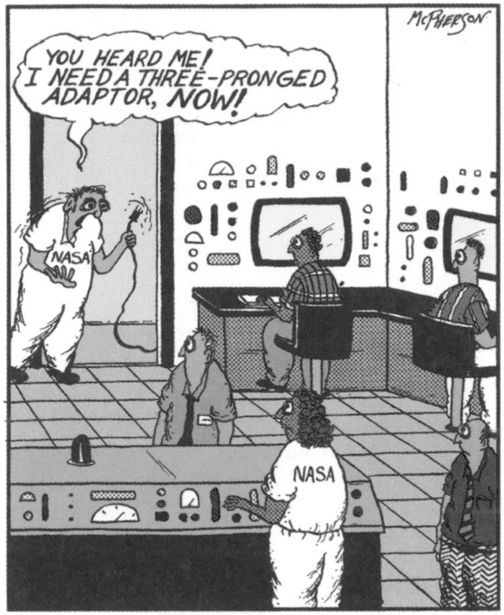
McPHERSON
YOU HEARD ME!
I NEED A THREE-PRONGED
ADAPTOR, NOW!
NASA
NASA

Stricken by a sudden emergency,
NASA scraps yet another shuttle flight.

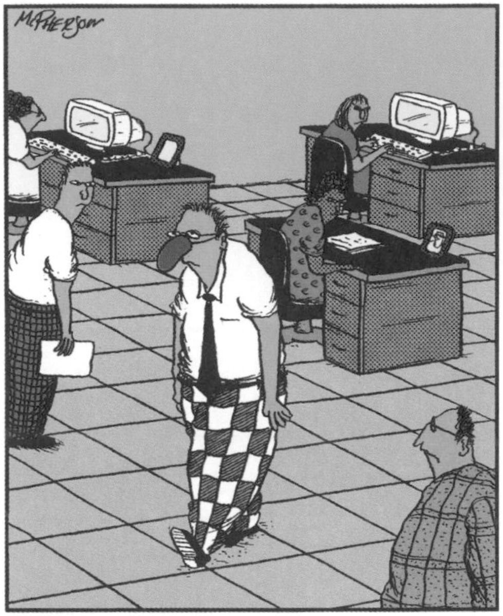
McPHERSON

Caught kissing up to the boss one too many times,
Dale is forced to wear the Brown Nose of Dishonor.

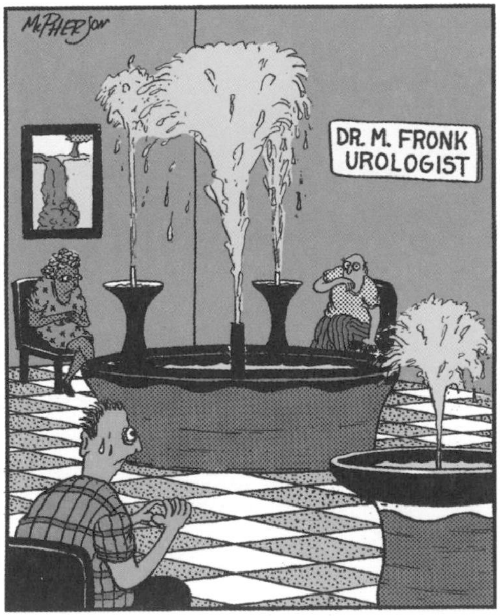
McPHERSON
DR. M. FRONK
UROLOGIST

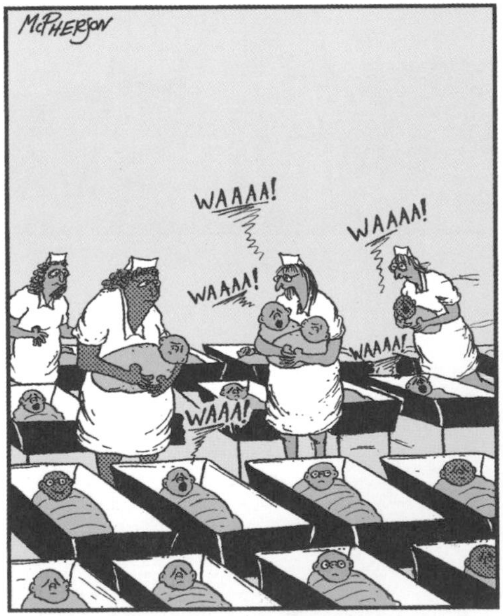
McPHERSON
WAAAA!
WAAAA!
WAAAA!
WAAAA!
WAAA!

"We've got four times as many babies in here
as usual. I did some research and found out that
cable was out for a week nine months ago."

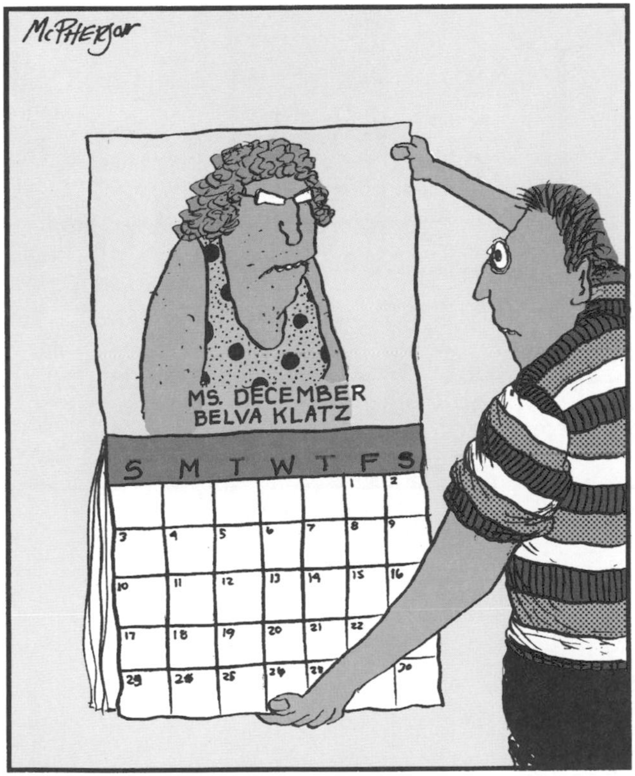
MS. DECEMBER
BELVA KLATZ
S M T W T F S

Glamour calendars that bombed: Women of the DMV

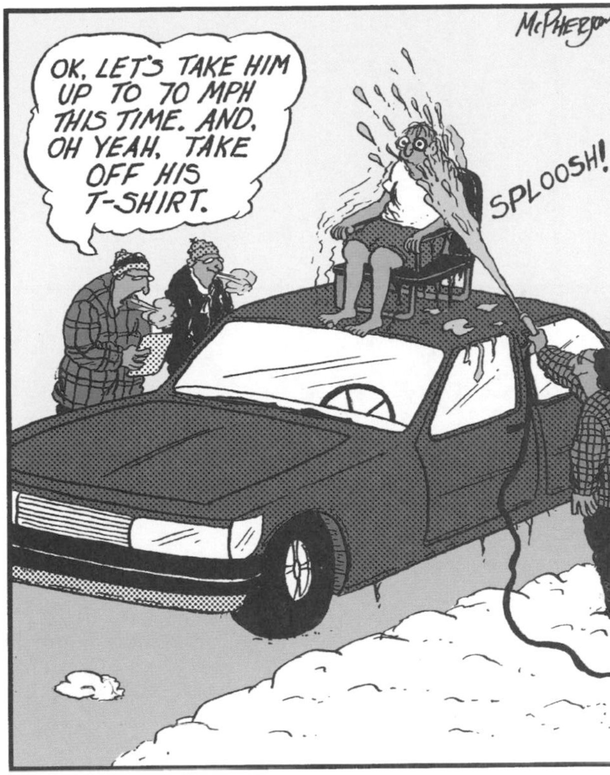
OK, LET'S TAKE HIM UP TO 70 MPH THIS TIME. AND, OH YEAH, TAKE OFF HIS T-SHIRT.
SPLOOSH!

Testing how people get colds

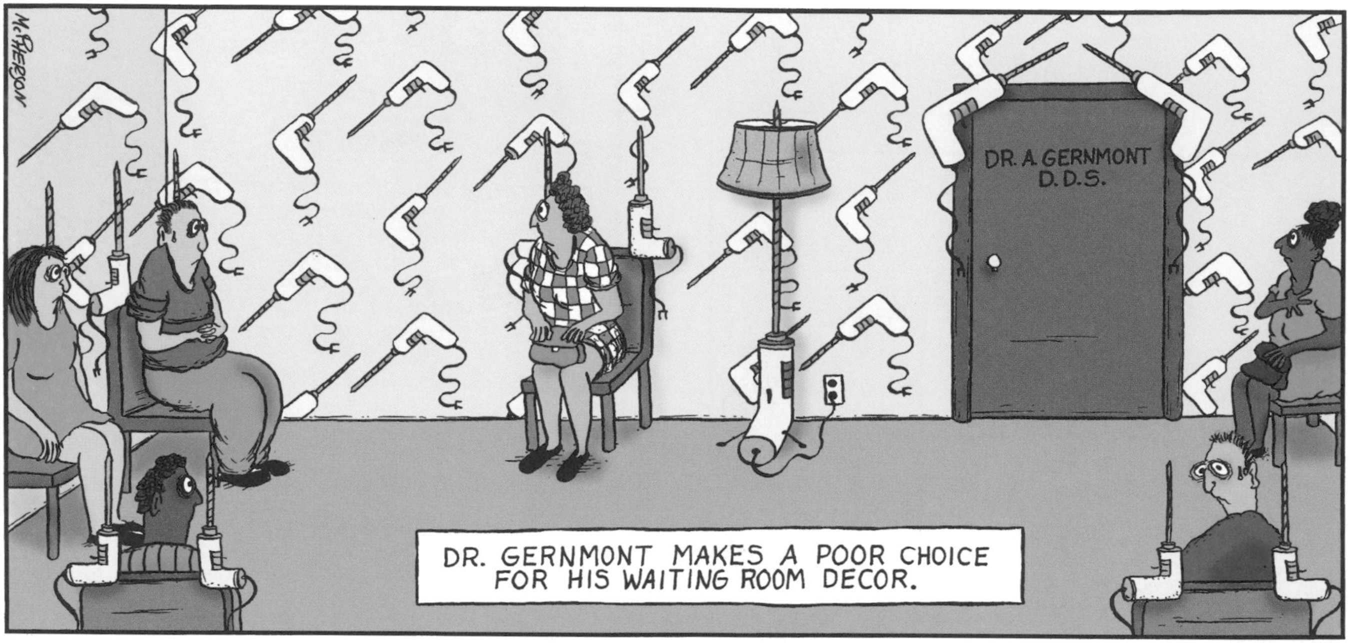
McPHERSON
DR. A. GERNMONT
D.D.S.
DR. GERNMONT MAKES A POOR CHOICE FOR HIS WAITING ROOM DECOR.

At the funeral of the Amazing Voltar

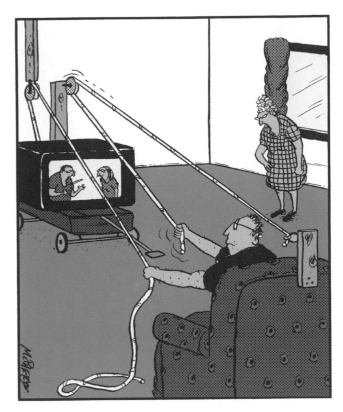

"For cryin' out loud, would it bankrupt us to buy a new remote?!"

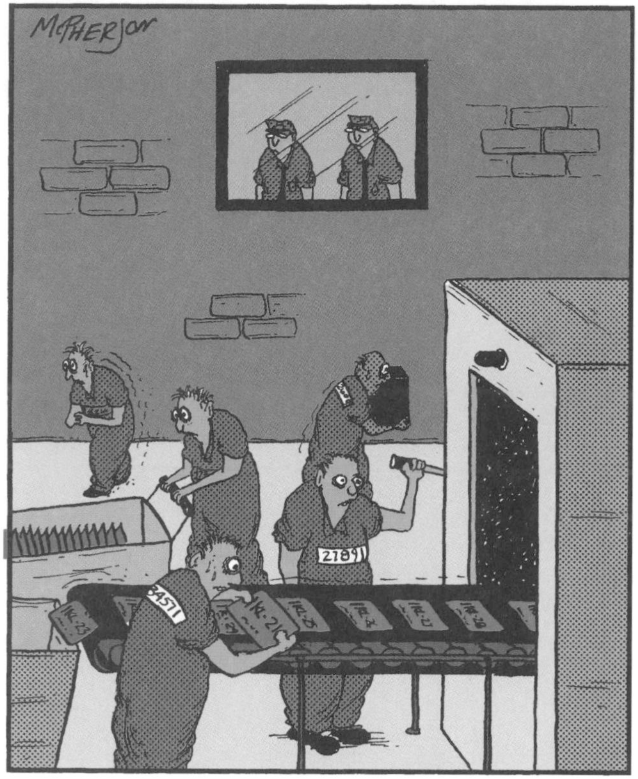

New Hampshire State Prison officials were concerned that producing 100,000 license plates with the motto "LIVE FREE OR DIE!" was severely affecting the prisoners' morale.

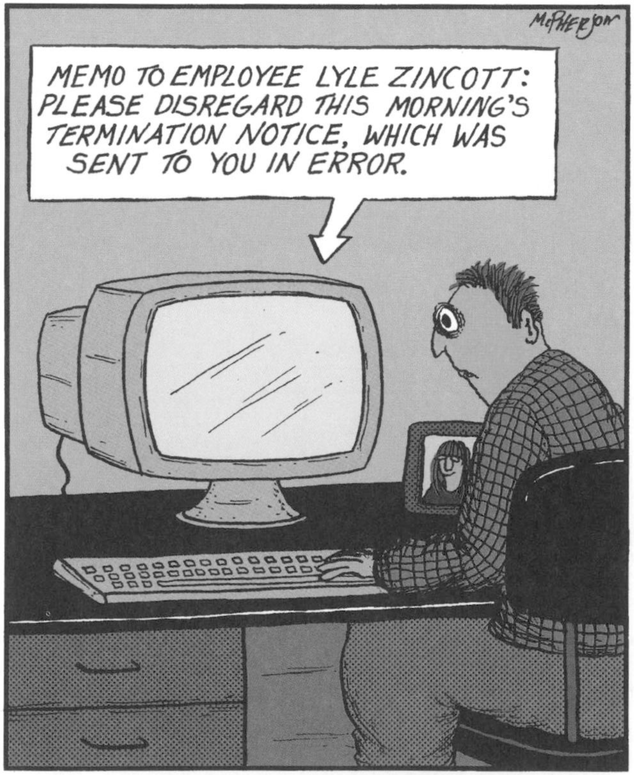
MEMO TO EMPLOYEE LYLE ZINCOTT: PLEASE DISREGARD THIS MORNING'S TERMINATION NOTICE, WHICH WAS SENT TO YOU IN ERROR.

Unfortunately, Lyle had already sent nasty e-mails to his boss, three vice presidents, and the CEO.

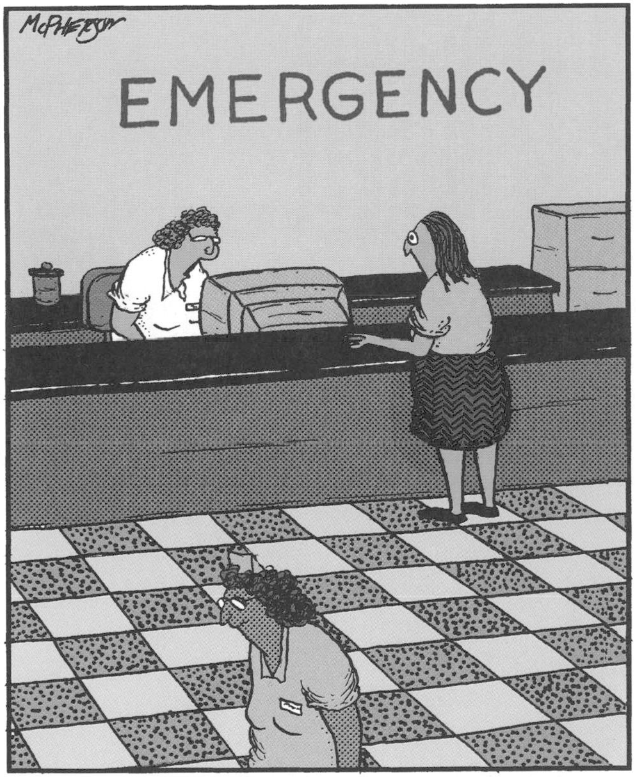
McPHERSON
EMERGENCY

"Let's see . . . Lloyd Young . . . sat on by elephant . . . he's in rooms 23, 24, and 25.

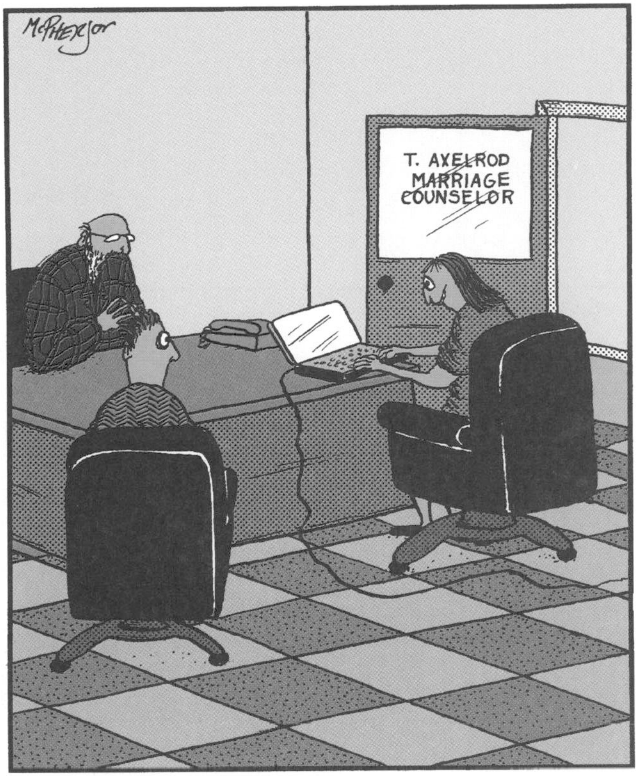
McPHERSON
T. AXELROD
MARRIAGE
COUNSELOR

"Carol, do you understand how your obsession with Internet chat rooms might make Frank uncomfortable? . . . Carol?"

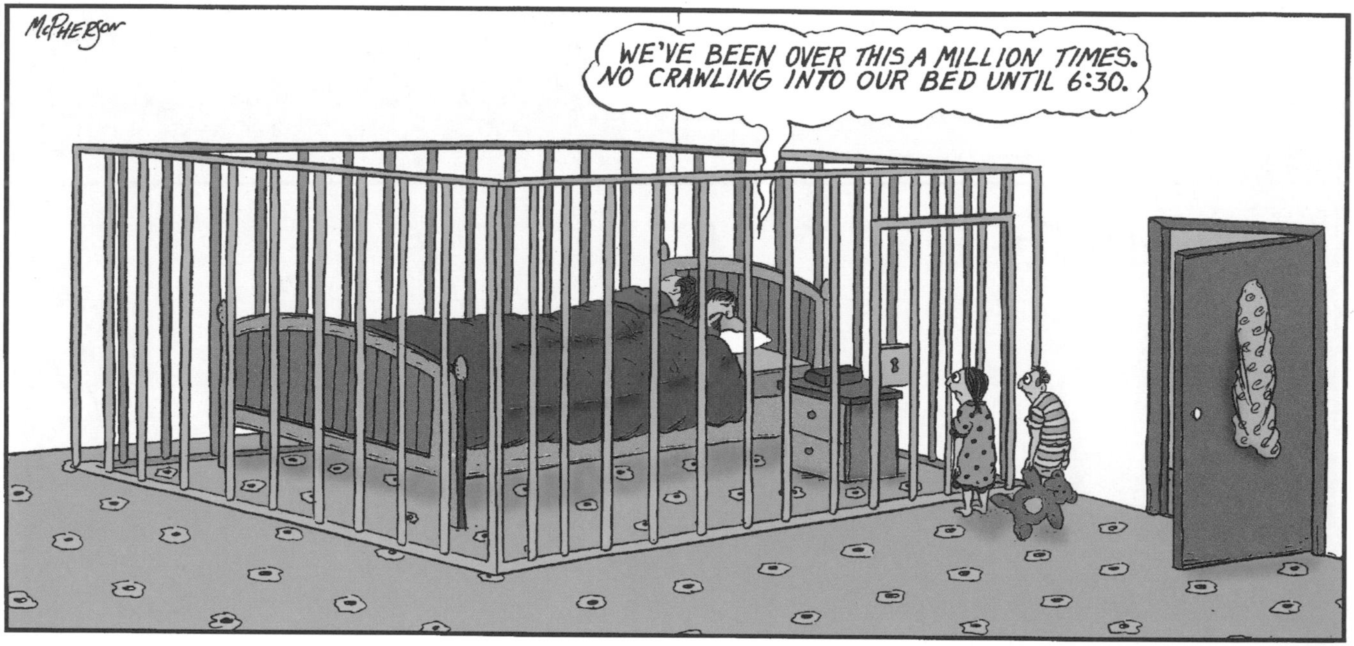
McPHERSON
WE'VE BEEN OVER THIS A MILLION TIMES. NO CRAWLING INTO OUR BED UNTIL 6:30.

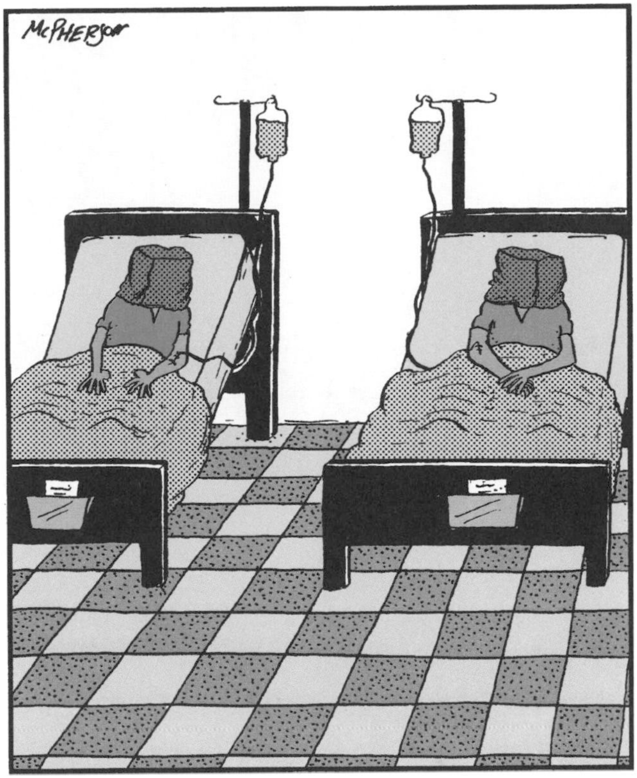
McPHERSON

"This isn't what I had in mind when I asked for a semiprivate room."

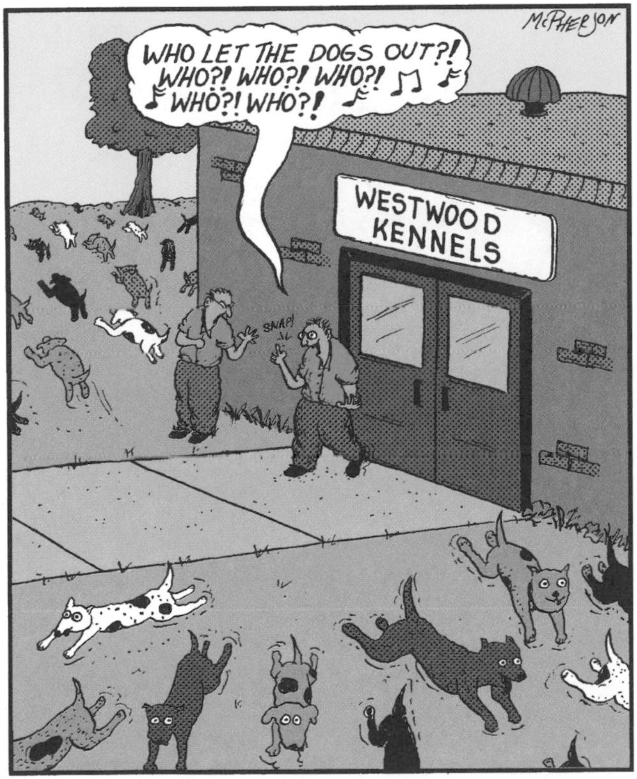
McPHERSON
WHO LET THE DOGS OUT?! WHO?! WHO?! WHO?! WHO?! WHO?!
WESTWOOD KENNELS
SNAP!

"Will you knock it off with that stupid song! We are in serious trouble here, Eddie!"

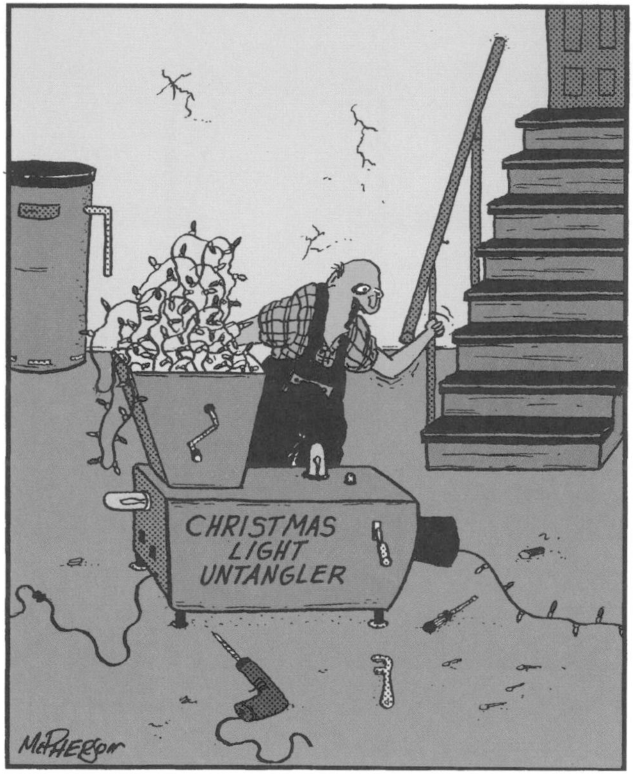
CHRISTMAS
LIGHT
UNTANGLER
McPHERSON

Working tirelessly in his basement since 1979, Wilbur Futslan creates one of the greatest inventions of the twenty-first century.

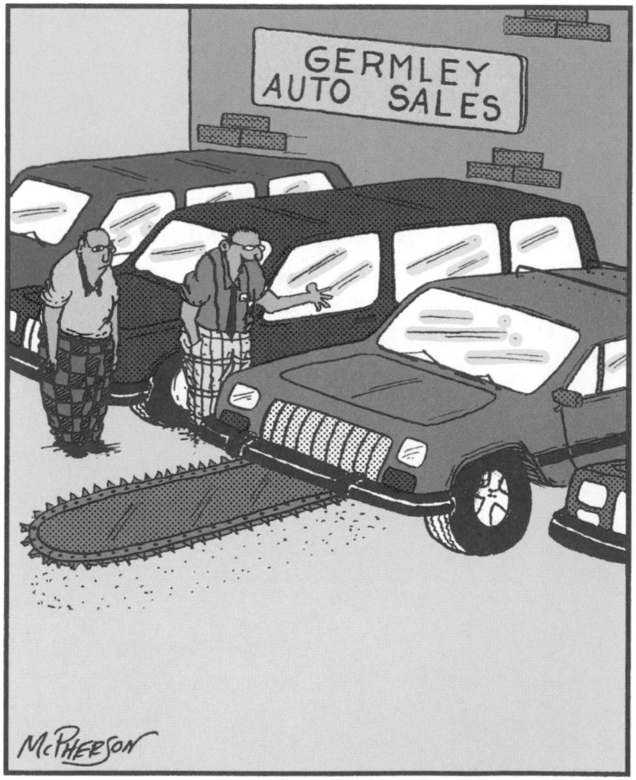
GERMLEY
AUTO SALES
McPHERSON

"Now, if you're looking for an SUV that can literally go anywhere, *this* is the vehicle for you!"

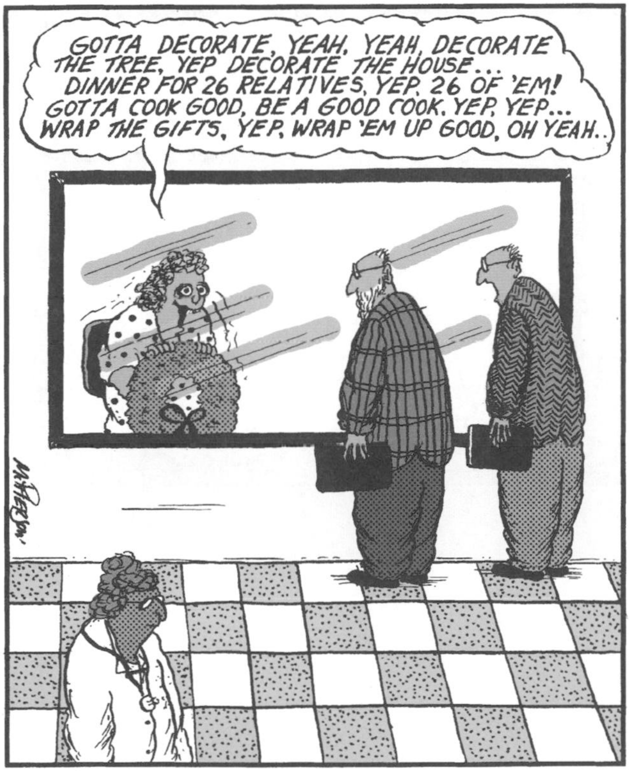
GOTTA DECORATE, YEAH, YEAH, DECORATE THE TREE, YEP DECORATE THE HOUSE... DINNER FOR 26 RELATIVES, YEP, 26 OF 'EM! GOTTA COOK GOOD, BE A GOOD COOK, YEP, YEP... WRAP THE GIFTS, YEP, WRAP 'EM UP GOOD, OH YEAH..

"Worst case of Holiday Burnout Syndrome I've ever seen."

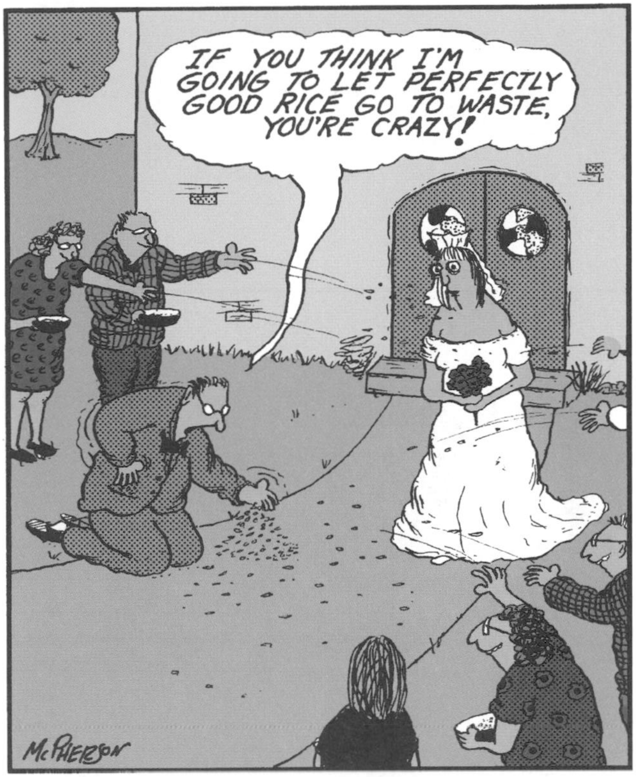
IF YOU THINK I'M GOING TO LET PERFECTLY GOOD RICE GO TO WASTE, YOU'RE CRAZY!
McPHERSON

Carolyn gets the first glimpse of the excessive frugality that would define the next forty-two years of her life.

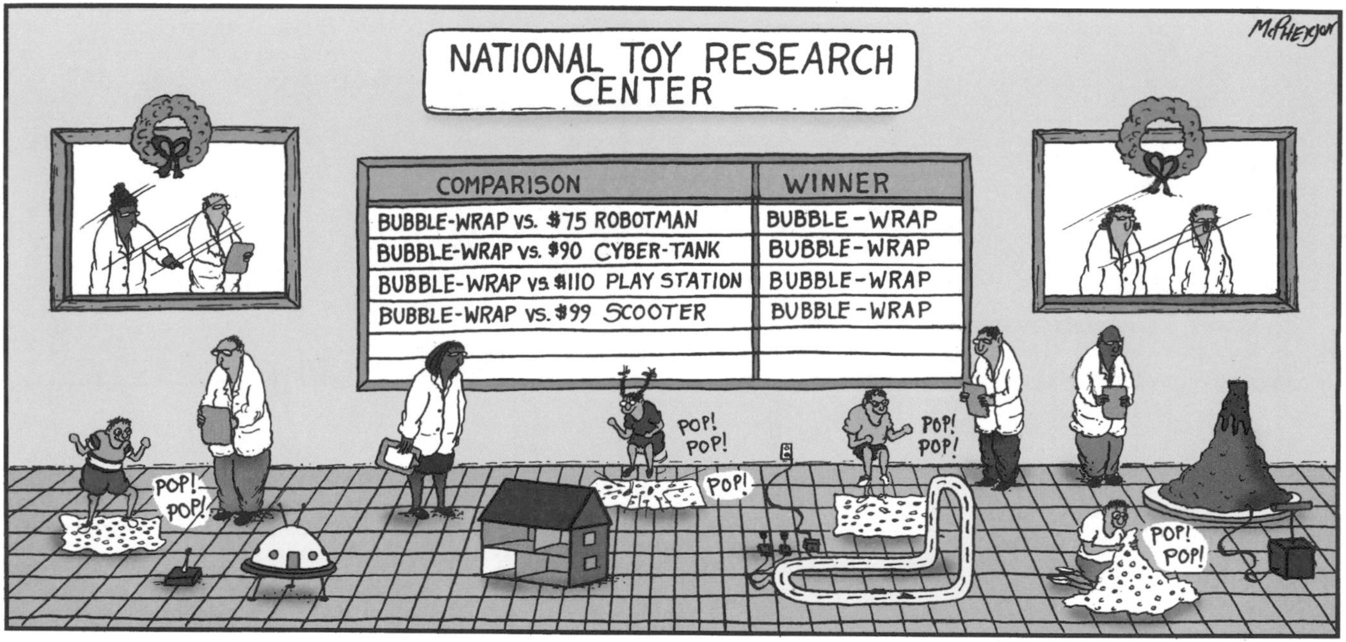
McPherson
NATIONAL TOY RESEARCH CENTER
COMPARISON
WINNER
BUBBLE-WRAP VS. $75 ROBOTMAN
BUBBLE-WRAP
BUBBLE-WRAP VS. $90 CYBER-TANK
BUBBLE-WRAP
BUBBLE-WRAP VS. $110 PLAY STATION
BUBBLE-WRAP
BUBBLE-WRAP VS. $99 SCOOTER
BUBBLE-WRAP
POP! POP!
POP! POP!
POP!
POP! POP!
POP! POP!

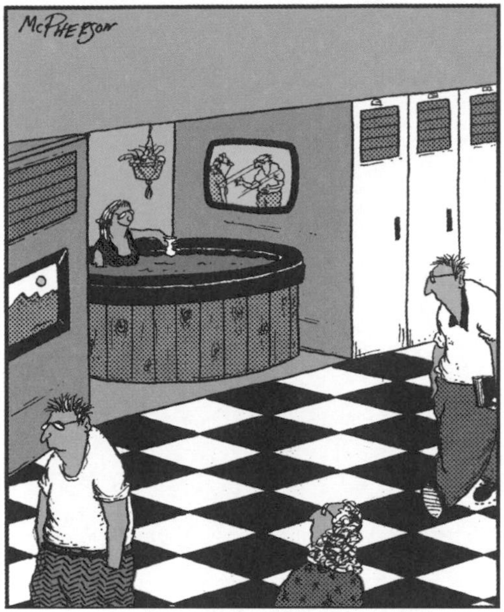
McPHERSON

Crystal lucks into being assigned the legendary locker number 379.

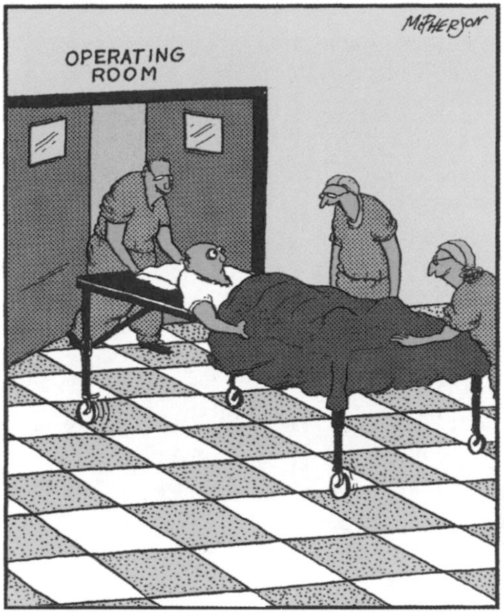
McPHERSON
OPERATING
ROOM

"Can I interest you in our Frequent Operation Program? For every five hundred stitches you pay for, you'll receive one hundred bonus stitches absolutely free!"

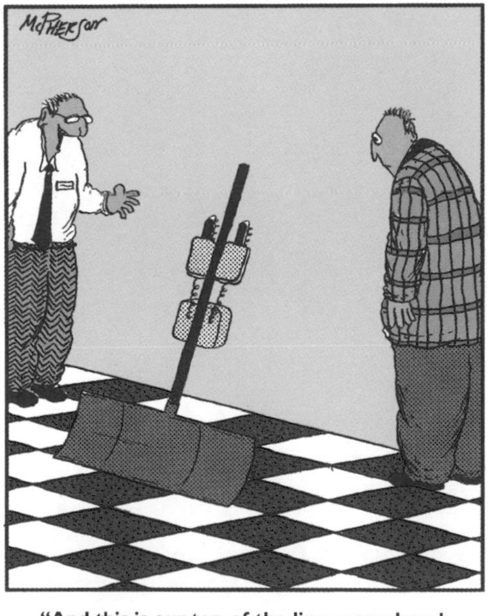
McPHERSON

"And this is our top-of-the-line snow shovel, complete with a pair of defibrillation paddles."

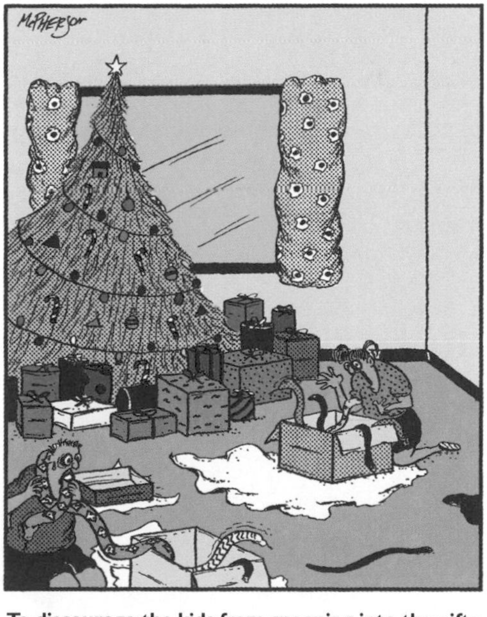
McPHERSON

To discourage the kids from snooping into the gifts before Christmas, the Milnaks filled a few decoy gifts with a variety of snakes.

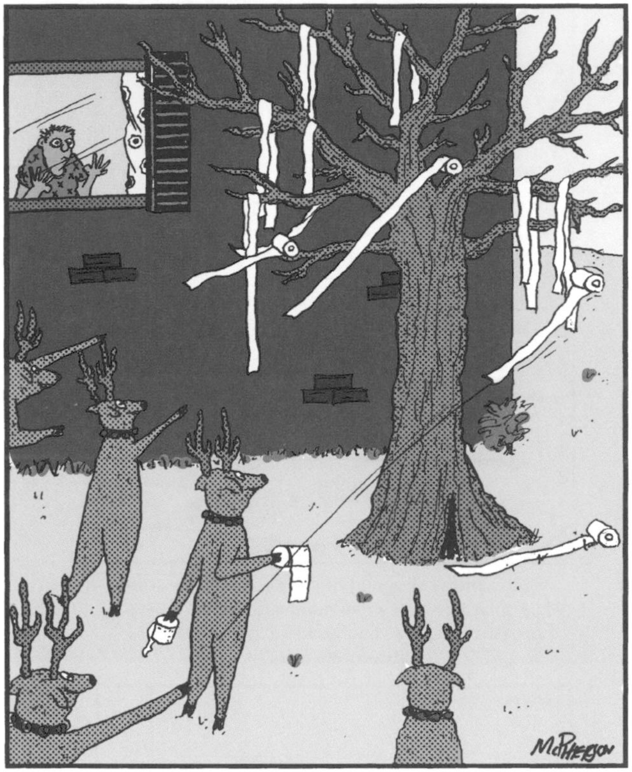

How to tell when you're on Santa's naughty list

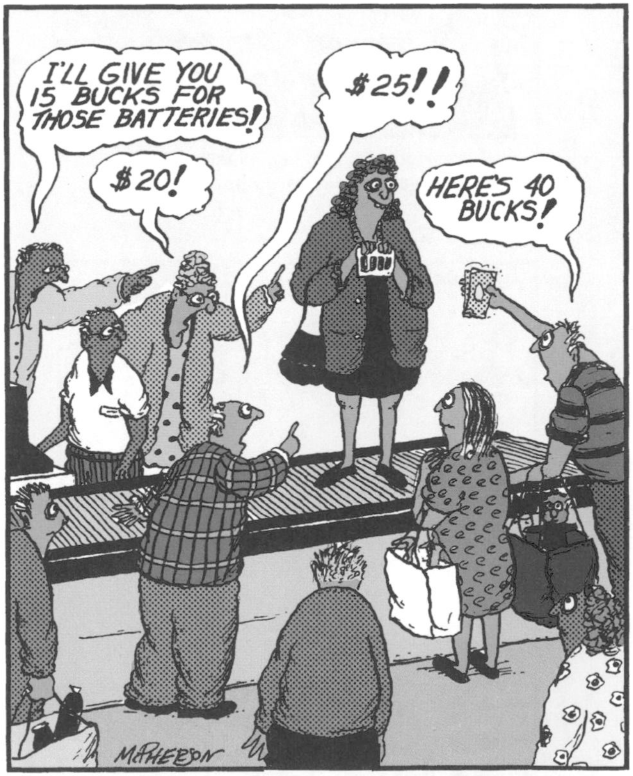
I'LL GIVE YOU 15 BUCKS FOR THOSE BATTERIES!
$25!!
$20!
HERE'S 40 BUCKS!

Having purchased the last package of AA batteries with only one shopping day left before Christmas, Glenda finds herself in a unique position.

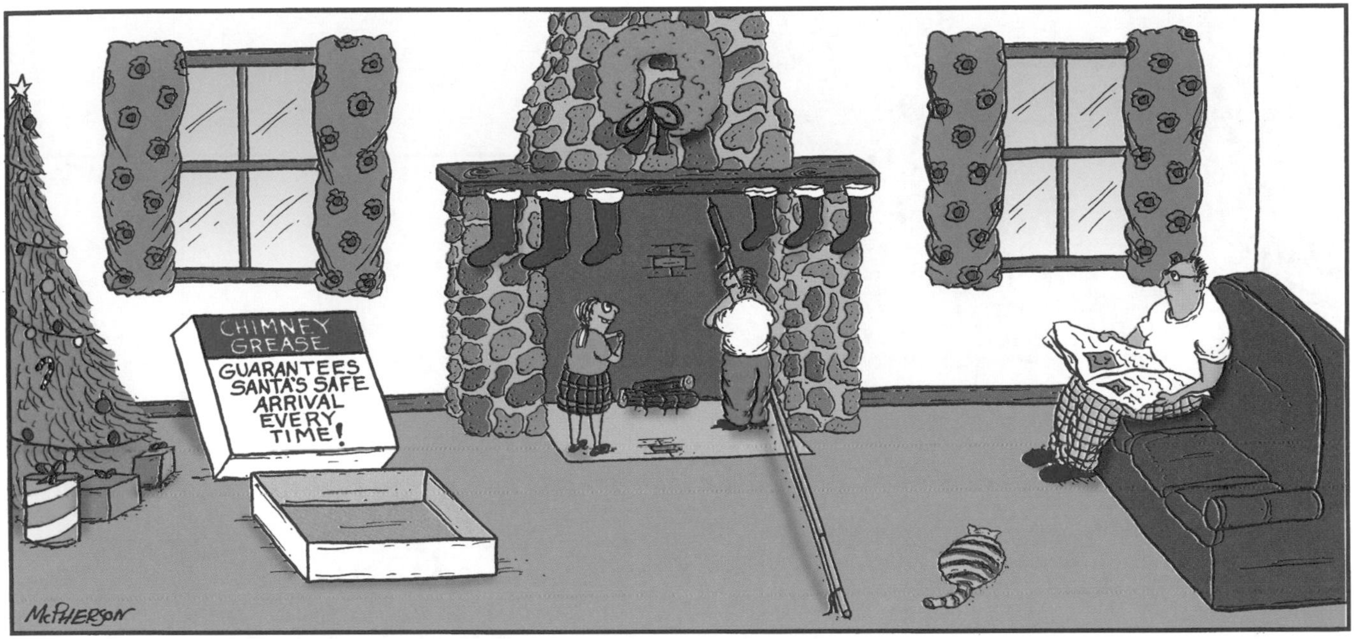
CHIMNEY
GREASE
GUARANTEES
SANTA'S SAFE
ARRIVAL
EVERY
TIME!
McPHERSON

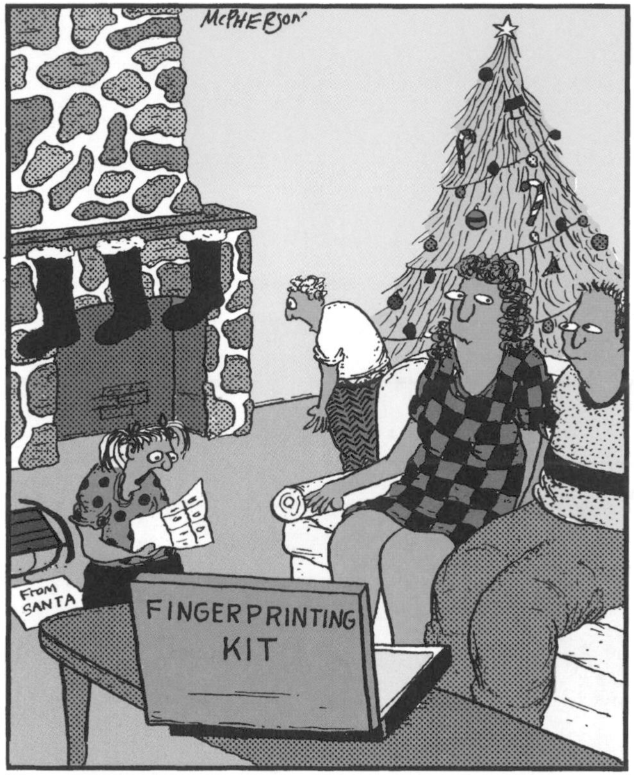
McPHERSON
FROM SANTA
FINGERPRINTING KIT

The Wurtner kids' suspicions grew when the fingerprints on their new sleds matched their parents' and the delicate thread they had strung across the fireplace had not been broken.

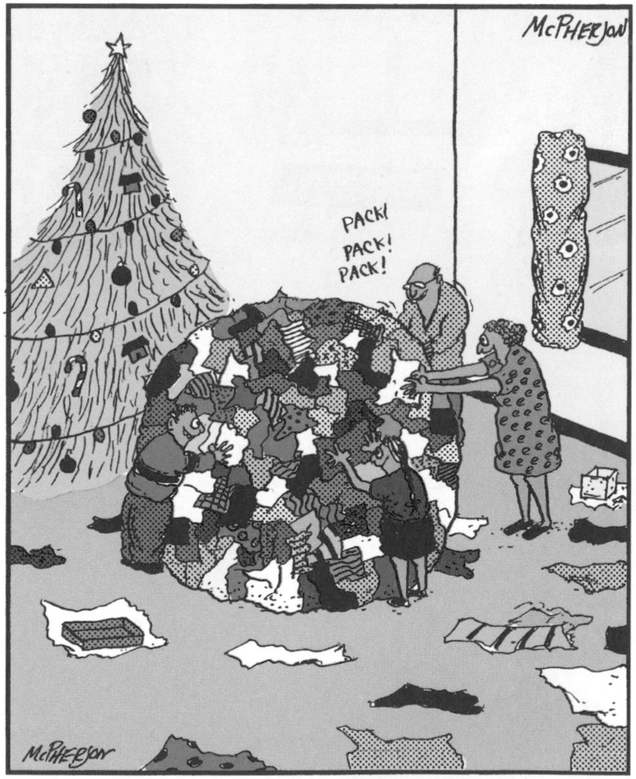
McPHERSON
PACK!
PACK!
PACK!
McPHERSON

Each year as part of their holiday traditions, the Milmonts would add more to their Christmas wrapping paper ball.

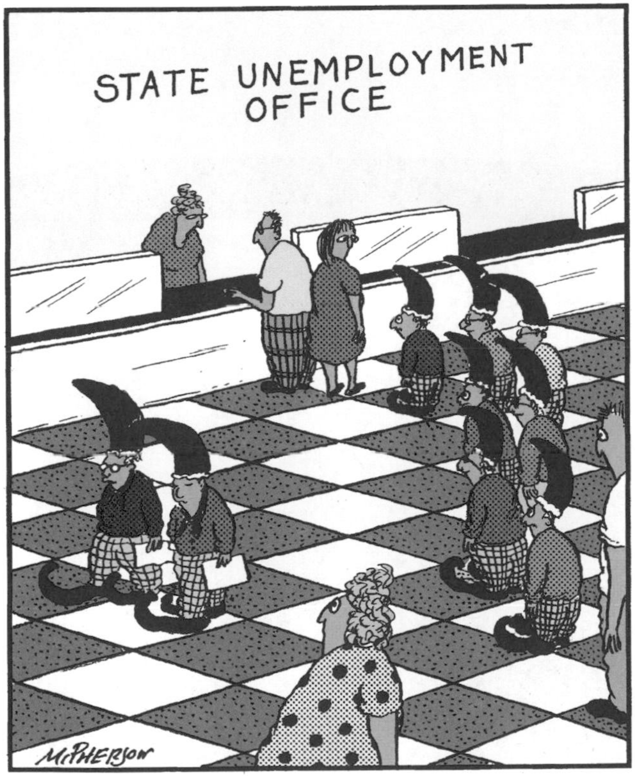
STATE UNEMPLOYMENT
OFFICE
McPHERSON

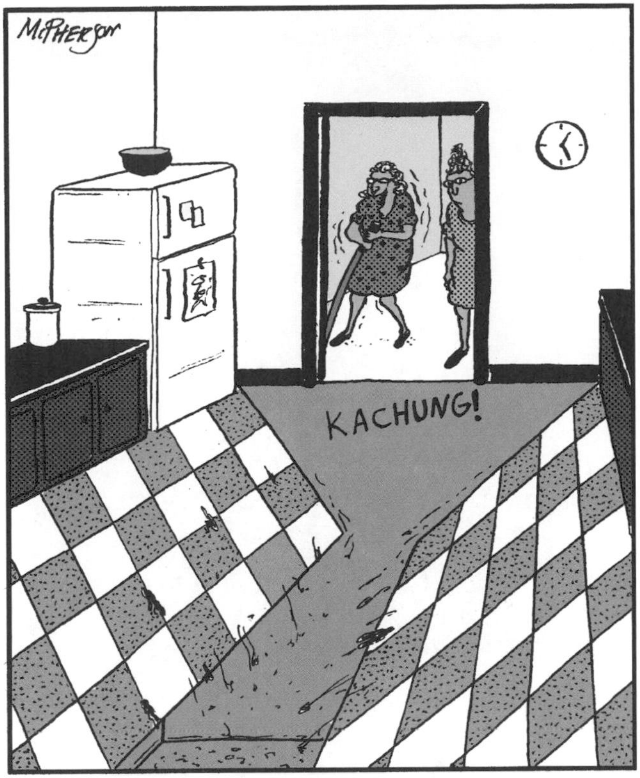
McPHERSON
KACHUNG!

"I'm tellin' ya, Brenda, this new floor is great! Crumbs, dirt, and spills are gone with the switch of a lever!"

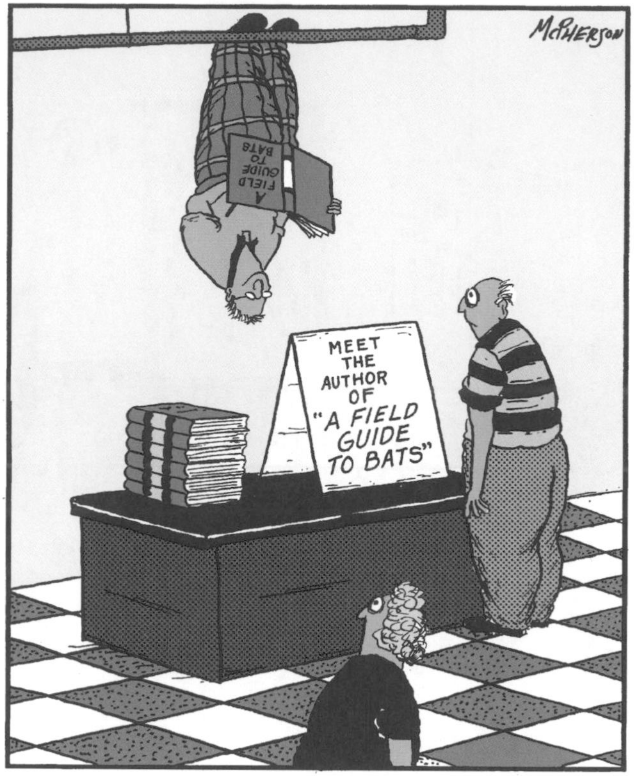
McPHERSON
A FIELD GUIDE TO BATS
MEET THE AUTHOR OF "A FIELD GUIDE TO BATS"

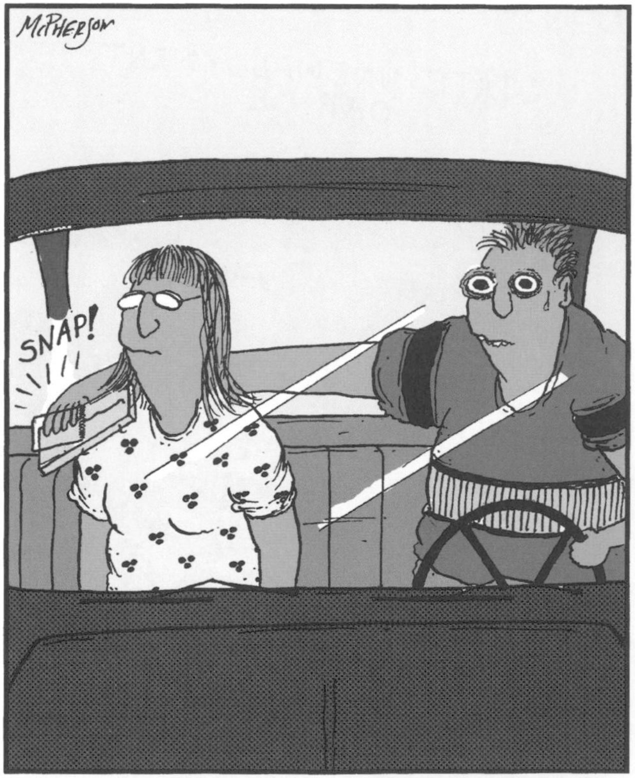
McPHERSON
SNAP!

Carol lets Brian know that she wants to keep their relationship platonic.

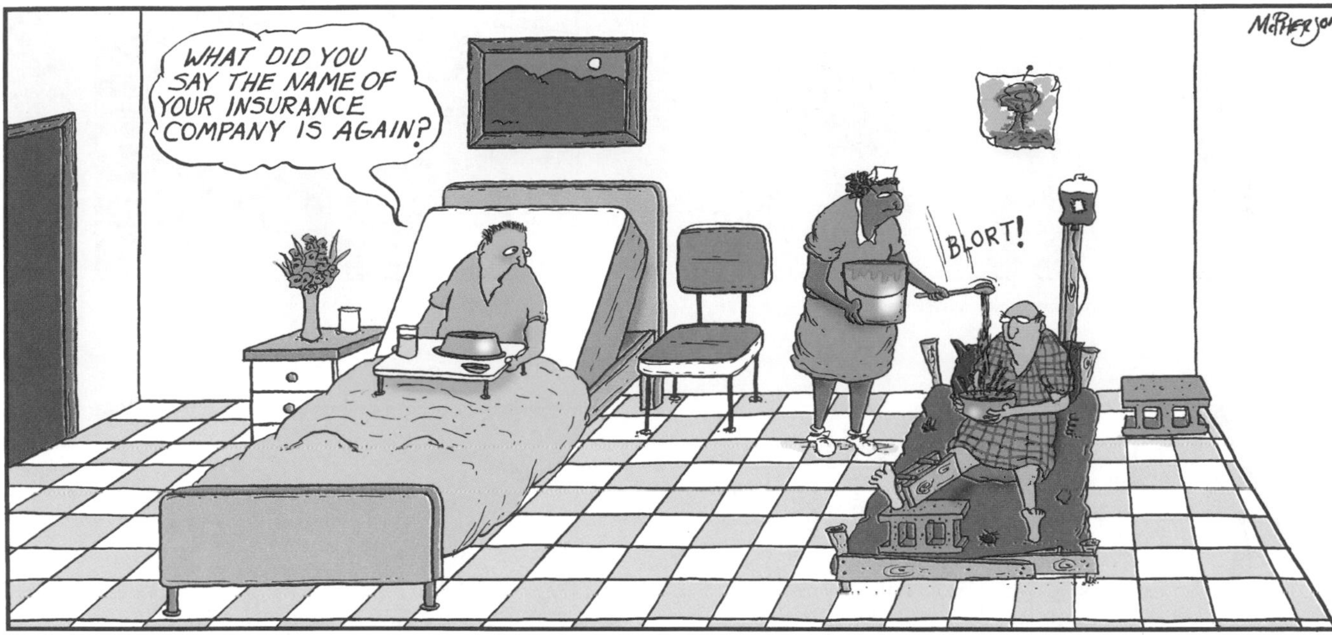
McPHERSON
WHAT DID YOU SAY THE NAME OF YOUR INSURANCE COMPANY IS AGAIN?
BLORT!

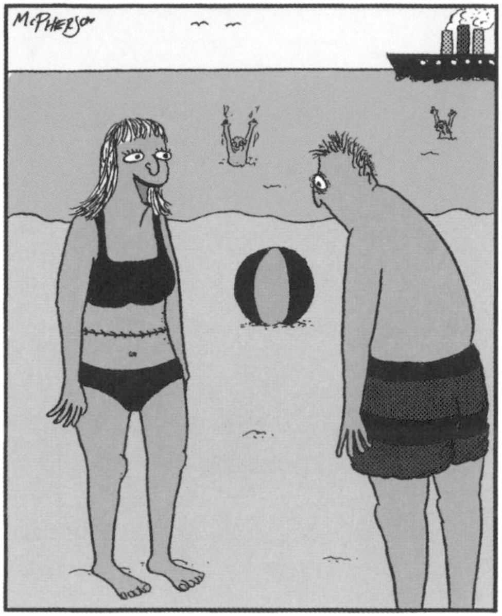

"Me? I'm a magician's assistant."

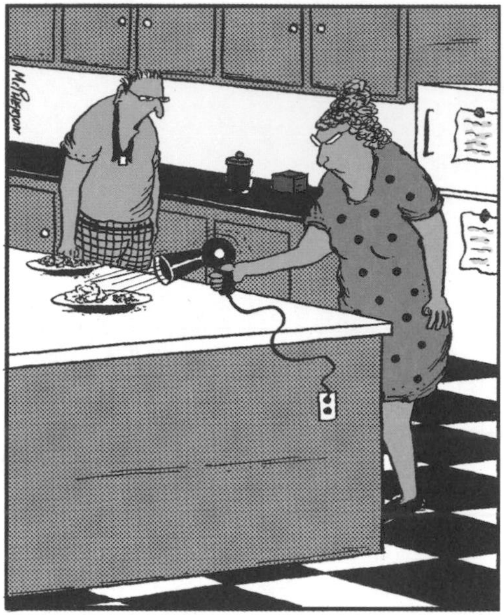

"OK! OK! We can buy a microwave!"

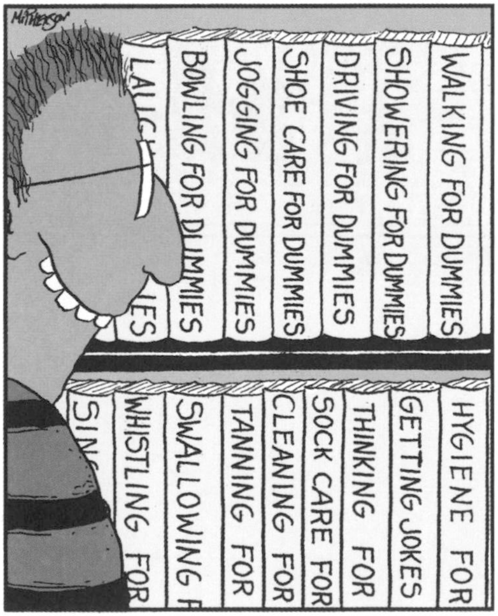
BOWLING FOR DUMMIES
JOGGING FOR DUMMIES
SHOE CARE FOR DUMMIES
DRIVING FOR DUMMIES
SHOWERING FOR DUMMIES
WALKING FOR DUMMIES
WHISTLING FOR
SWALLOWING
TANNING FOR
CLEANING FOR
SOCK CARE FOR
THINKING FOR
GETTING JOKES
HYGIENE FOR

**At home with Lester Culdoon:
The World's Dumbest Man**

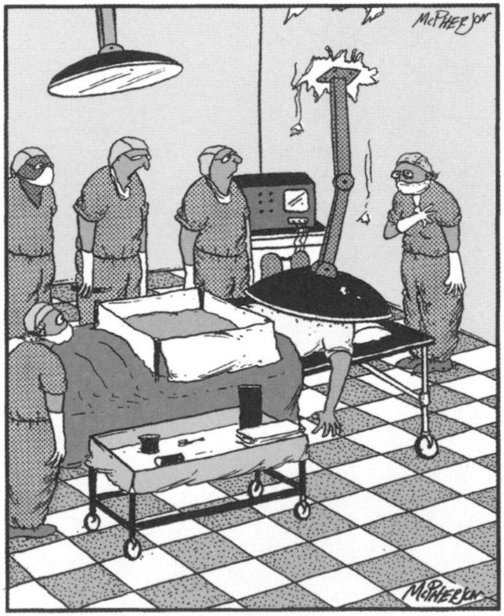

"Ten to one that when he comes to he tells one of those stories about seeing a bright light at the end of a tunnel."

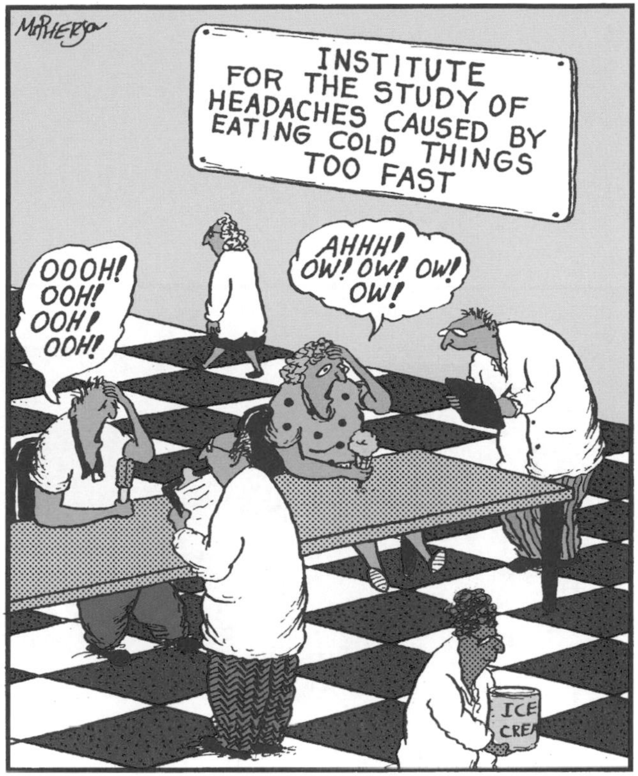
McPHERSON
INSTITUTE FOR THE STUDY OF HEADACHES CAUSED BY EATING COLD THINGS TOO FAST
OOOH! OOH! OOH! OOH!
AHHH! OW! OW! OW! OW!
ICE CREA

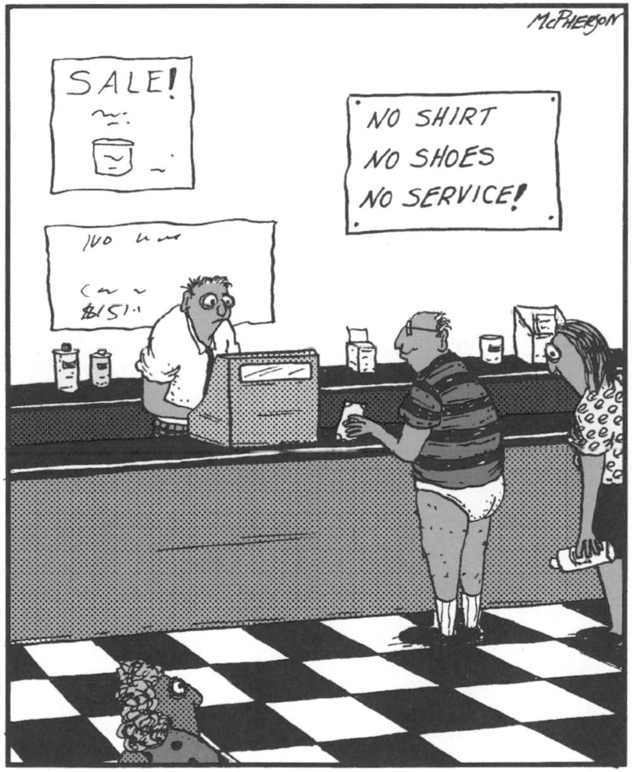
McPHERSON
SALE!
NO SHIRT
NO SHOES
NO SERVICE!

IT WAS BILL'S LAST REQUEST. ALL HIS LIFE HE SUFFERED FROM CLAUSTROPHOBIA.
McPHERSON

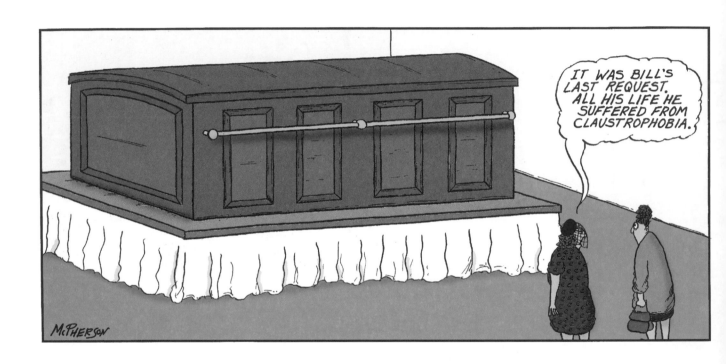

MCPHERSON

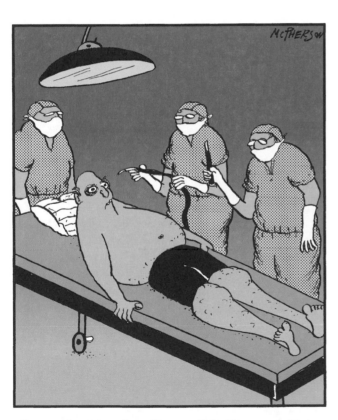

Overestimating the effects of his fitness regimen, Warren becomes the first person ever to require surgical removal of bicycle shorts.

MCPHERSON
SMASH!

"Use words, Hon."

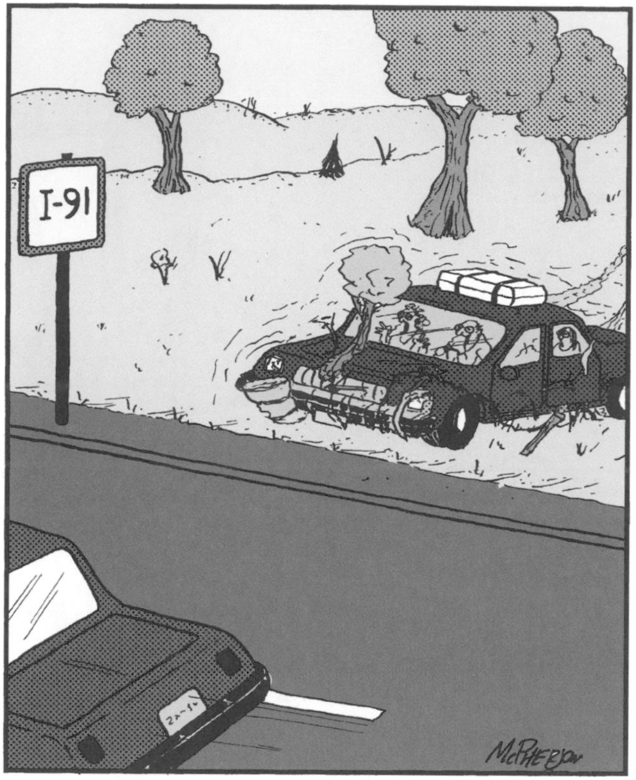
I-91

"Ha! I *told* you I could find my way back to the interstate without stopping to ask directions!"

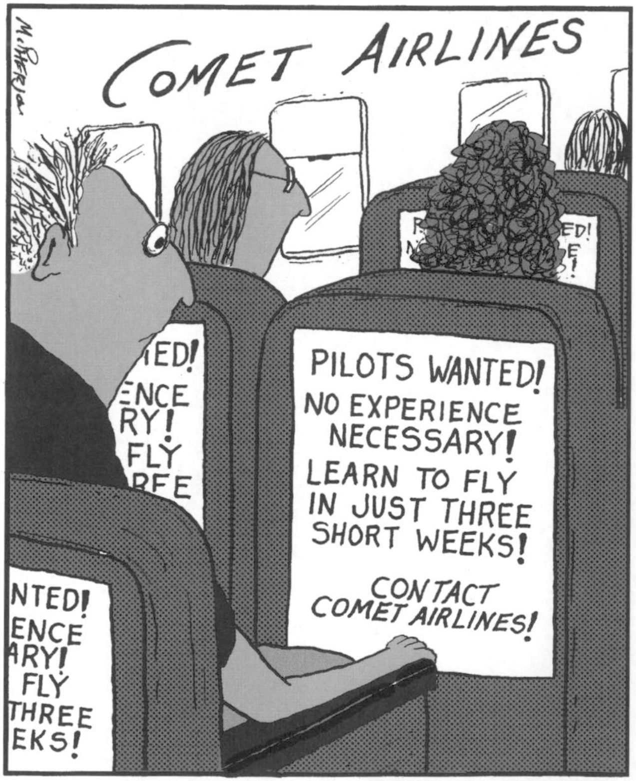
COMET AIRLINES
PILOTS WANTED!
NO EXPERIENCE NECESSARY!
LEARN TO FLY IN JUST THREE SHORT WEEKS!
CONTACT COMET AIRLINES!

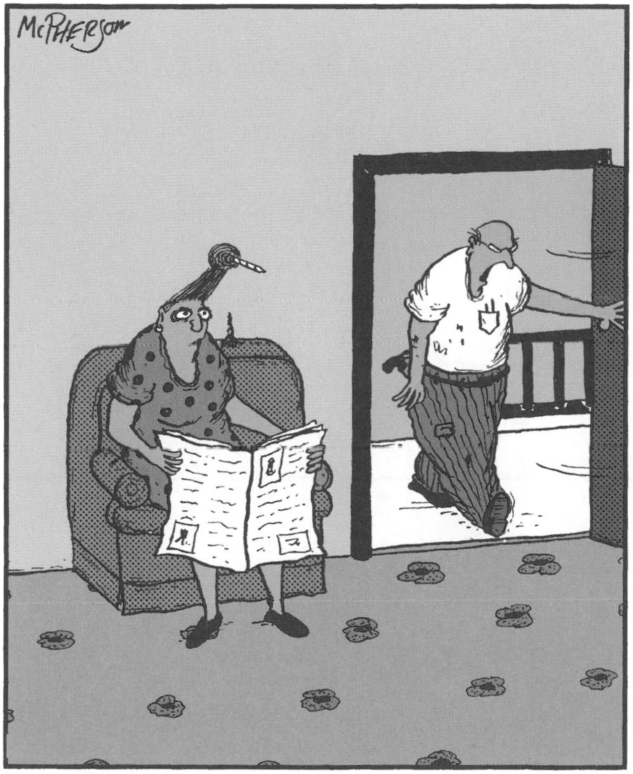
McPHERSON

"Stupid piece-of-junk drill! I drill a simple hole for the new porch light and the useless thing gets jammed!"

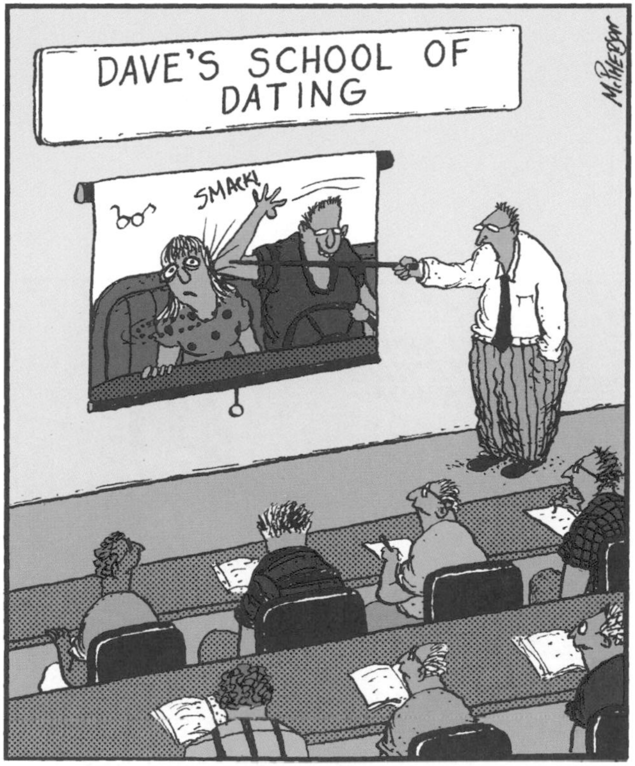
DAVE'S SCHOOL OF DATING
SMACK!
McPHERSON

"So what does Marty do wrong here? He comes in with an arm trajectory that's too low and . . . BAM! Say good-bye to a second date!"

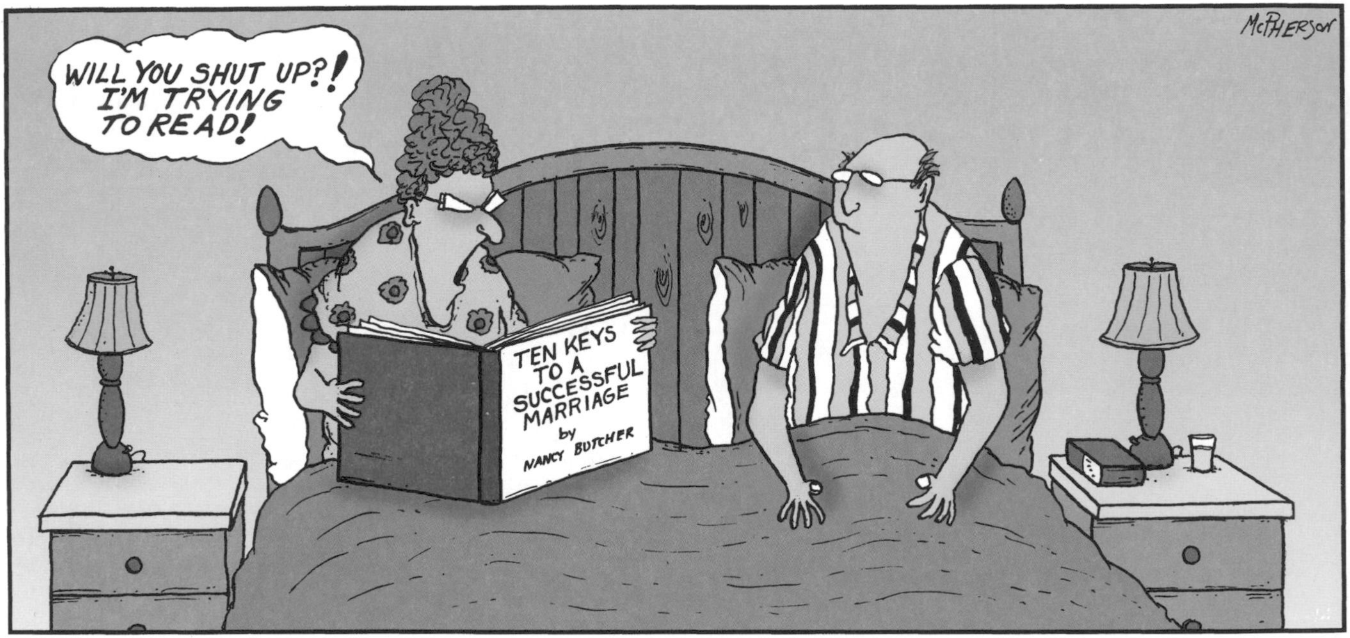
McPHERSON
WILL YOU SHUT UP?! I'M TRYING TO READ!
TEN KEYS TO A SUCCESSFUL MARRIAGE by NANCY BUTCHER

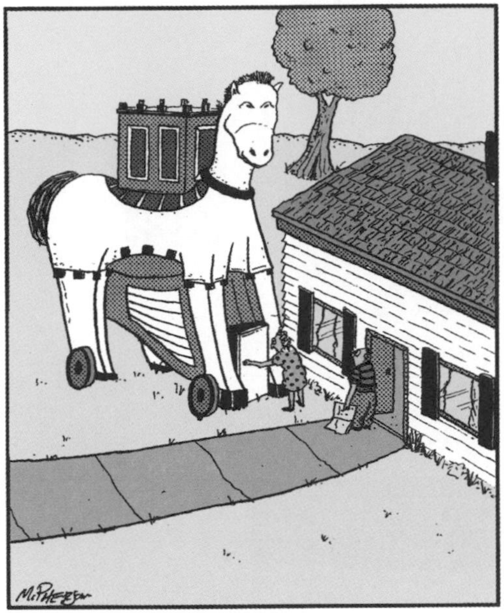
McPHERSON

Overcome by curiosity, the Feeglemans open the door to the Trojan horse and unwittingly allow their three grown children to move back home.

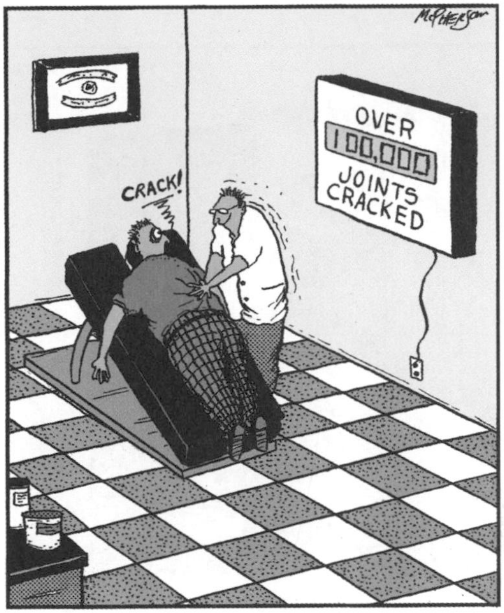
McPHERSON
CRACK!
OVER
100,000
JOINTS
CRACKED

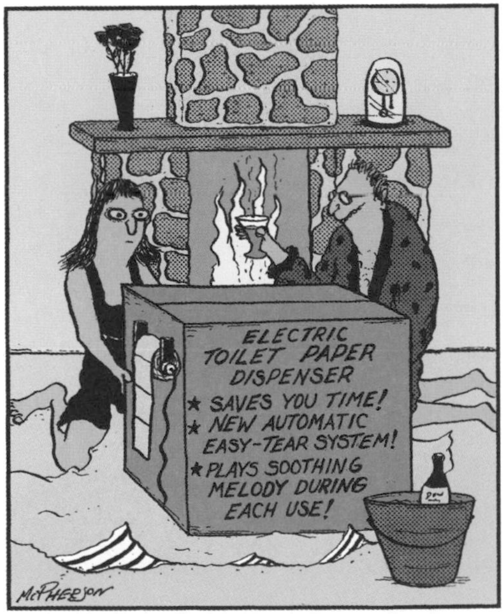
ELECTRIC
TOILET PAPER
DISPENSER
★ SAVES YOU TIME!
★ NEW AUTOMATIC
EASY-TEAR SYSTEM!
★ PLAYS SOOTHING
MELODY DURING
EACH USE!
McPHERSON

The Willmans' ten-year-anniversary celebration takes a sudden nosedive.

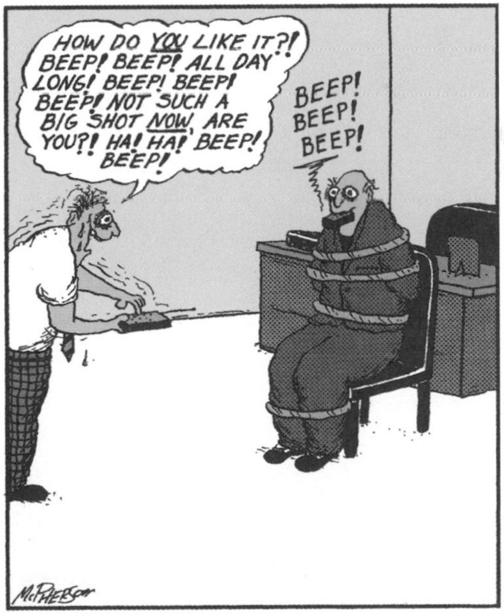
HOW DO YOU LIKE IT?! BEEP! BEEP! ALL DAY LONG! BEEP! BEEP! BEEP! NOT SUCH A BIG SHOT NOW, ARE YOU?! HA! HA! BEEP! BEEP!
BEEP! BEEP! BEEP!
McPHERSON

Twelve years of being constantly on call finally push Larry Zench over the edge.

"I told you it was a bad idea to stop and get doughnuts first."

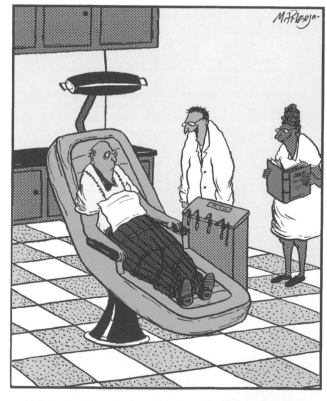

"Unfortunately, we are all out of laughing gas. So in lieu of that, Ms. Keser will read aloud an assortment of Henny Youngman jokes."

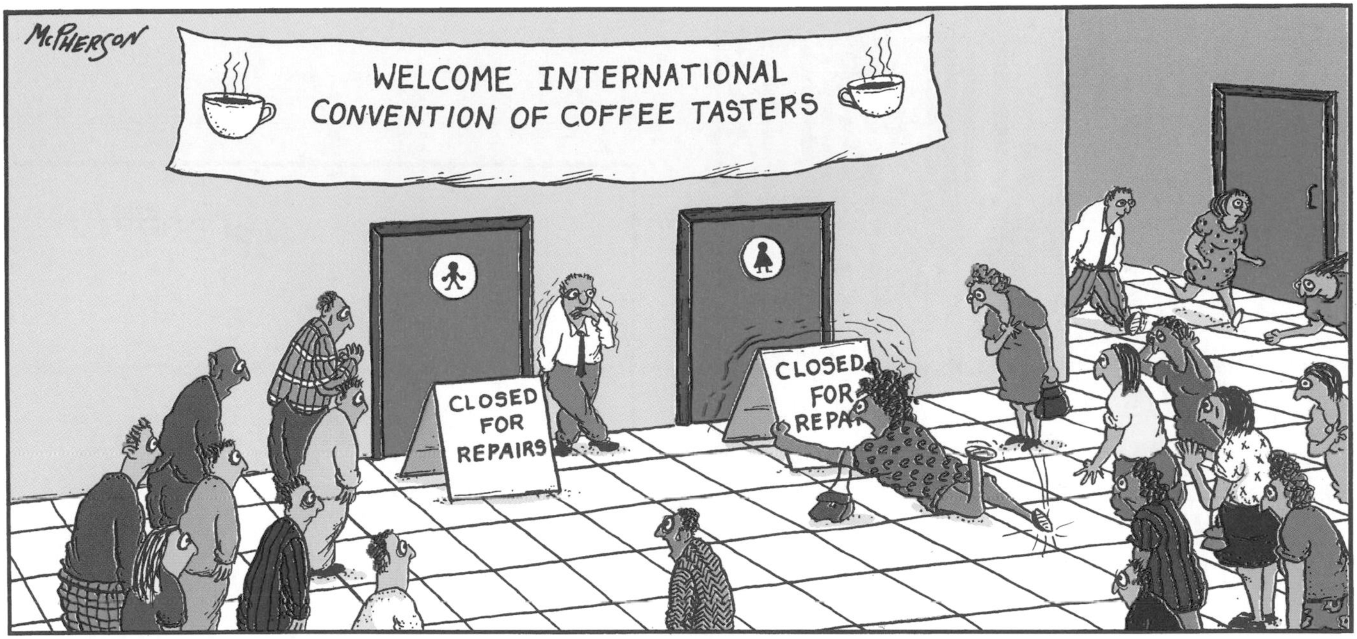
McPHERSON
WELCOME INTERNATIONAL
CONVENTION OF COFFEE TASTERS
CLOSED
FOR
REPAIRS
CLOSED
FOR
REPA

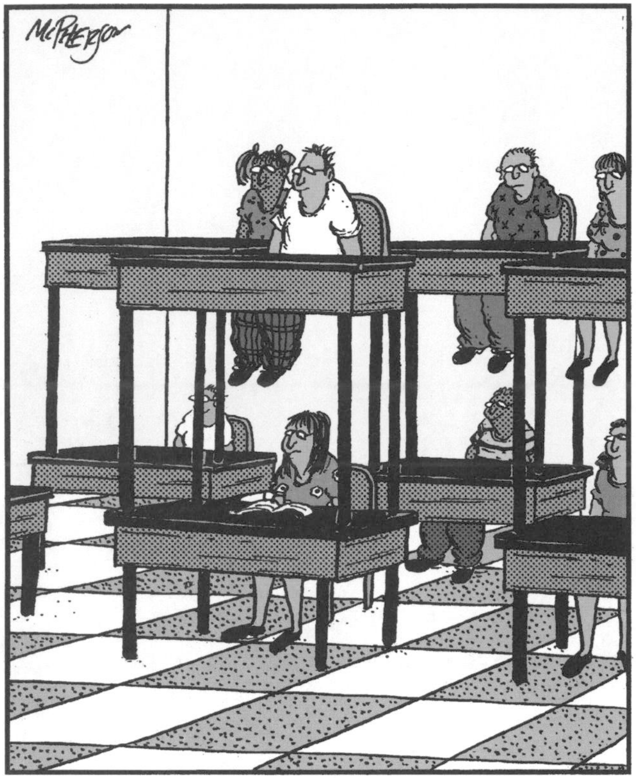

Winston Central School District finds a solution to overcrowded classrooms.

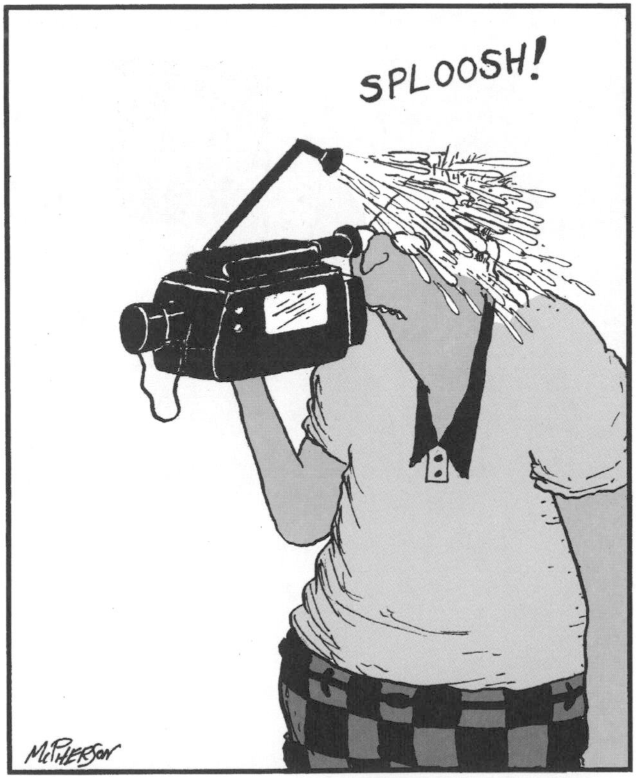
SPLOOSH!

Lenny's new Sony Idiot-Proof 3000 camcorder alerts him to the fact that his lens cap is still on.

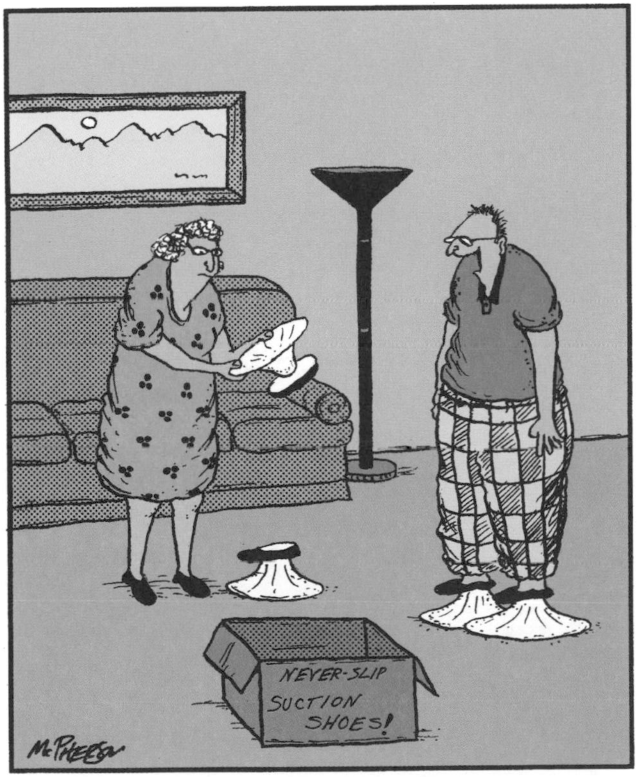
NEVER-SLIP
SUCTION
SHOES!
McPHERSON

"We can get a half percent off our homeowner's insurance if we'll wear these every time we shower."

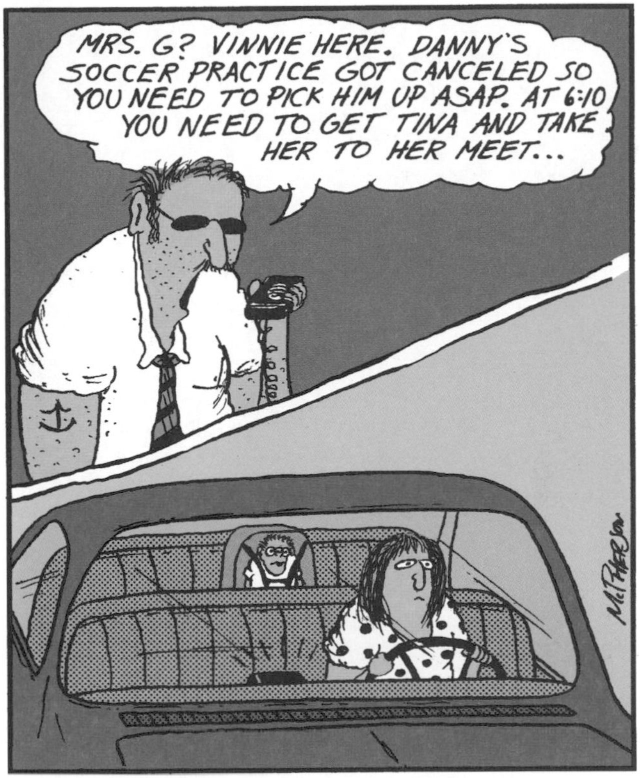
MRS. G? VINNIE HERE. DANNY'S SOCCER PRACTICE GOT CANCELED SO YOU NEED TO PICK HIM UP ASAP. AT 6:10 YOU NEED TO GET TINA AND TAKE HER TO HER MEET...
McPHERSON

As a mother of three active teenagers, Marilyn Gilcrest relied on a professional dispatcher to help coordinate her day.

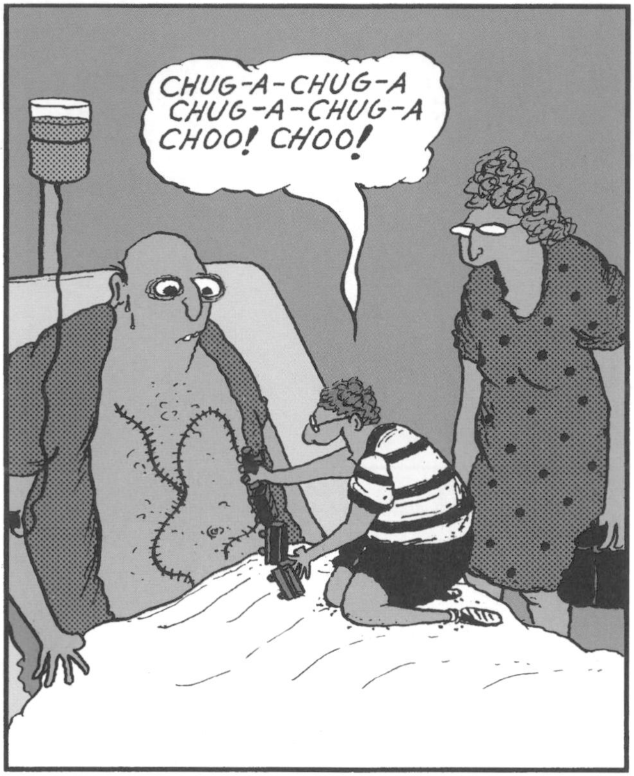
CHUG-A-CHUG-A
CHUG-A-CHUG-A
CHOO! CHOO!

"Oh, for heaven's sake, let your son have some fun! You're always being such a spoilsport!"

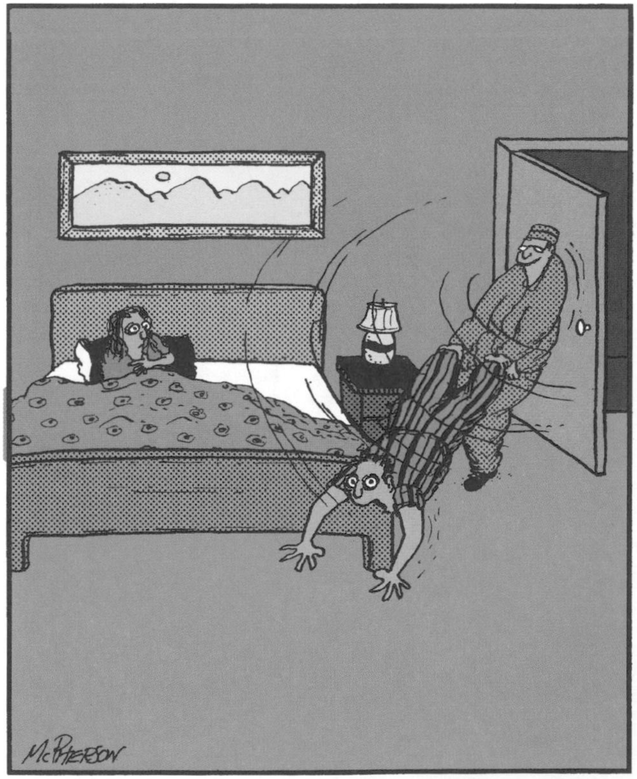
McPHERSON

The Grand Coronado Hotel quickly gained notoriety for its unique wake-up service.

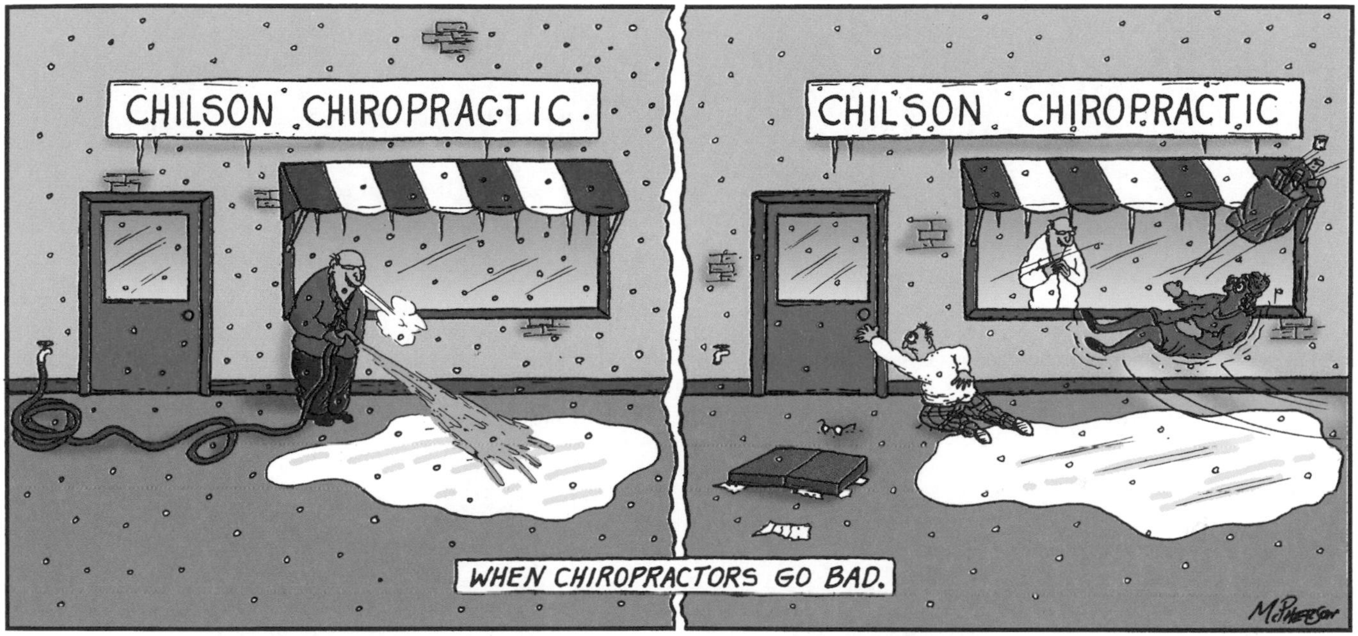

CHILSON CHIROPRACTIC
CHILSON CHIROPRACTIC
WHEN CHIROPRACTORS GO BAD.
McPHERSON

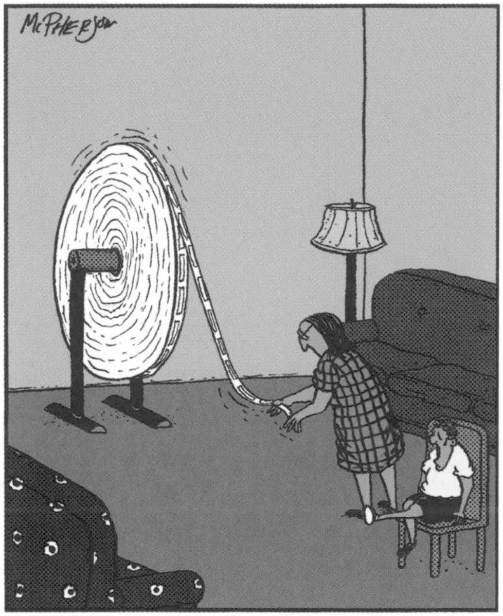

As the parents of five children, the Wortleys wisely bought Band-Aid bandages in quarter-mile-long rolls.

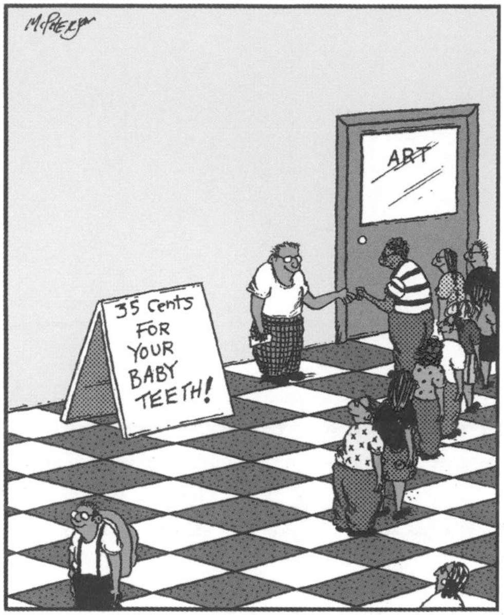
ART
35 Cents FOR YOUR BABY TEETH!

Knowing that he could make fifty cents a tooth from the "Tooth Fairy," Alan makes a killing at school.

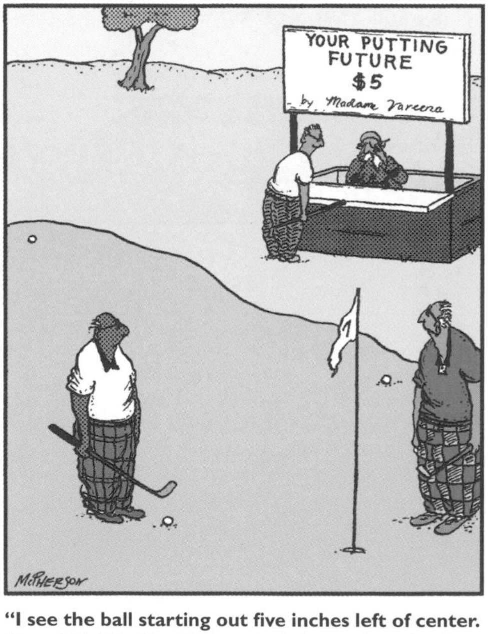
YOUR PUTTING FUTURE
$5

"I see the ball starting out five inches left of center. Struck lightly, it gathers speed down a long incline, bends right . . . and into the cup."

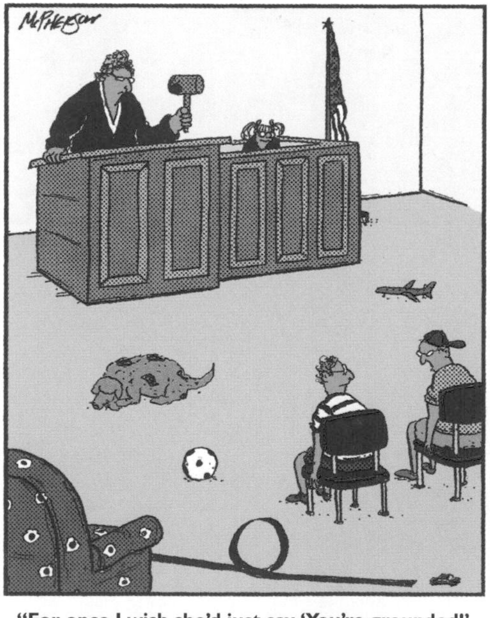

"For once I wish she'd just say, 'You're grounded!' and be done with it."

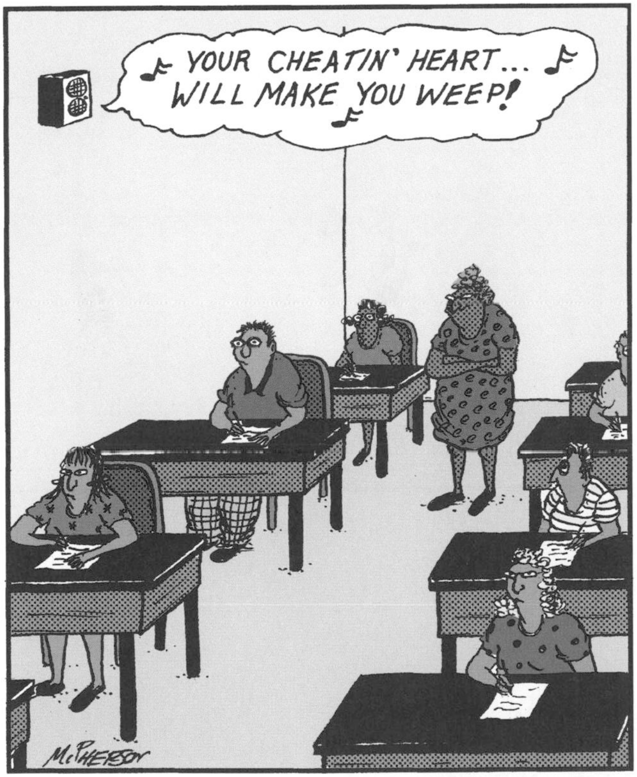
YOUR CHEATIN' HEART... WILL MAKE YOU WEEP!
McPHERSON

With the help of Hank Williams, Mrs. Slatchner sends a subtle message to her students during midterms.

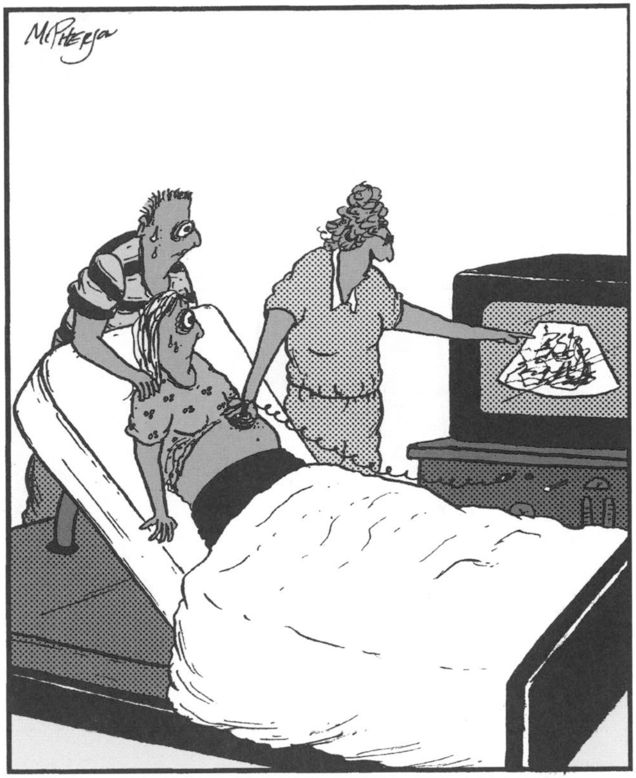

". . . and over *here* you can see the *sixth* baby's head! . . . Just kidding! There are only five babies."

FRANK LLOYD WRIGHT, AGE 10

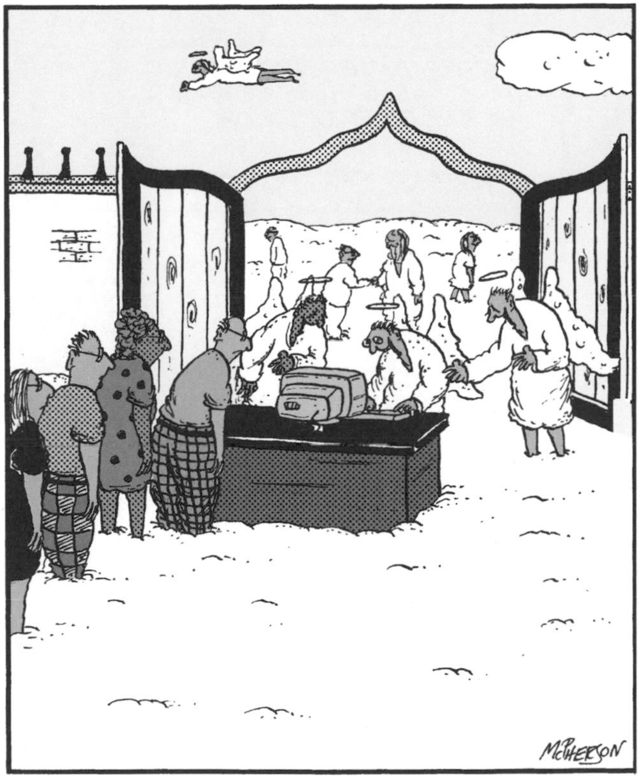
McPHERSON

"OK, if you *really* want to know. . . . You spent $29,137 on late video rental fees, $18,578 on overdue library books, $23,481 on unredeemed soda bottle deposits . . ."

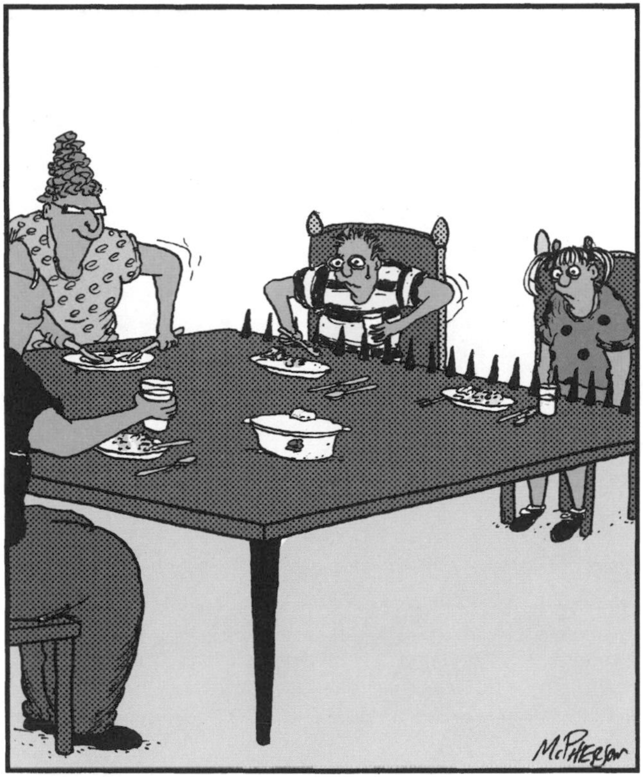
McPHERSON

Mrs. Stimpson gets serious about the "no elbows on the table" rule.

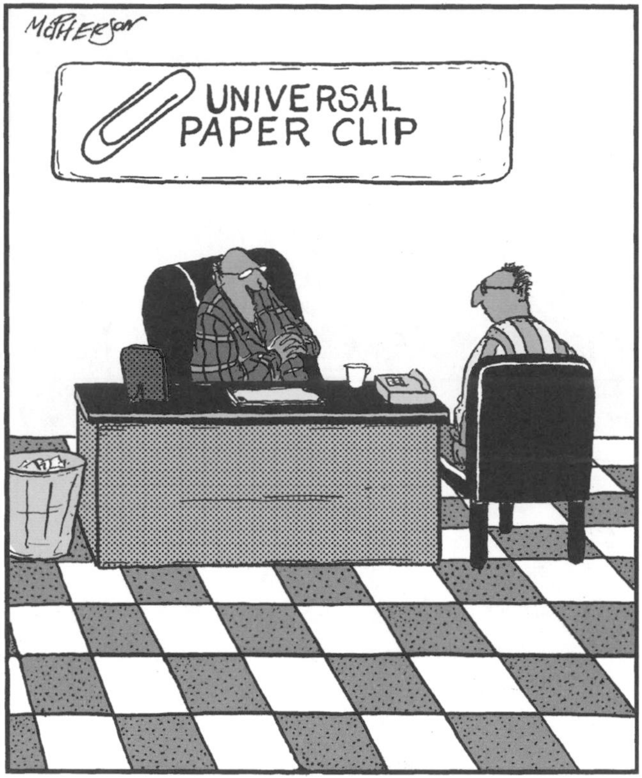
McPHERSON
UNIVERSAL PAPER CLIP

"We're looking for a creative, innovative individual to head up our new Research and Development Department."

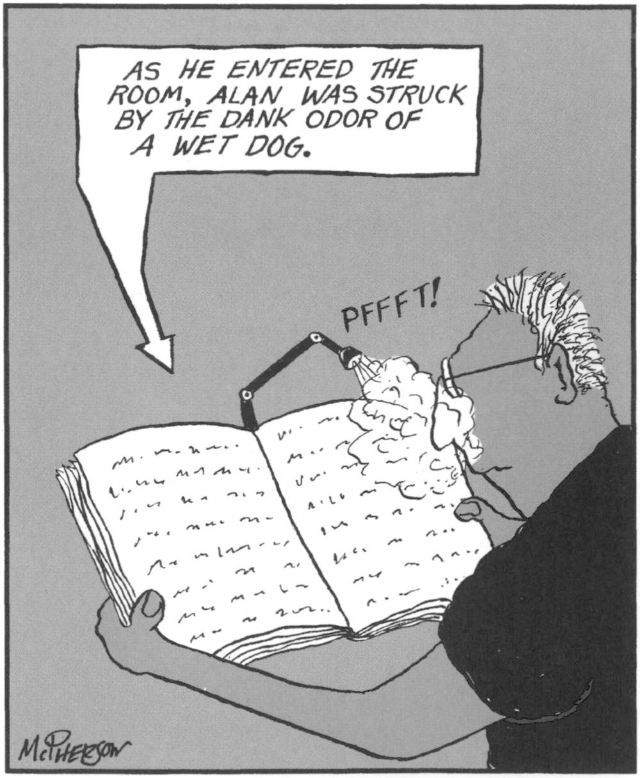
AS HE ENTERED THE ROOM, ALAN WAS STRUCK BY THE DANK ODOR OF A WET DOG.
PFFFT!
McPHERSON

A major breakthrough in book publishing: aromatic books

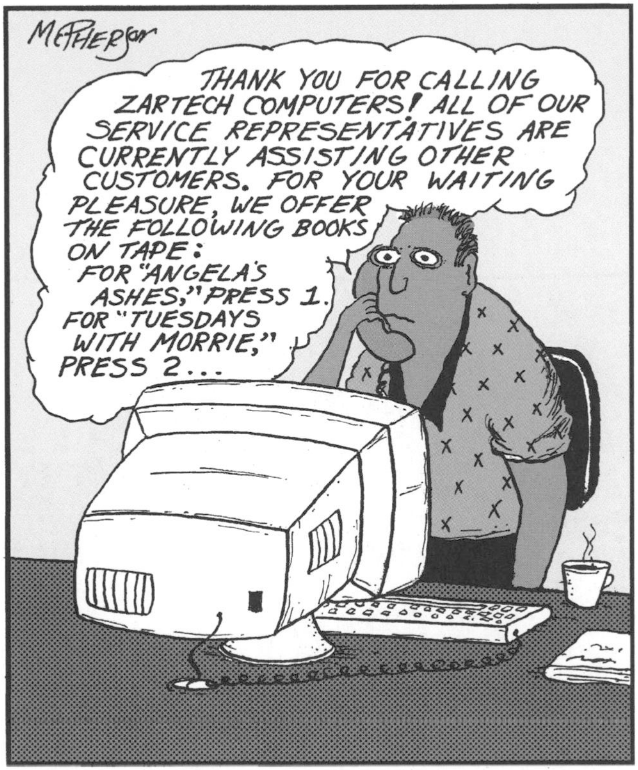
McPherson
THANK YOU FOR CALLING ZARTECH COMPUTERS! ALL OF OUR SERVICE REPRESENTATIVES ARE CURRENTLY ASSISTING OTHER CUSTOMERS. FOR YOUR WAITING PLEASURE, WE OFFER THE FOLLOWING BOOKS ON TAPE: FOR "ANGELA'S ASHES," PRESS 1. FOR "TUESDAYS WITH MORRIE," PRESS 2...

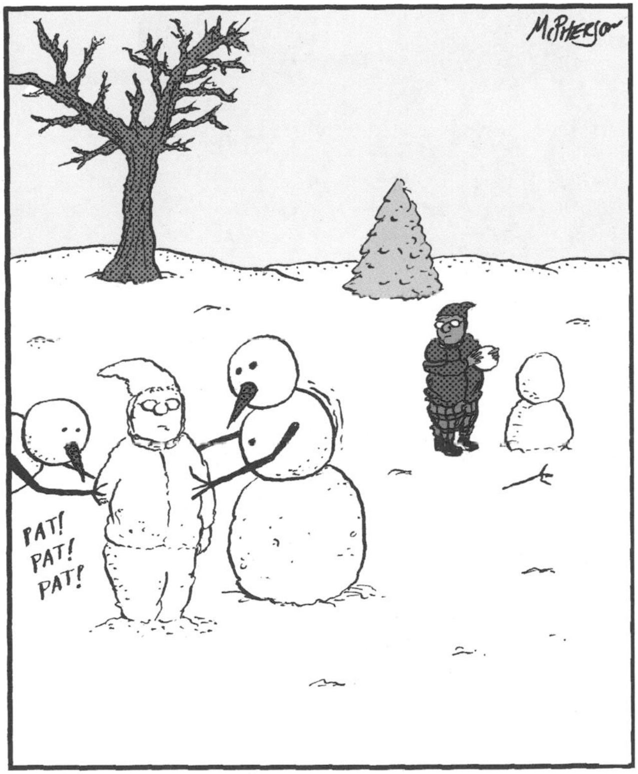
McPherson
PAT! PAT! PAT!

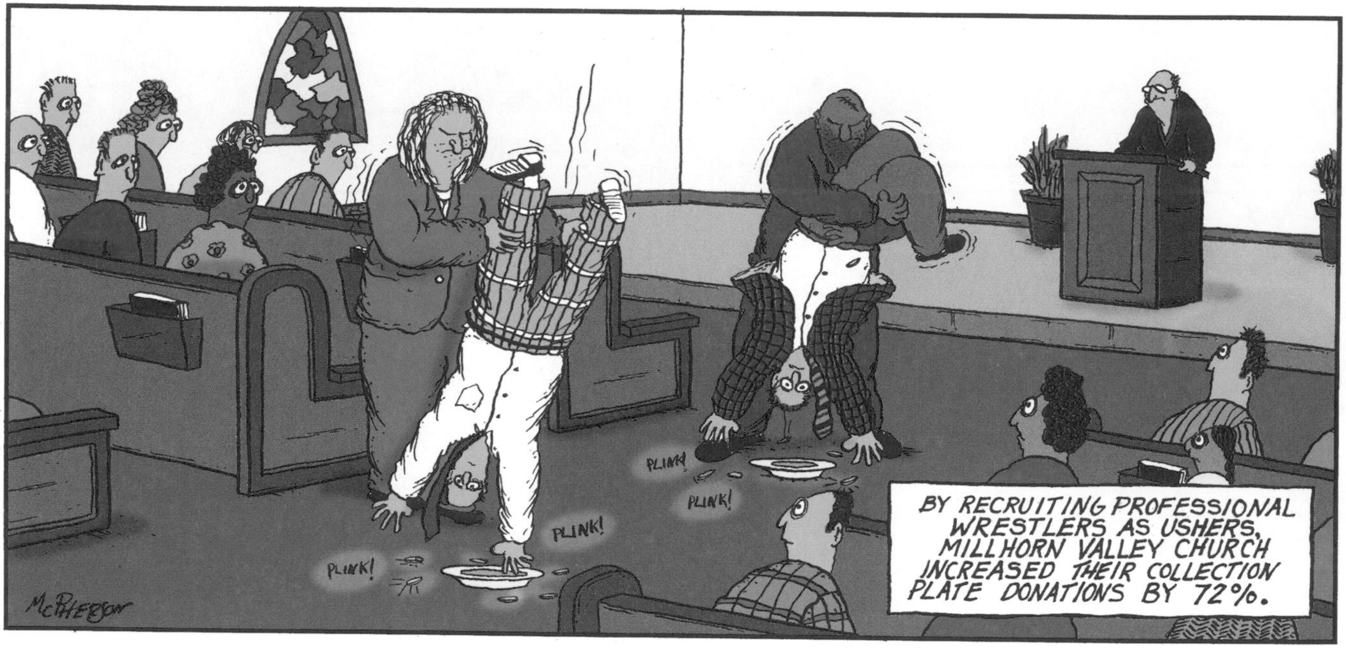

PLINK!
PLINK!
PLINK!
PLINK!
BY RECRUITING PROFESSIONAL WRESTLERS AS USHERS, MILLHORN VALLEY CHURCH INCREASED THEIR COLLECTION PLATE DONATIONS BY 72%.
McPHERSON

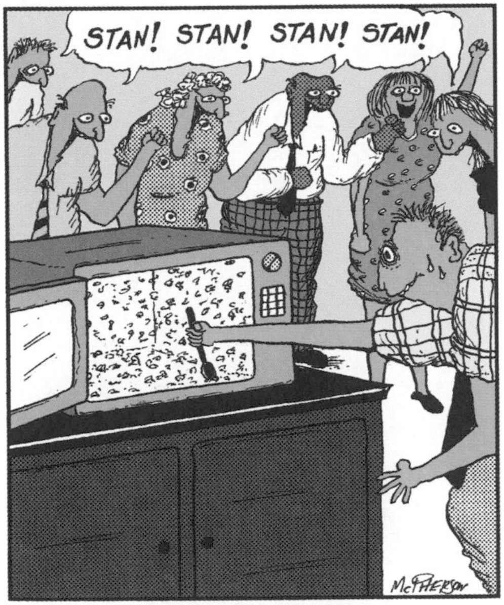
STAN! STAN! STAN! STAN!
McPHERSON

Eager to earn the $200 that had been raised by his coworkers, Stan attempts to eat every spec of crud from the inside of the break-room microwave.

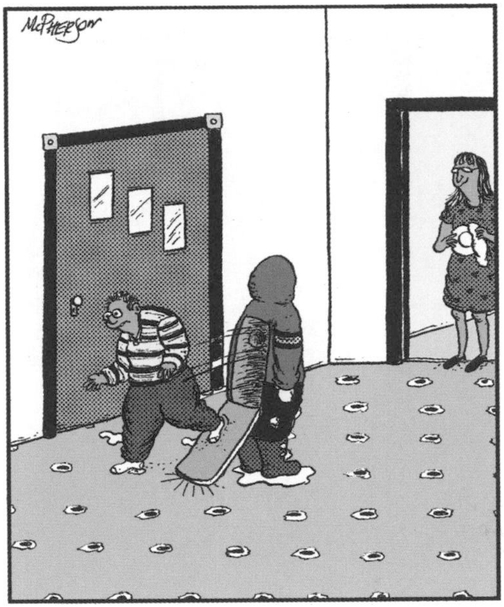
McPHERSON

Donny's snowsuit escape hatch made trips to the restroom a piece of cake.

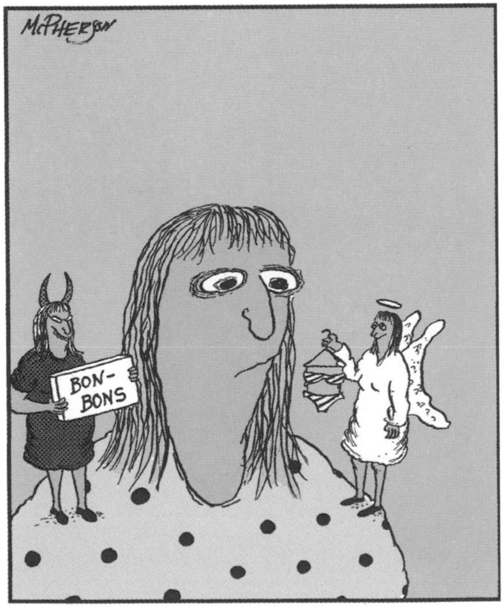
McPHERSON
BON-
BONS

Francesca's annual Valentine's Day dilemma

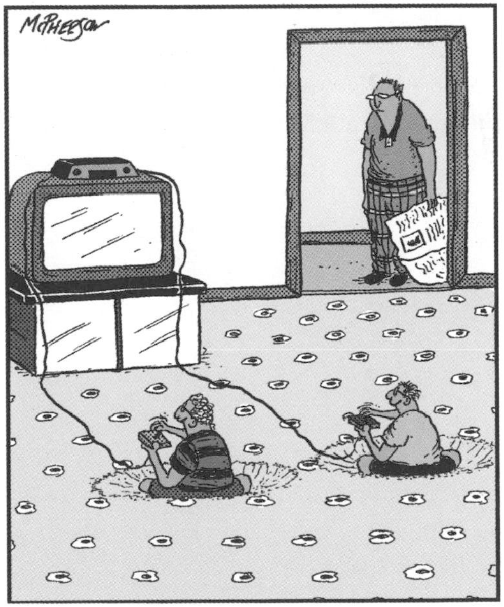
McPHERSON

How to tell when your kids are playing too much Sony PlayStation

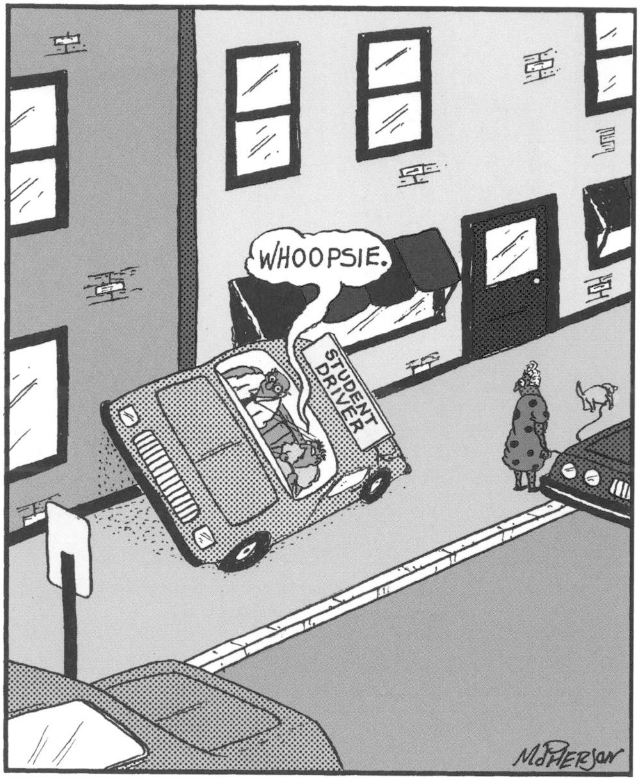
WHOOPSIE.
STUDENT DRIVER
McPHERSON

Wally fails the parallel parking portion of his exam.

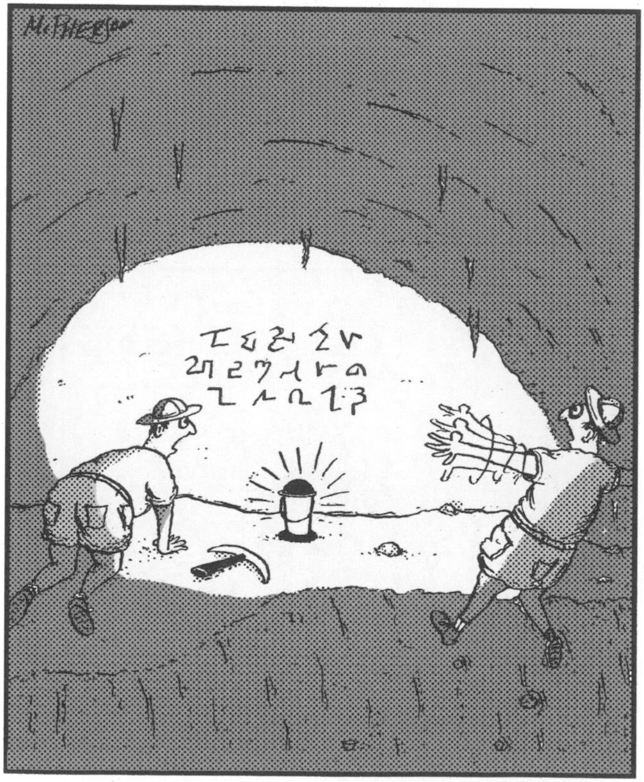

"It says, 'W-A-T-C-H . . . Y-O-U-R . . . S-T-E-P!'"

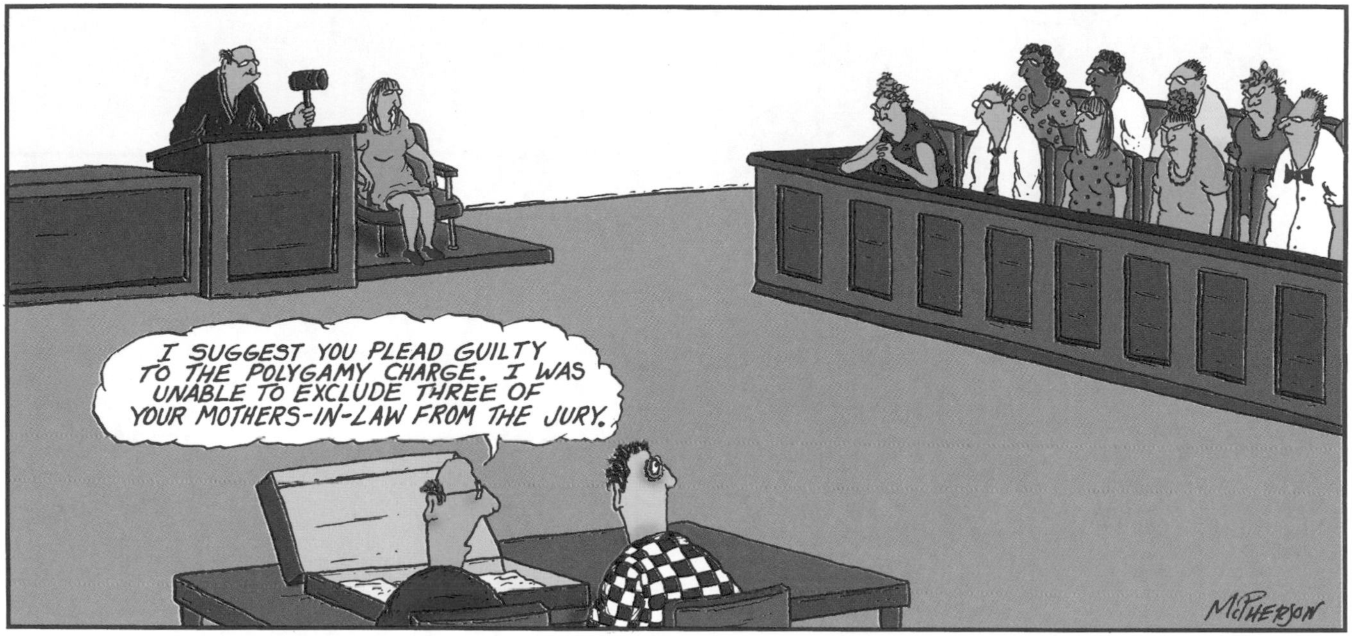
I SUGGEST YOU PLEAD GUILTY TO THE POLYGAMY CHARGE. I WAS UNABLE TO EXCLUDE THREE OF YOUR MOTHERS-IN-LAW FROM THE JURY.
McPHERSON

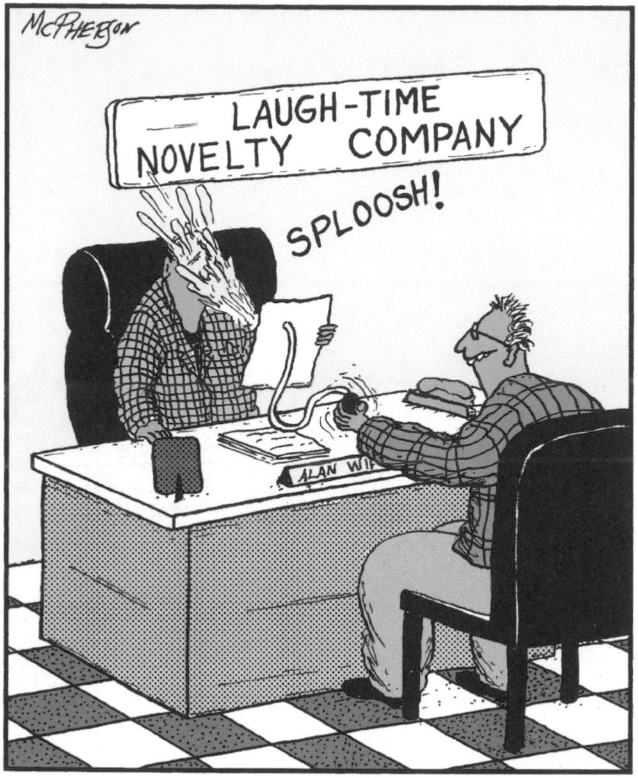
McPHERSON
LAUGH-TIME NOVELTY COMPANY
SPLOOSH!

Just moments into the interview, Eric scores big points with the director of personnel.

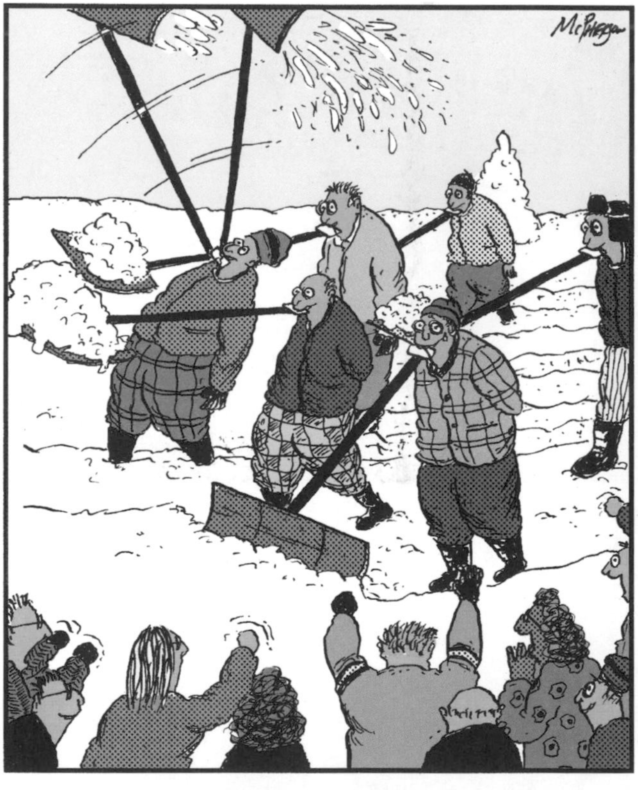
McPherson

At the Sheboygan, Wisconsin, No-Hands-Allowed Snow Shoveling Contest

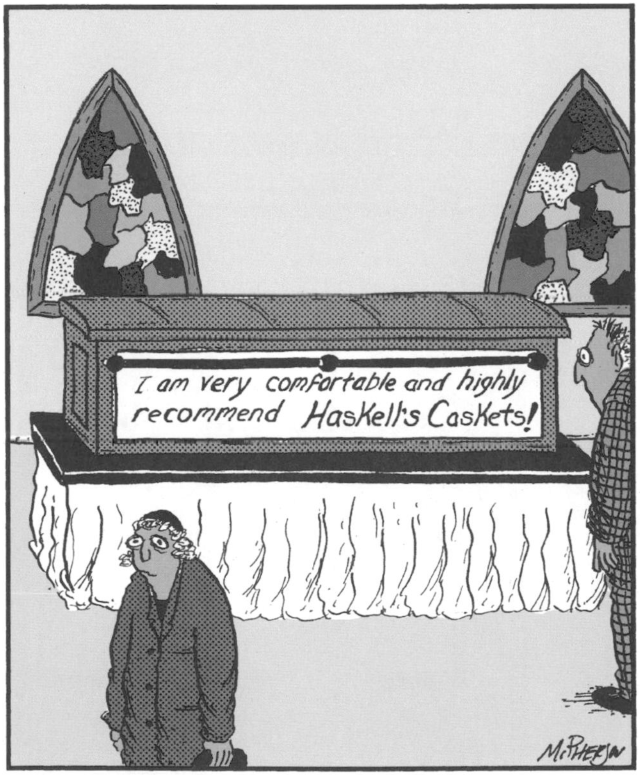
I am very comfortable and highly recommend Haskell's Caskets!
McPHERSON

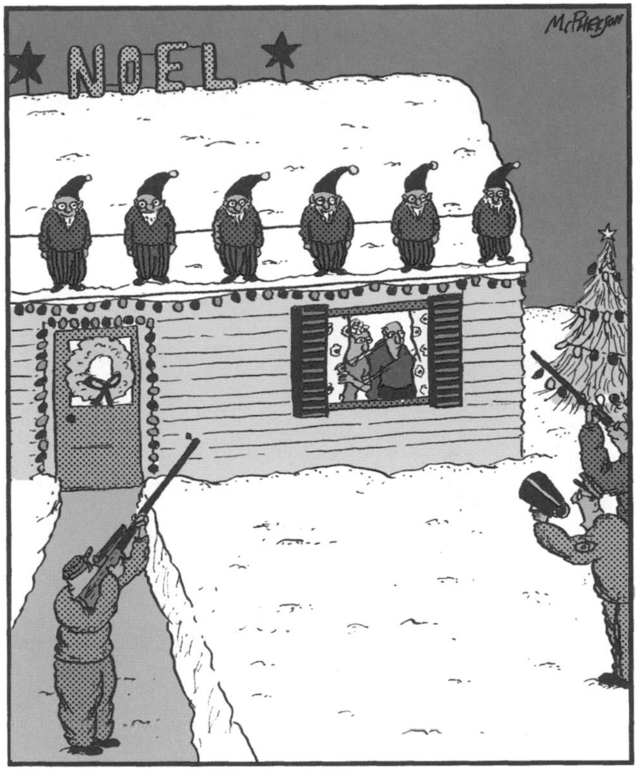
McPHERSON
NOEL

"Mr. Hays, you are violating city ordinance number 3110: leaving Christmas lights up past February 15! You have ten minutes to start removing them, or our sharpshooters will begin taking out your elves one by one!"

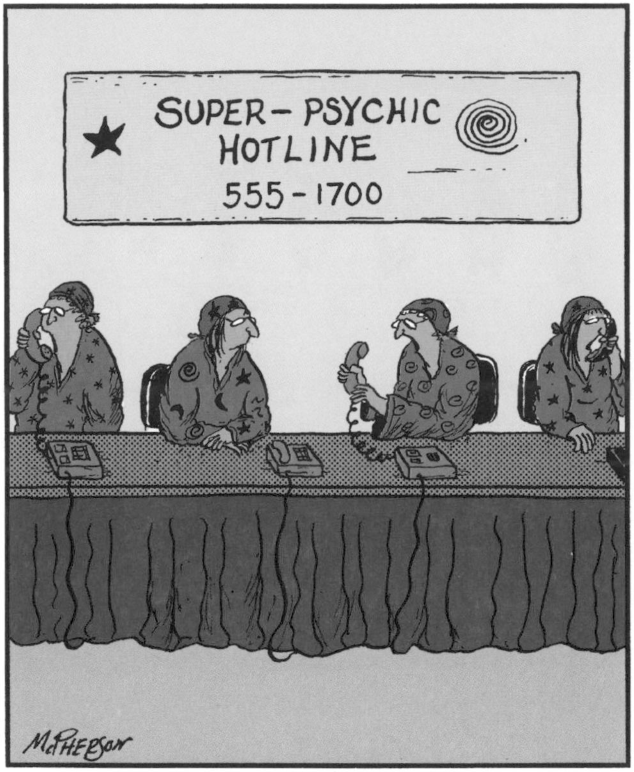
SUPER-PSYCHIC HOTLINE
555-1700
McPHERSON

"It's your broker. He says that hot new stock of yours just tanked."

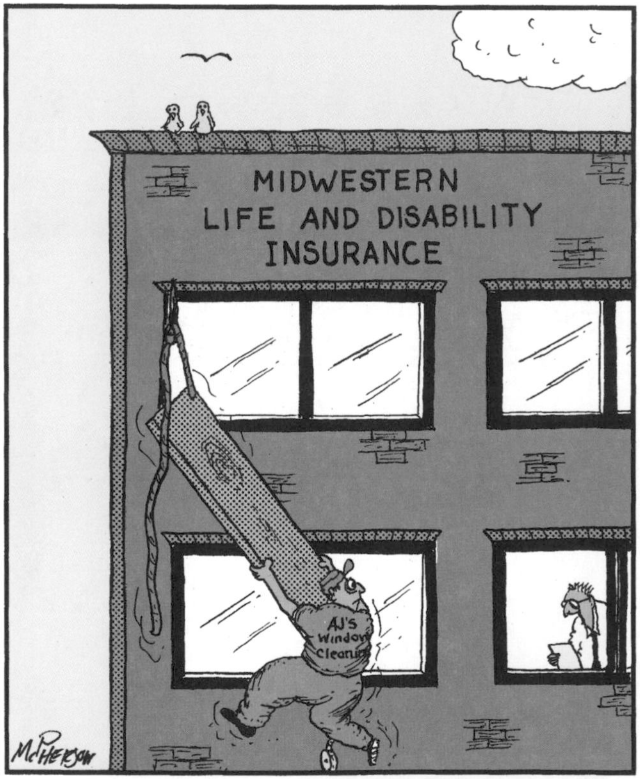
MIDWESTERN
LIFE AND DISABILITY
INSURANCE
McPHERSON

"Boy, how quickly things change. If you had asked me five minutes ago to give you a quote on disability insurance, it would have been $128 per month. Now it's . . . who-weee! You don't even want to know!"

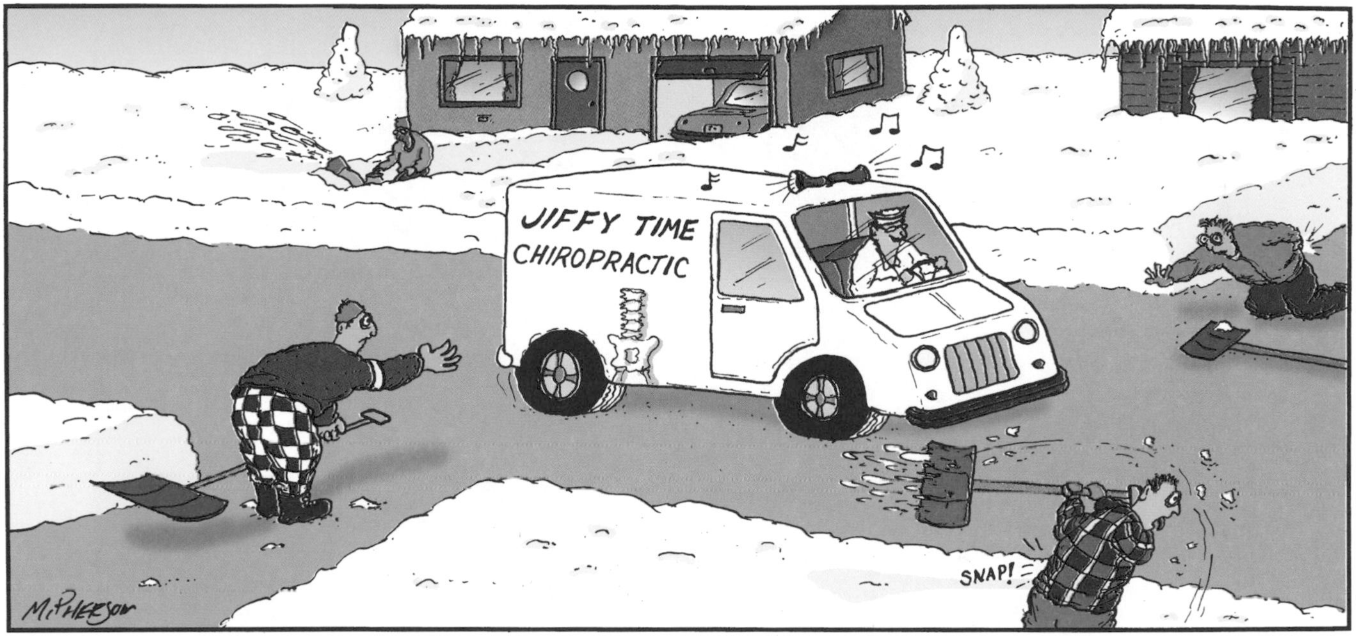
JIFFY TIME
CHIROPRACTIC
SNAP!
McPHERSON

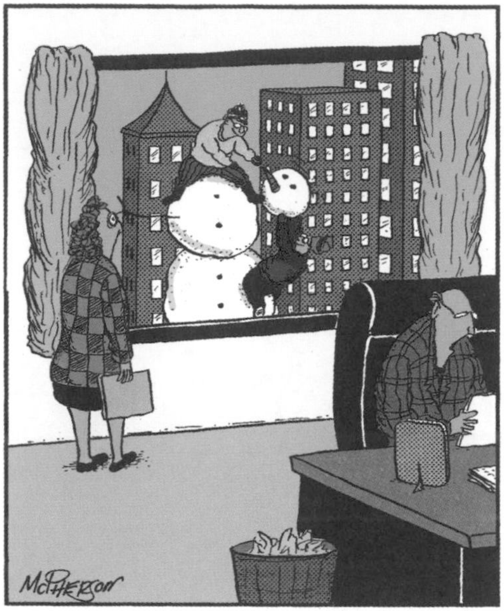
McPHERSON

"What floor are we on?! The twelfth, of course! What the heck are you asking me that for?"

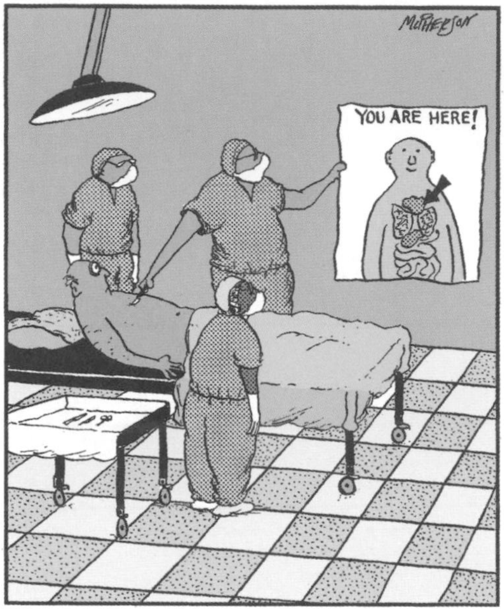
McPHERSON
YOU ARE HERE!

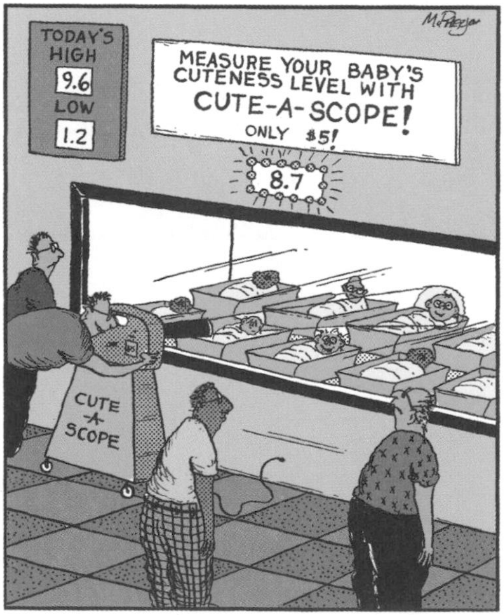
McPHERSON
TODAY'S HIGH
9.6
LOW
1.2
MEASURE YOUR BABY'S CUTENESS LEVEL WITH
CUTE-A-SCOPE!
ONLY $5!
8.7
CUTE -A- SCOPE

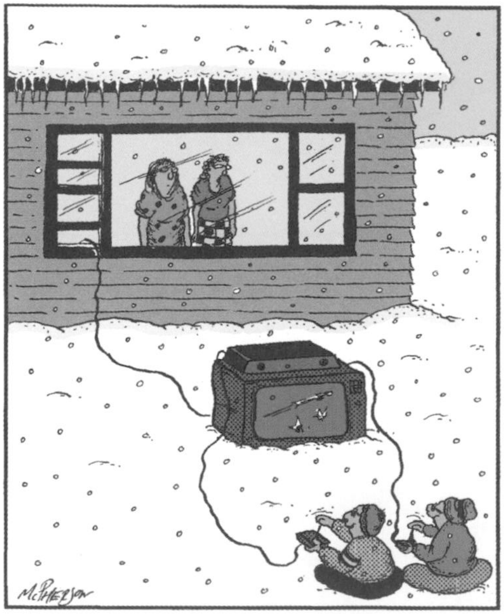
McPHERSON

"It's the only way we can get them to play outside."

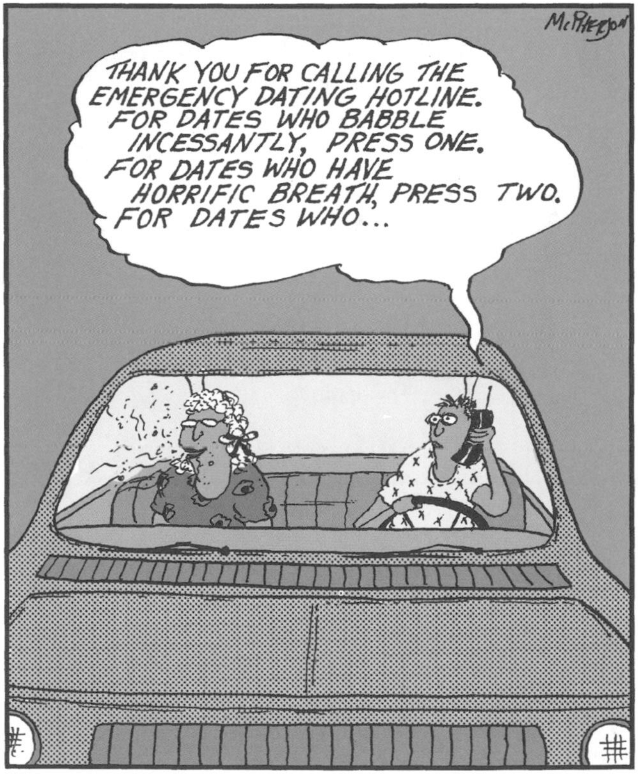

McPherson
THANK YOU FOR CALLING THE EMERGENCY DATING HOTLINE. FOR DATES WHO BABBLE INCESSANTLY, PRESS ONE. FOR DATES WHO HAVE HORRIFIC BREATH, PRESS TWO. FOR DATES WHO...

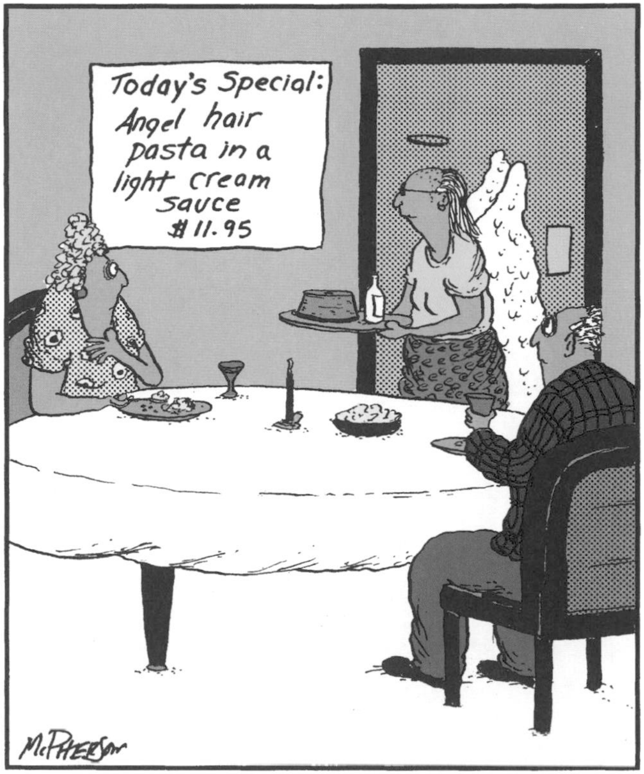

Today's Special: Angel hair pasta in a light cream sauce $11.95
McPherson

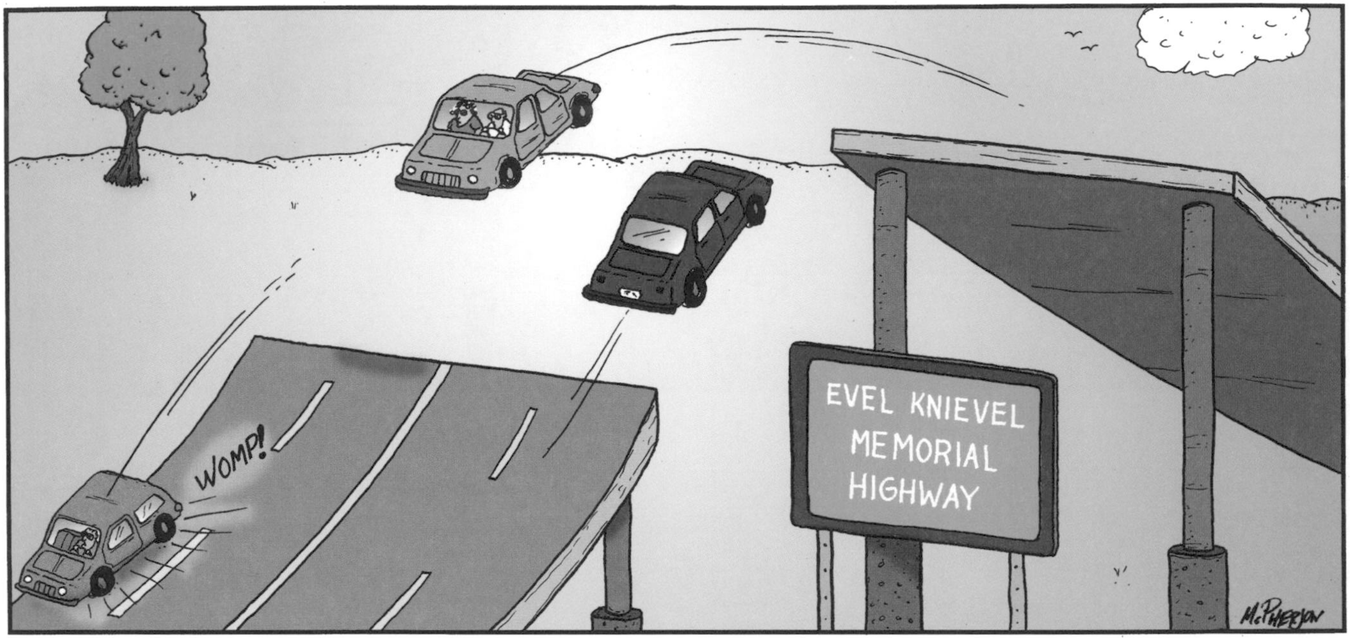
WOMP!
EVEL KNIEVEL
MEMORIAL
HIGHWAY
McPHERSON

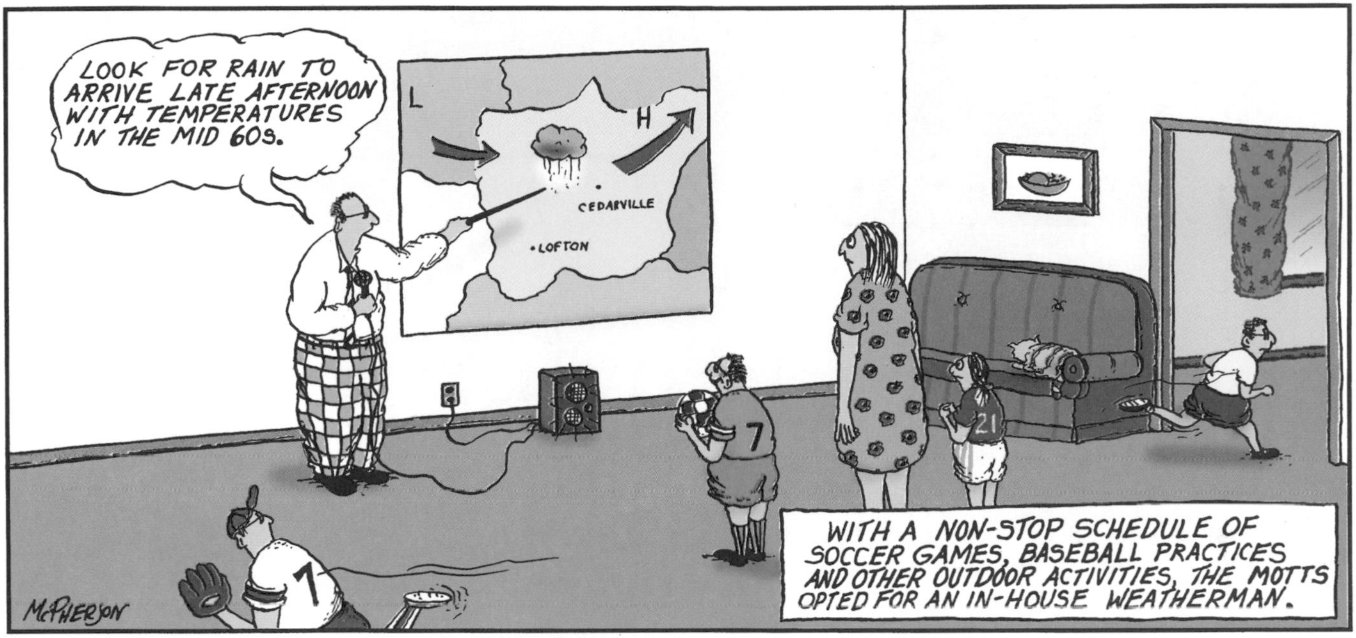
LOOK FOR RAIN TO ARRIVE LATE AFTERNOON WITH TEMPERATURES IN THE MID 60s.
L
H
CEDARVILLE
LOFTON
7
7
21
WITH A NON-STOP SCHEDULE OF SOCCER GAMES, BASEBALL PRACTICES AND OTHER OUTDOOR ACTIVITIES, THE MOTTS OPTED FOR AN IN-HOUSE WEATHERMAN.
McPHERSON

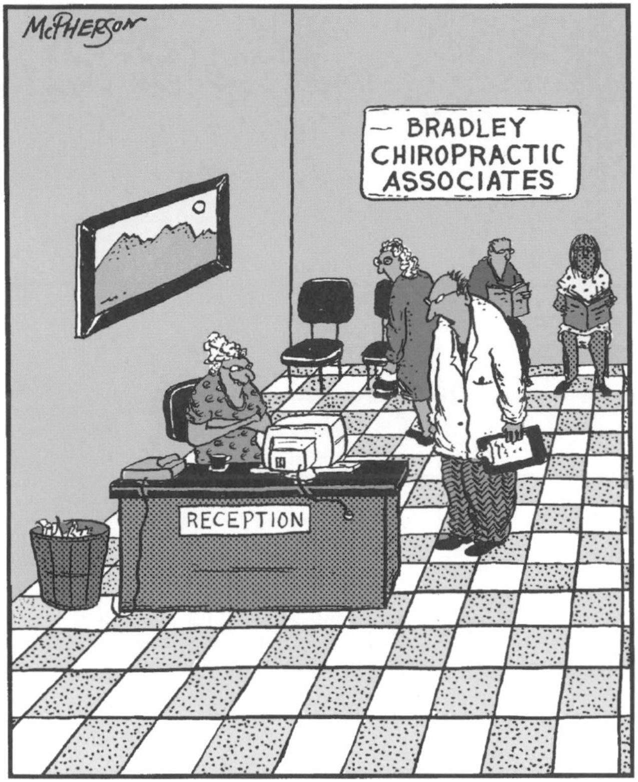
McPHERSON
BRADLEY
CHIROPRACTIC
ASSOCIATES
RECEPTION

"Gloria, I would appreciate it if you would stop greeting the patients with 'Welcome to the Crack House!'"

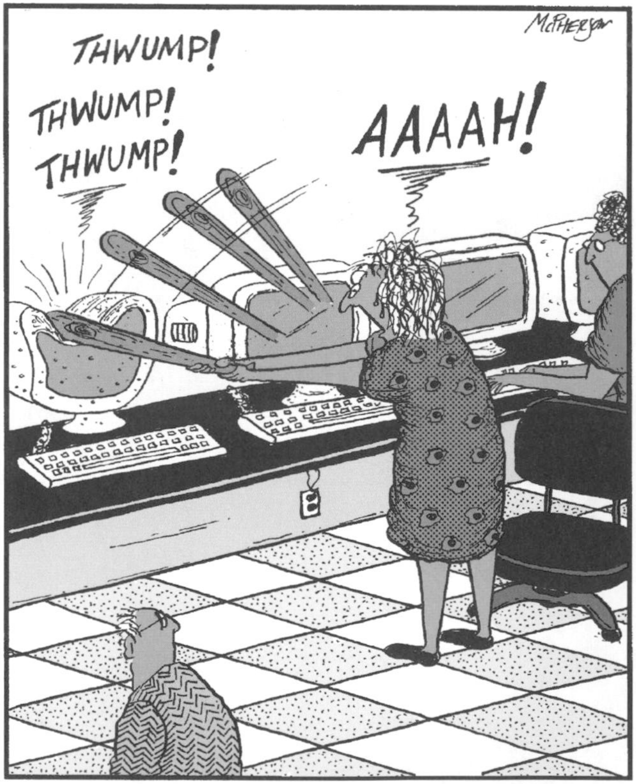
McPHERSON
THWUMP!
THWUMP!
THWUMP!
AAAAH!

The company's new rubber decoy PCs allowed employees to vent their frustrations without ruining vital equipment.

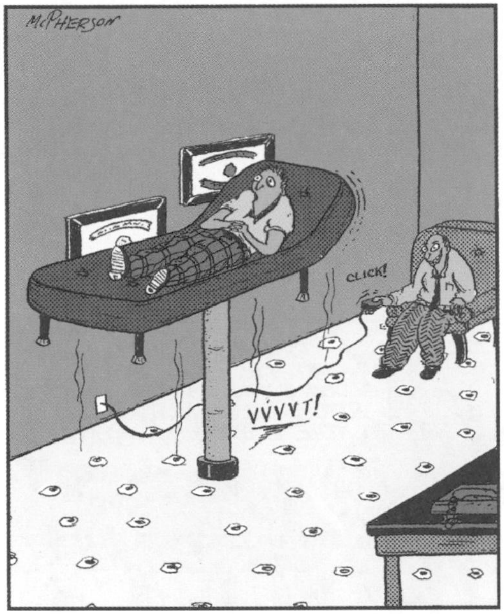
McPHERSON
CLICK!
VVVVT!

"When did it begin? I dunno, I guess my fear of heights started when my dad used to make me clean the leaves out of the rain gutters."

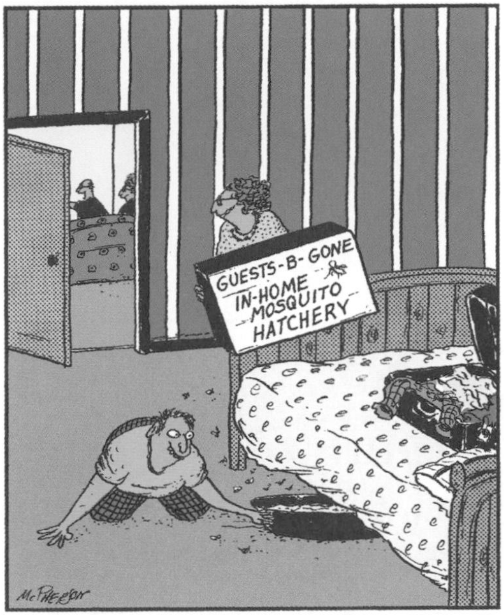
GUESTS-B-GONE
IN-HOME
MOSQUITO
HATCHERY
McPHERSON

With their annoying relatives momentarily distracted, the Bigelows went to work.

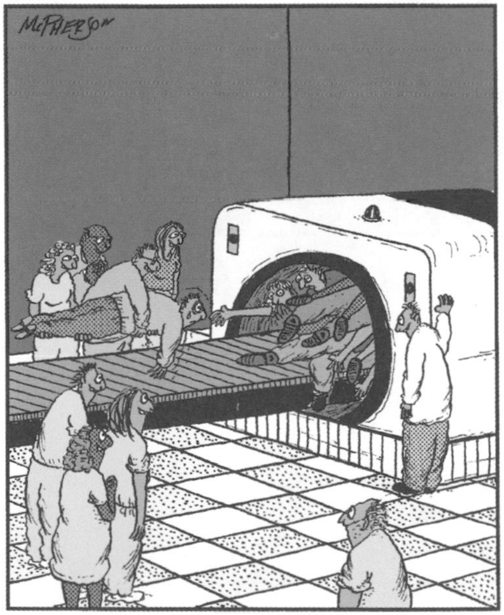
McPHERSON

Fogburn Hospital's annual tradition of seeing how many interns they can fit into an MRI

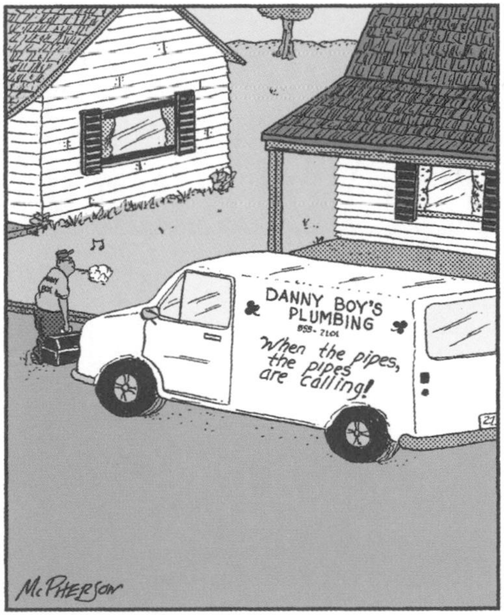
DANNY BOY'S
PLUMBING
When the pipes,
the pipes
are calling!
McPHERSON

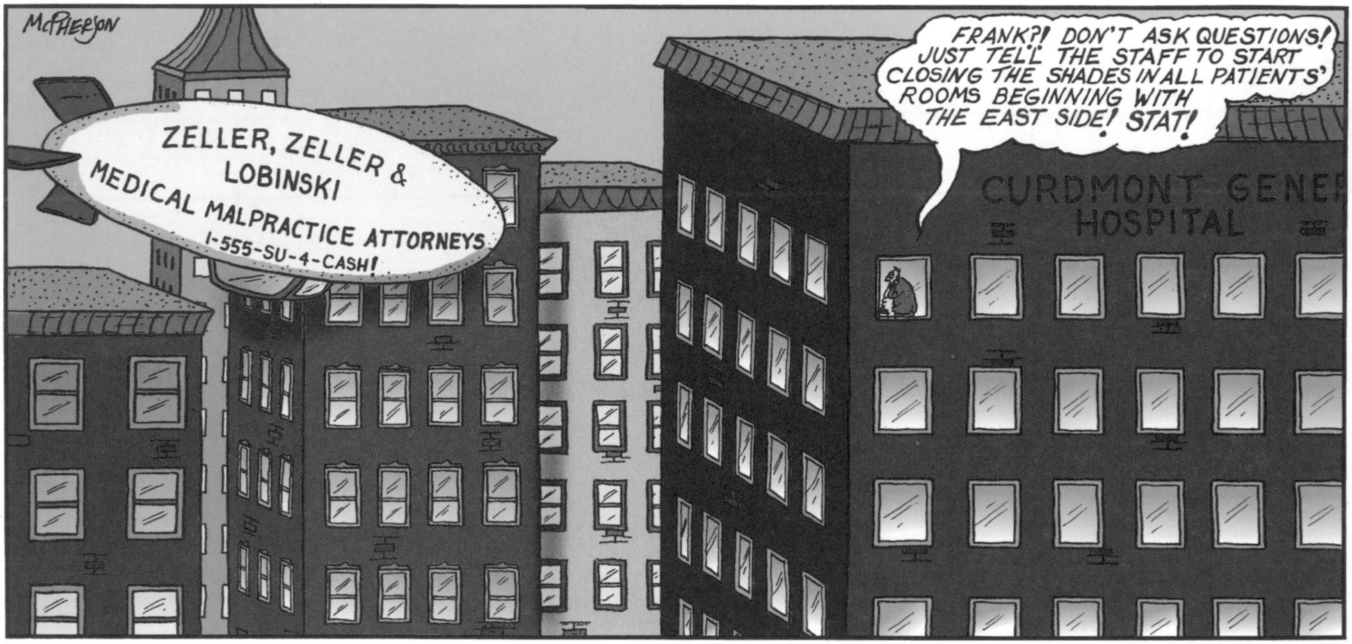
McPHERSON
ZELLER, ZELLER & LOBINSKI
MEDICAL MALPRACTICE ATTORNEYS
1-555-SU-4-CASH!
FRANK?! DON'T ASK QUESTIONS! JUST TELL THE STAFF TO START CLOSING THE SHADES IN ALL PATIENTS' ROOMS BEGINNING WITH THE EAST SIDE! STAT!
CURDMONT GENER
HOSPITAL

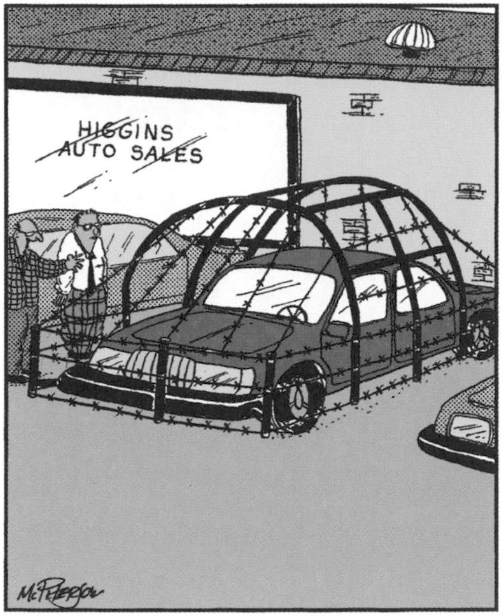
HIGGINS
AUTO SALES
McPHERSON

"And here, for just $700, is our *deluxe* security system!"

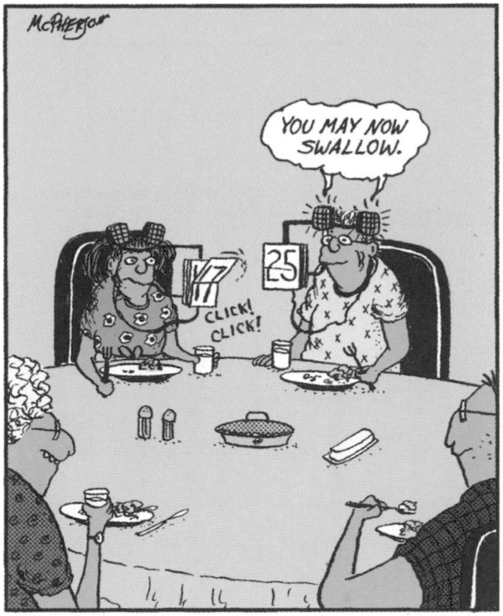
McPHERSON
YOU MAY NOW SWALLOW.
CLICK! CLICK!

Thanks to the Chew-O-Matic 4000™, the Kulp children never again unsafely wolfed down their food.

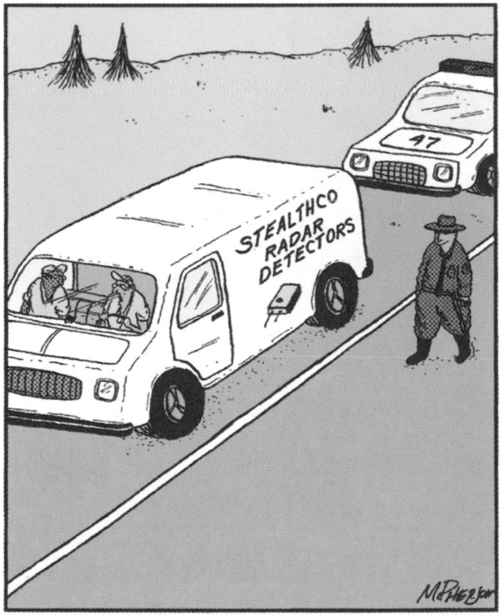
STEALTHCO RADAR DETECTORS
47
McPHERSON

"Something tells me this ain't gonna look good on our report."

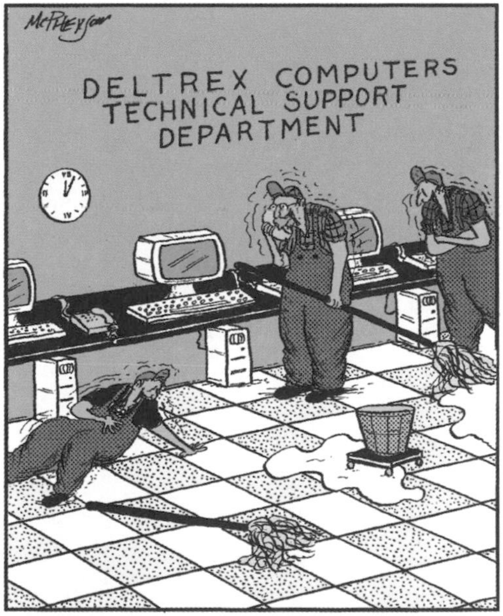
McPHERSON
DELTREX COMPUTERS
TECHNICAL SUPPORT
DEPARTMENT

"OK, open yer . . . watcha-call . . . hard drive, and find yer, uh . . . refragulation file . . . see it? Keep lookin' . . . not there?! Oooo, you got troubles! OK, try this . . . hit the 'C' key 187 times as fast as you can!"

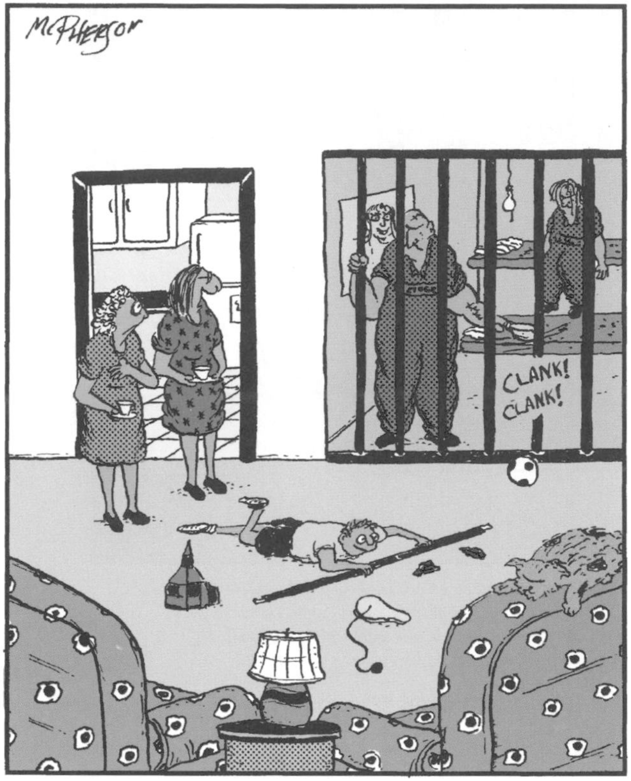
McPHERSON
CLANK!
CLANK!

"We've been needing some extra income. Then Don read about prison overcrowding and a program called the Private Citizens Convict Boarding Inititative . . ."

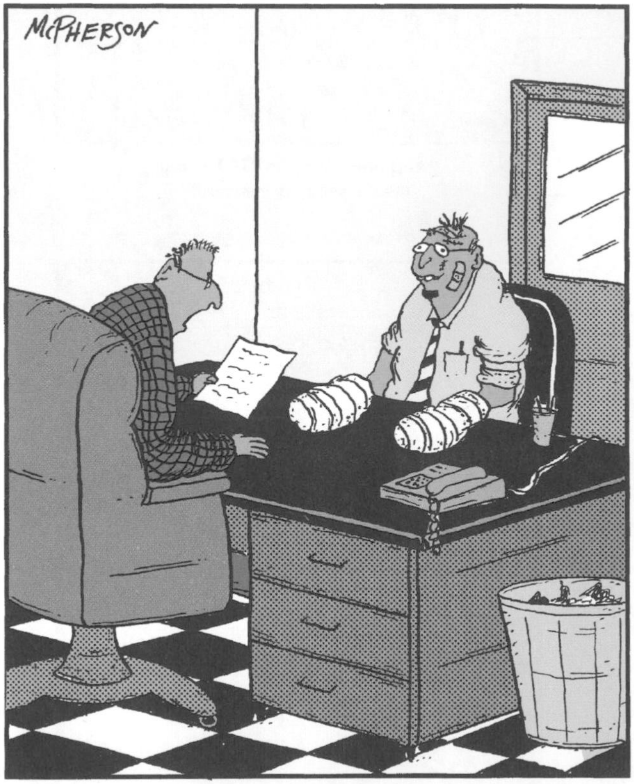
McPHERSON

"Thirteen years as a quality-control technician for International Barbed Wire Inc. Impressive! Tell me a bit more about that position and why you've decided to move on."

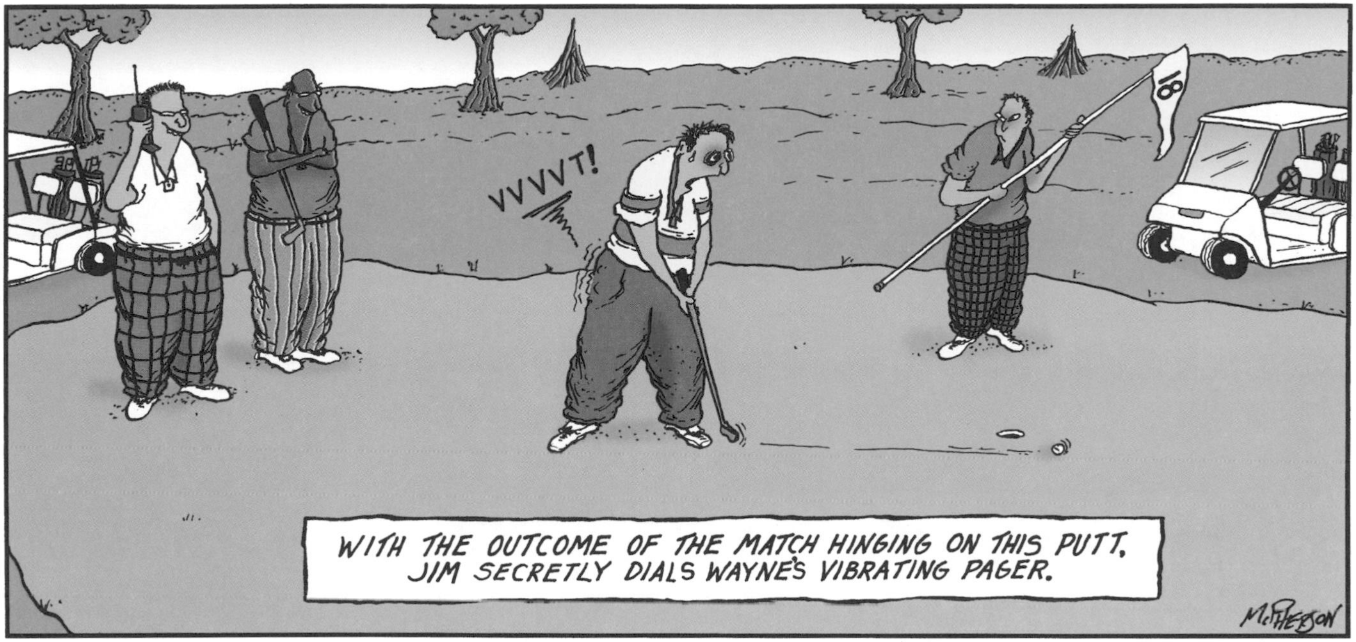
VVVVT!
18
WITH THE OUTCOME OF THE MATCH HINGING ON THIS PUTT, JIM SECRETLY DIALS WAYNE'S VIBRATING PAGER.
McPHERSON

"Those morons down in 2-C had a
skylight installed!"

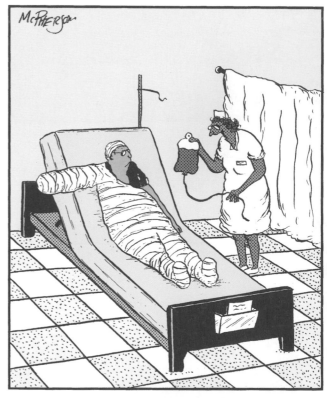

"Good news! It's Bottomless IV day! Drink up!
There's plenty more where this came from!"

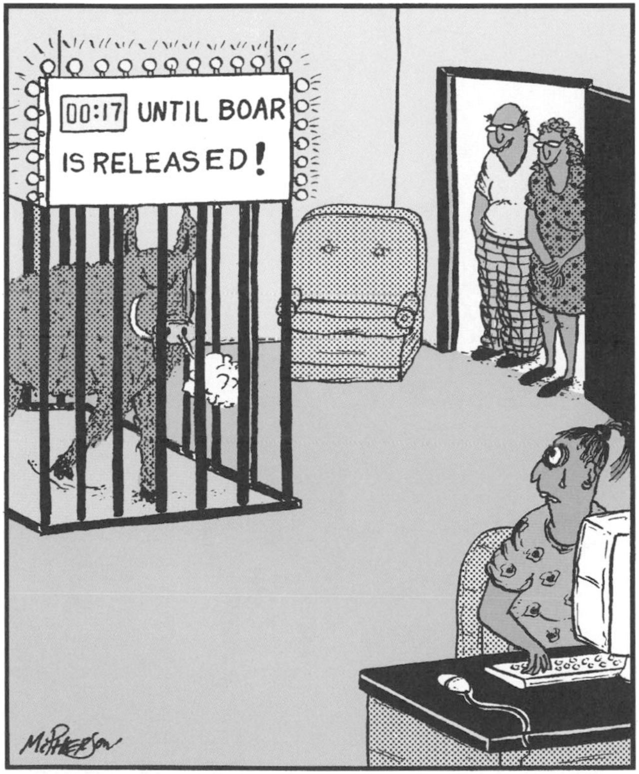
00:17 UNTIL BOAR IS RELEASED!
McPHERSON

At last the Hillmans found an effective way to limit their teen's computer use.

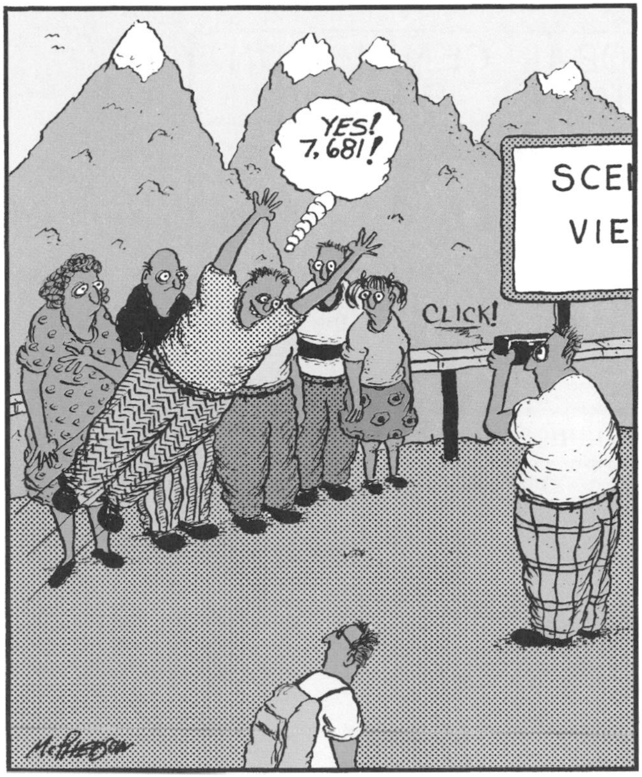
YES! 7,681!
CLICK!
McPHERSON

Barry's obsession with getting into as many tourist photos as possible continues.

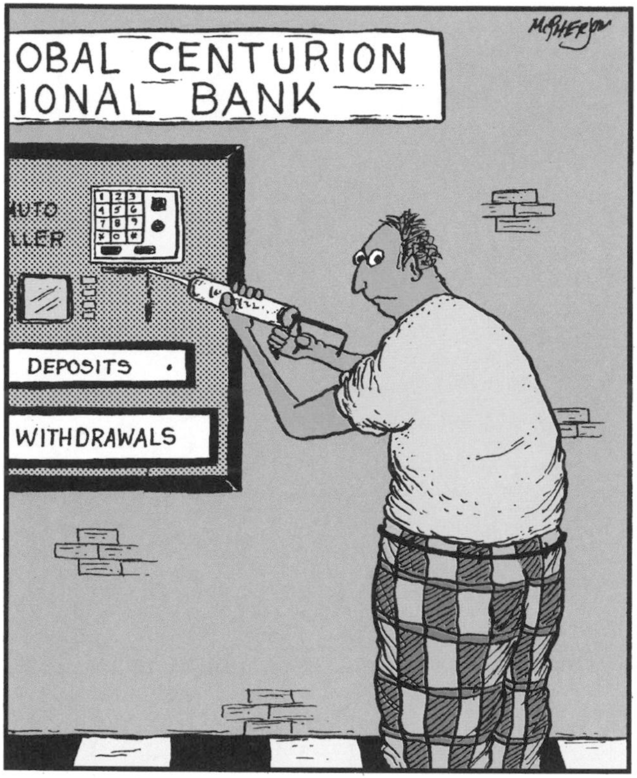

McPHERSON
OBAL CENTURION
IONAL BANK
DEPOSITS
WITHDRAWALS

With his wife's spending spree out of control, Ron desperately caulked the card slots on every ATM within ten miles of his house.

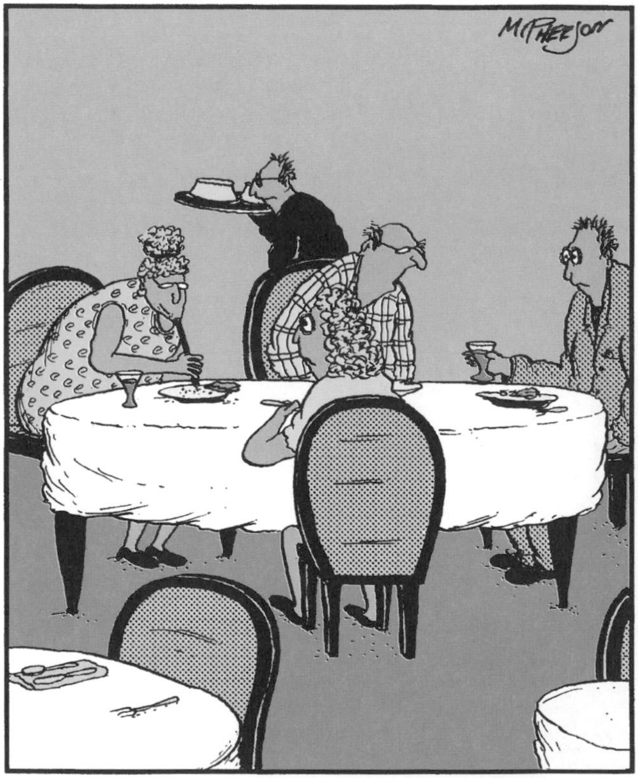

McPHERSON

"It's called the Straw Diet. Brenda eats only what she can cut up small enough to suck through a straw."

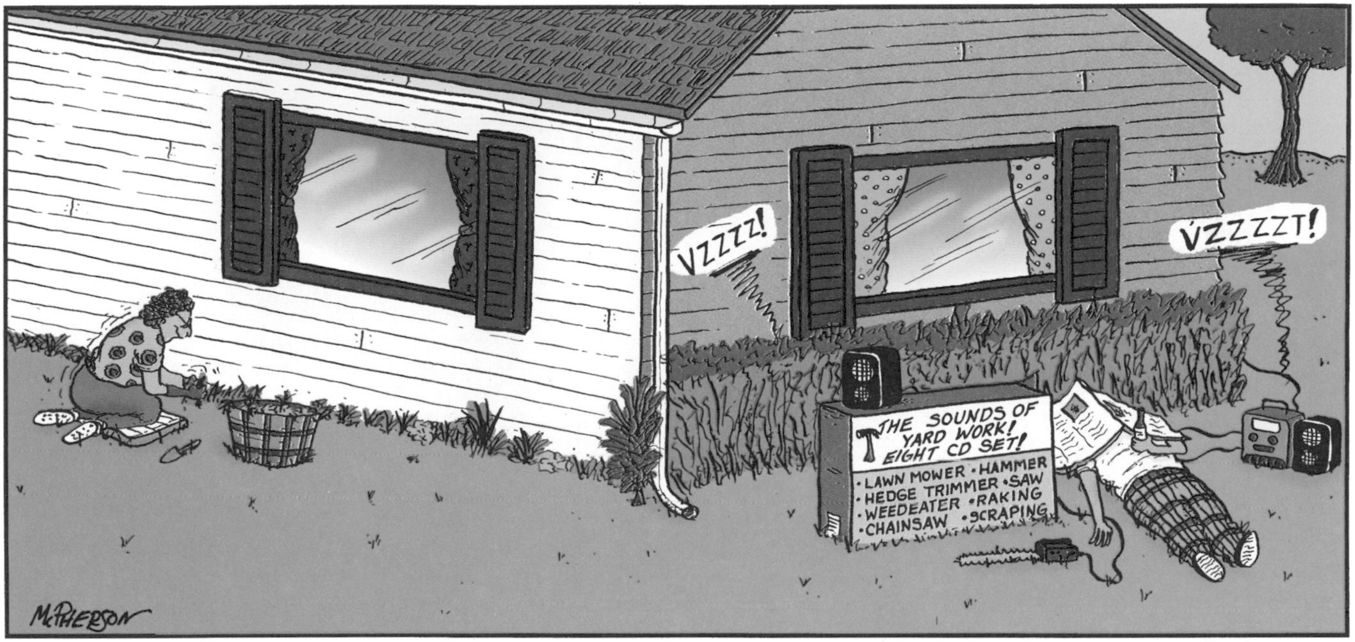
VZZZZ!
VZZZZZT!
THE SOUNDS OF YARD WORK! EIGHT CD SET!
• LAWN MOWER • HAMMER
• HEDGE TRIMMER • SAW
• WEEDEATER • RAKING
• CHAINSAW • SCRAPING
McPHERSON

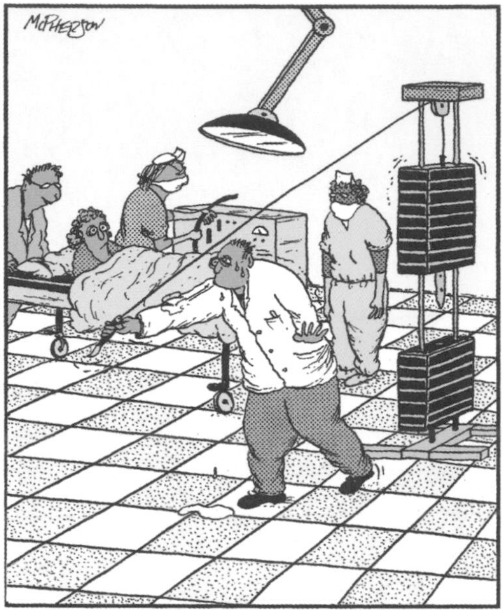
McPHERSON

Before performing any surgery, Dr. Lershman felt it was important to warm up on his Scalpel Master 2000™.

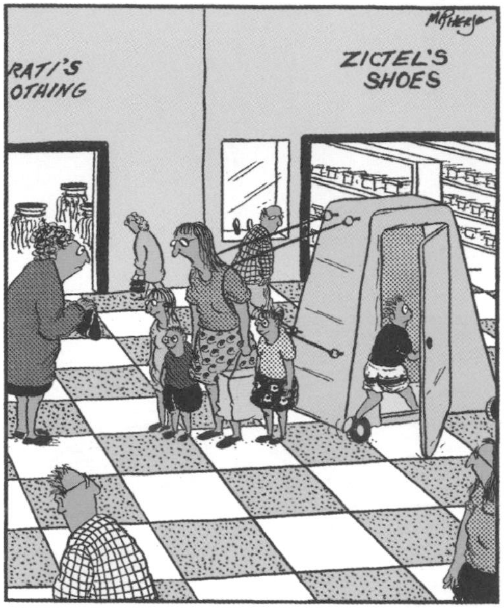
McPHERSON
RATI'S
OTHING
ZICTEL'S
SHOES

"With four kids under the age of six, it's really the only way I can get any shopping done."

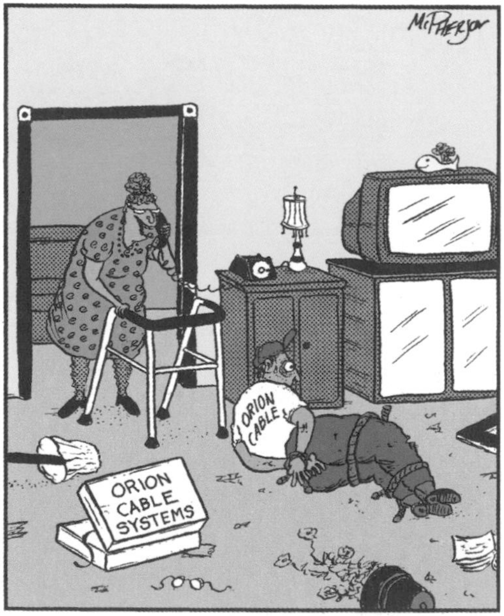
McPHERSON
ORION CABLE
ORION CABLE SYSTEMS

"Clara? I got the rascal! Yep, my cable's all hooked up! Tell Bernice and the others that as soon as he's done hooking you up, he'll be over!"

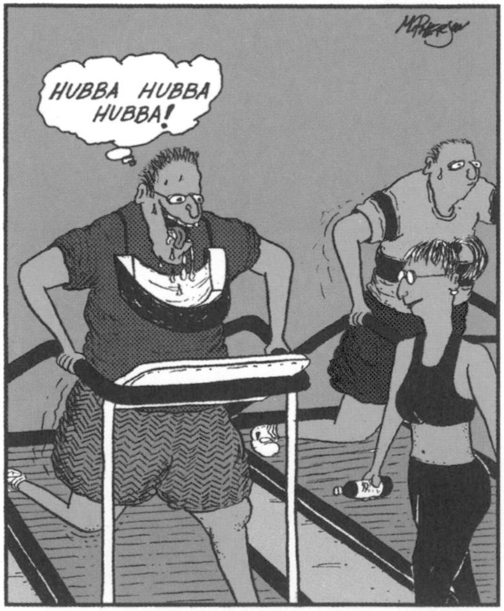
McPHERSON
HUBBA HUBBA HUBBA!

A compulsive ogler, Lanny never went to the gym without his drool guard.

**Wandering where he shouldn't have,
Larry Schmitz unwittingly stars in
Yellowstone's most infamous tragedy.**

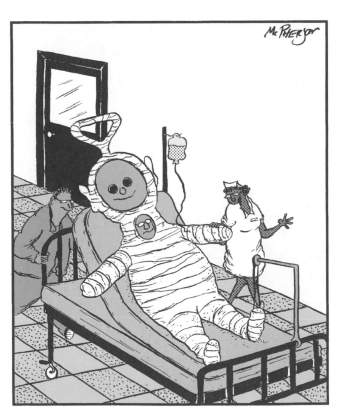

**"Thanks so much for agreeing to this, Mr. Foster.
The kids on the third floor are going to love it."**

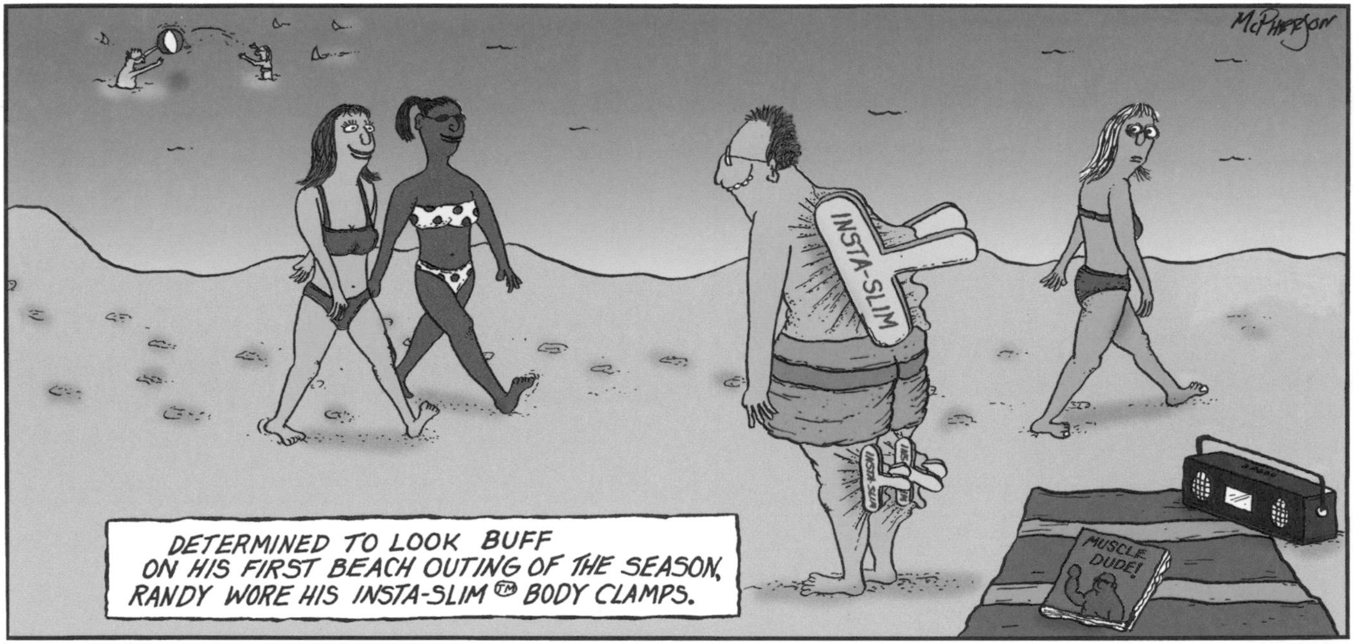
McPHERSON
INSTA-SLIM
MUSCLE DUDE!
DETERMINED TO LOOK BUFF
ON HIS FIRST BEACH OUTING OF THE SEASON,
RANDY WORE HIS INSTA-SLIM™ BODY CLAMPS.

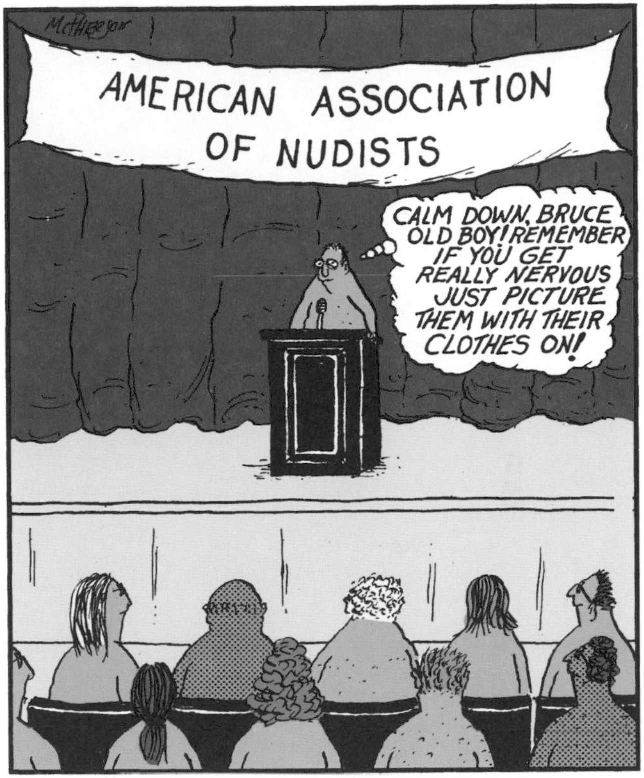
McPherson
AMERICAN ASSOCIATION OF NUDISTS
CALM DOWN, BRUCE OLD BOY! REMEMBER IF YOU GET REALLY NERVOUS JUST PICTURE THEM WITH THEIR CLOTHES ON!

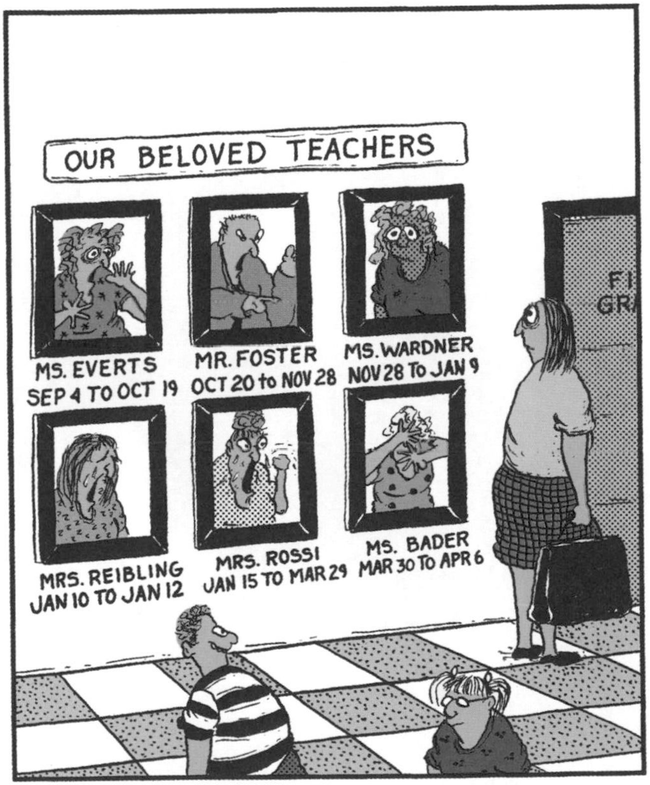
OUR BELOVED TEACHERS
MS. EVERTS SEP 4 TO OCT 19
MR. FOSTER OCT 20 to NOV 28
MS. WARDNER NOV 28 TO JAN 9
MRS. REIBLING JAN 10 TO JAN 12
MRS. ROSSI JAN 15 TO MAR 29
MS. BADER MAR 30 TO APR 6

Replacement teacher Ellen Twitchell has a sudden sense of foreboding.

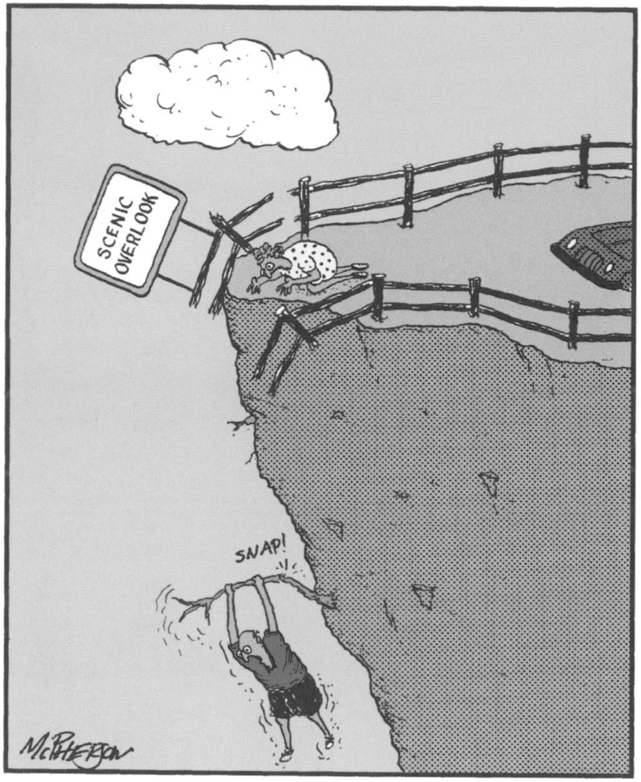
SCENIC OVERLOOK
SNAP!
McPHERSON

"Allan! Quick! Tell me how to drive a stick shift!"

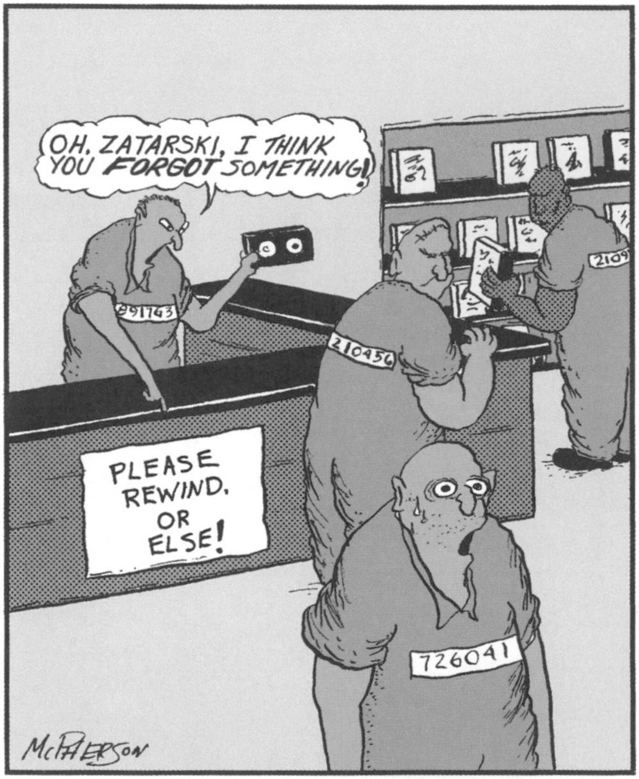
OH, ZATARSKI, I THINK YOU FORGOT SOMETHING!
891743
210456
2109
PLEASE REWIND, OR ELSE!
726041
McPHERSON

As he began to leave the prison's video store, Lionel realizes he has made a grave oversight.

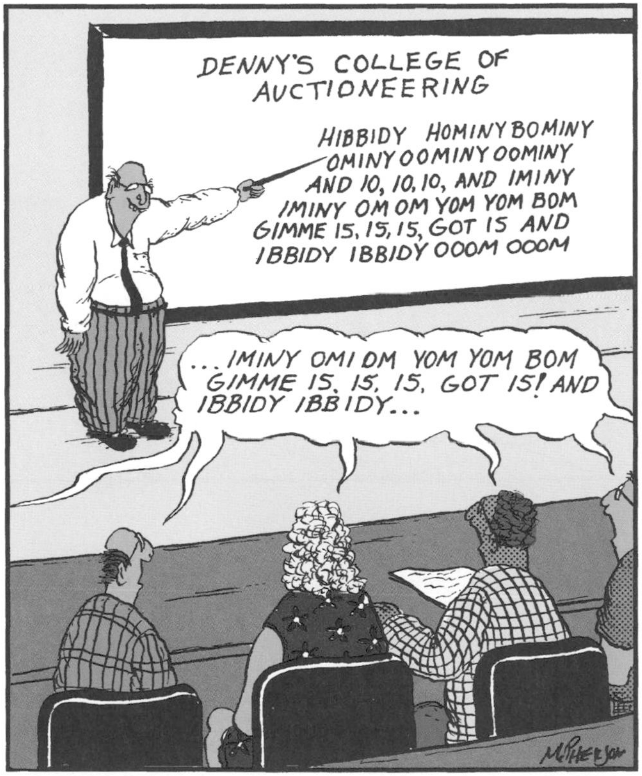
DENNY'S COLLEGE OF AUCTIONEERING
HIBBIDY HOMINY BOMINY OMINY OOMINY OOMINY AND 10, 10, 10, AND IMINY IMINY OM OM YOM YOM BOM GIMME 15, 15, 15, GOT 15 AND IBBIDY IBBIDY OOOM OOOM
...IMINY OM! OM YOM YOM BOM GIMME 15, 15, 15, GOT 15! AND IBBIDY IBBIDY...
McPHERSON

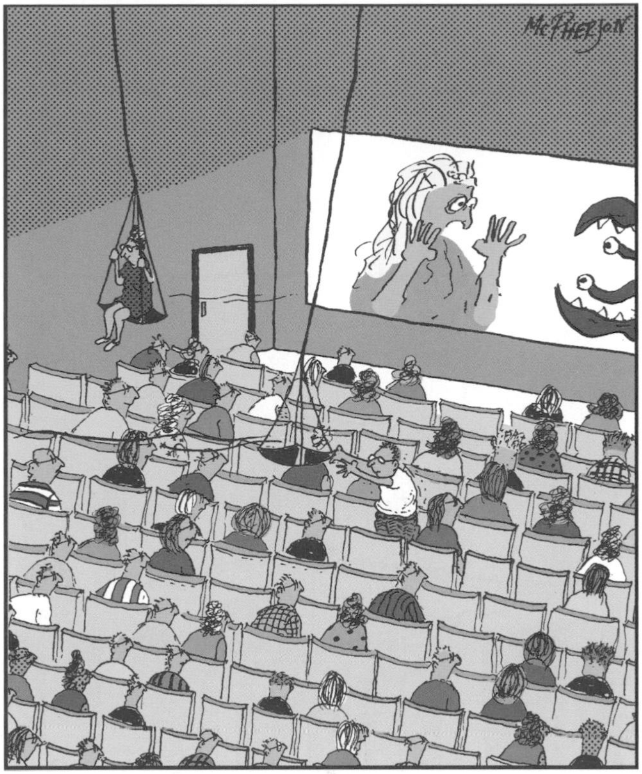
McPHERSON

As a convenience to their patrons located in the middle seats, many theaters have installed restroom sky chairs.

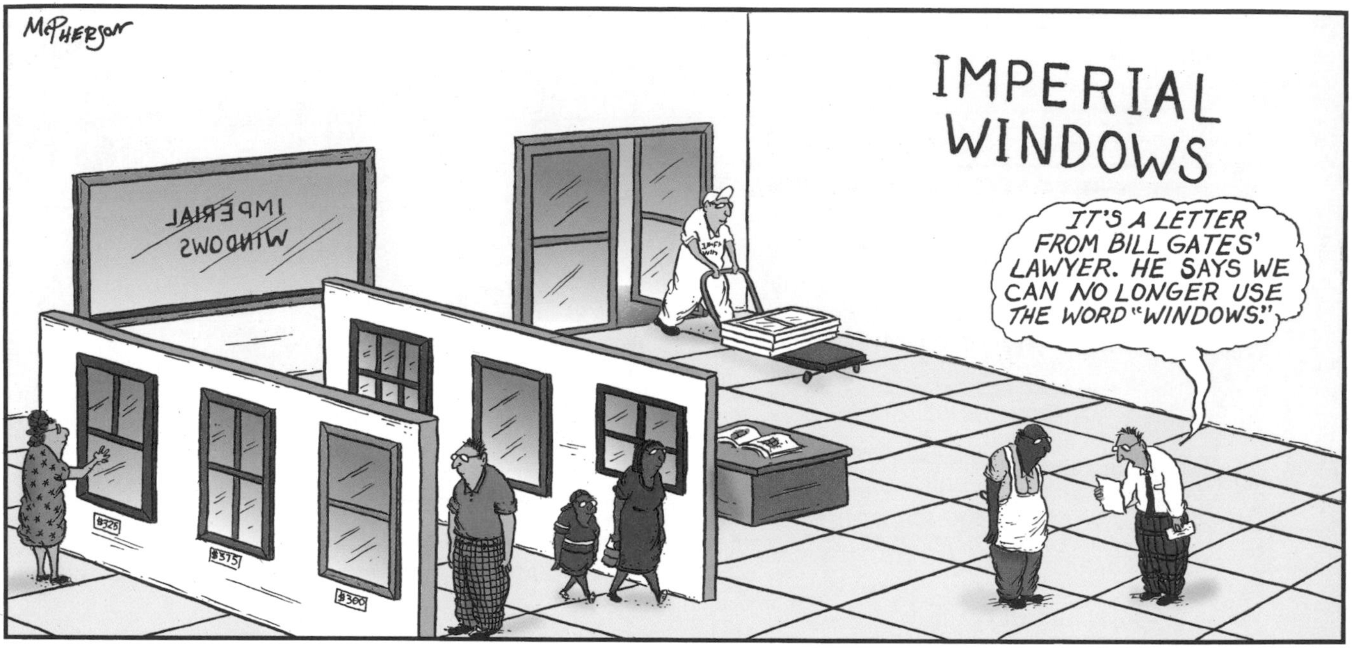
McPherson
IMPERIAL WINDOWS
$325
$375
$300
IT'S A LETTER FROM BILL GATES' LAWYER. HE SAYS WE CAN NO LONGER USE THE WORD "WINDOWS."

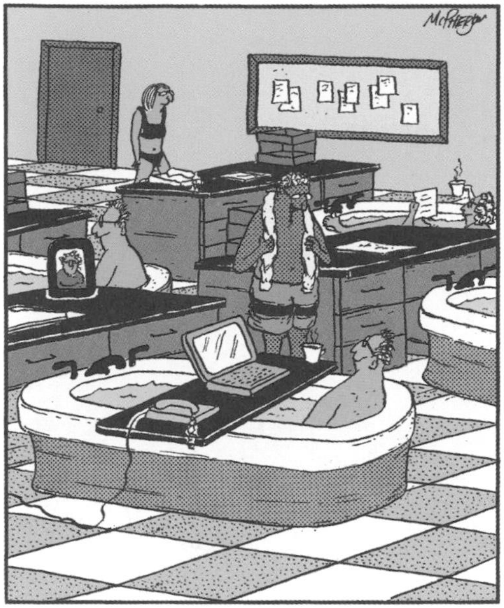

Having equipped all employees with their own Jacuzzi whirlpool tubs, Hutchinson Industries experienced an 87 percent reduction in absenteeism.

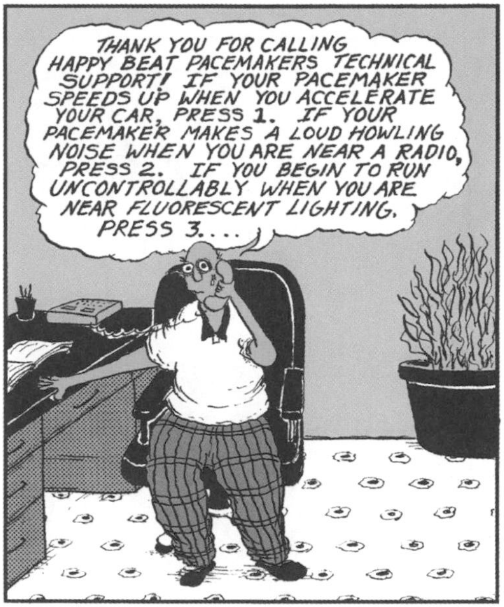
THANK YOU FOR CALLING HAPPY BEAT PACEMAKERS TECHNICAL SUPPORT! IF YOUR PACEMAKER SPEEDS UP WHEN YOU ACCELERATE YOUR CAR, PRESS 1. IF YOUR PACEMAKER MAKES A LOUD HOWLING NOISE WHEN YOU ARE NEAR A RADIO, PRESS 2. IF YOU BEGIN TO RUN UNCONTROLLABLY WHEN YOU ARE NEAR FLUORESCENT LIGHTING, PRESS 3....

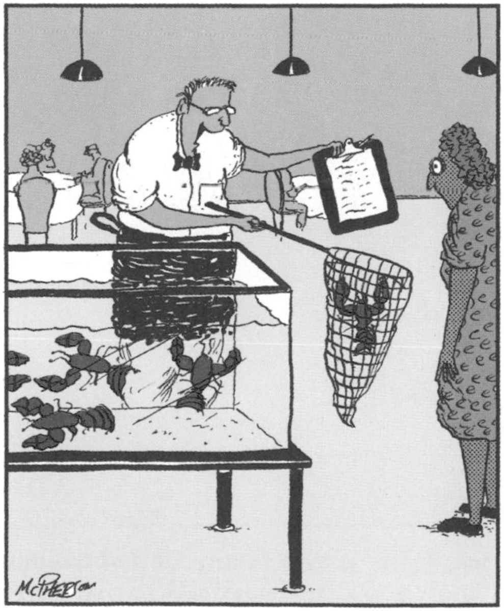

"Excellent choice, ma'am. Now if you'll just sign this death certificate for Wally the lobster, we'll have your meal to you in just twenty-five minutes.

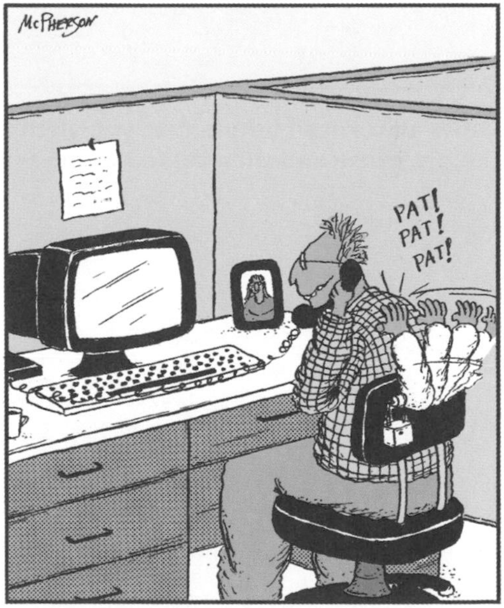
McPHERSON
PAT!
PAT!
PAT!

Thanks to the company's new pat-on-the-back devices, every employee who made a sale got an instant show of appreciation.

"Remember that recall notice that you glanced at during the big game and then tossed in the trash?"

"Jack, if you're ever in any kind of trouble, you know you can always talk to me, right?"

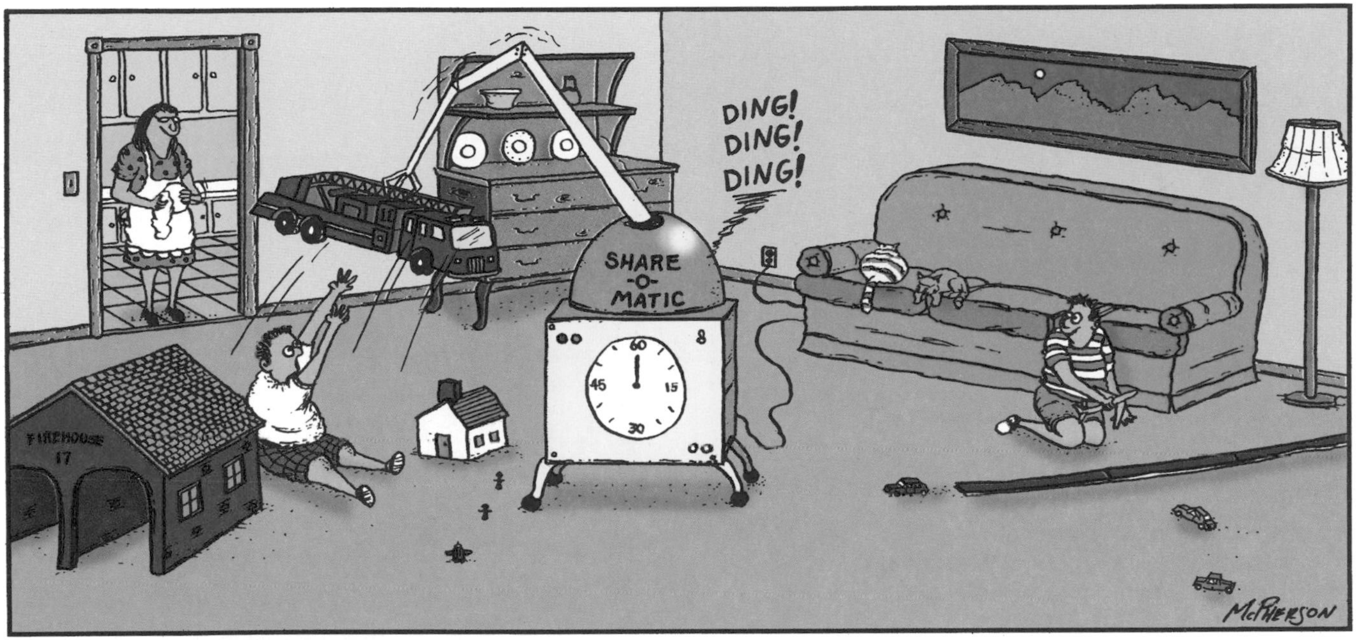
DING!
DING!
DING!
SHARE
-O-
MATIC
60
15
30
45
FIREHOUSE
17
McPHERSON

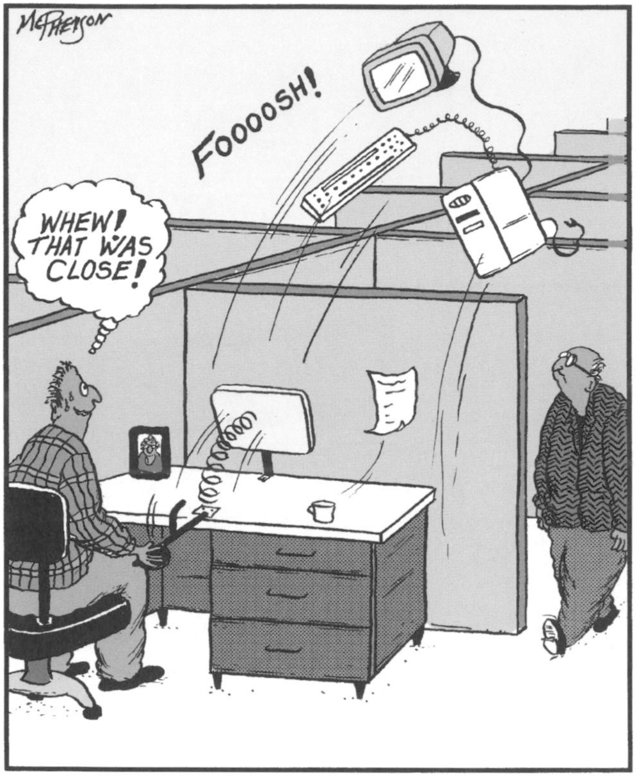
McPHERSON
FOOOOSH!
WHEW! THAT WAS CLOSE!

Surprised by his supervisor while he was viewing inappropriate Web sites, Dan quickly hit his homemade "boss button."

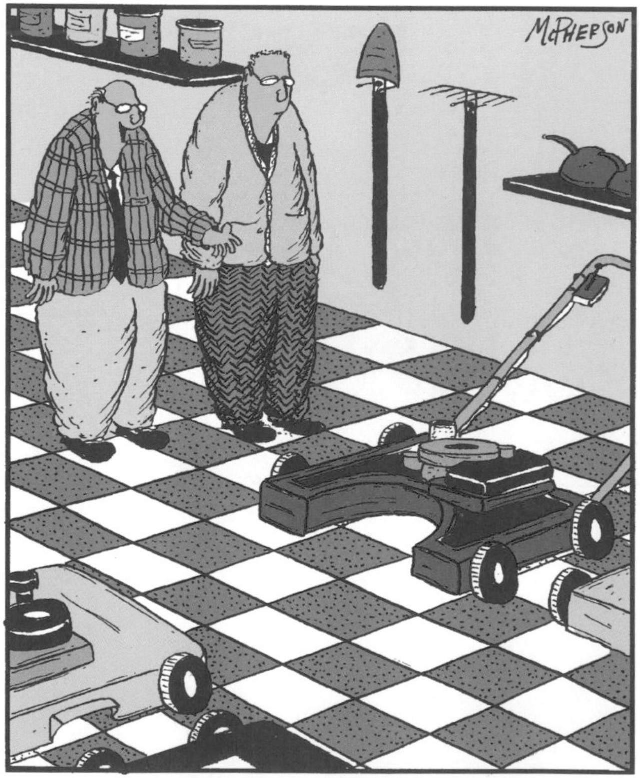
McPHERSON

"Hey, are you like me? Do you hate mowing around trees? Well, then *this* is the machine for you!"

 Oh, I know! I've been telling him for years that he
needs to take better care of himself, stop working
so hard, get some exercise . . . Oh, here he is now."

Disaster at the Rogaine plant

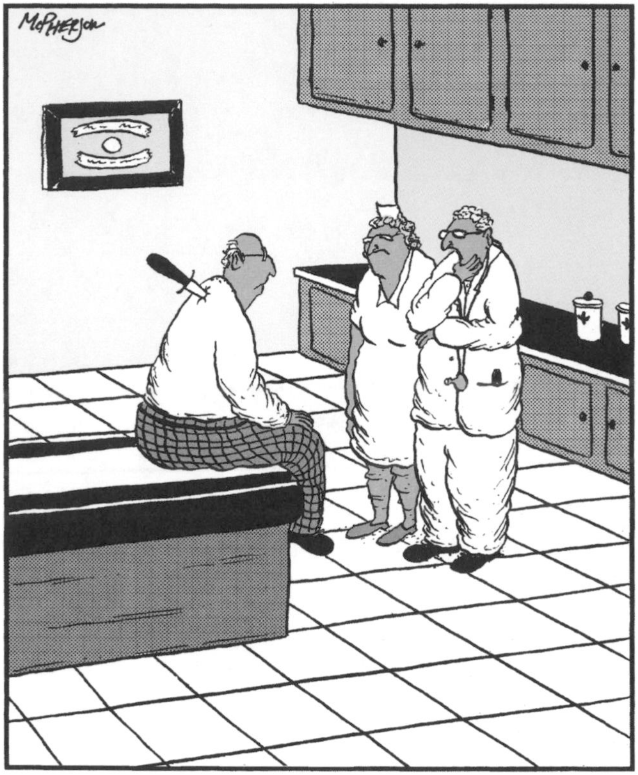
McPHERSON

"You say it's a sharp, stabbing pain. Hmmmm . . .
sharp . . . stabbing pain."

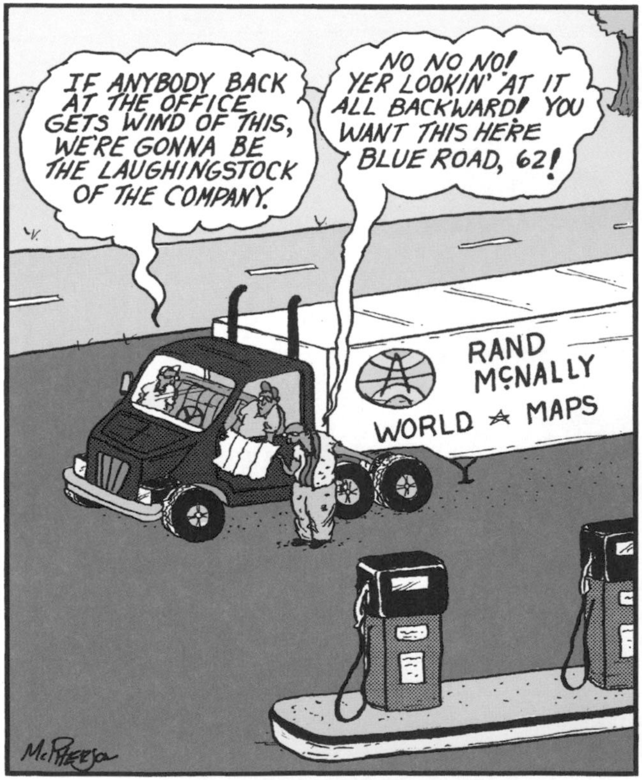
IF ANYBODY BACK AT THE OFFICE GETS WIND OF THIS, WE'RE GONNA BE THE LAUGHINGSTOCK OF THE COMPANY.
NO NO NO! YER LOOKIN' AT IT ALL BACKWARD! YOU WANT THIS HERE BLUE ROAD, 62!
RAND McNALLY
WORLD MAPS
McPHERSON

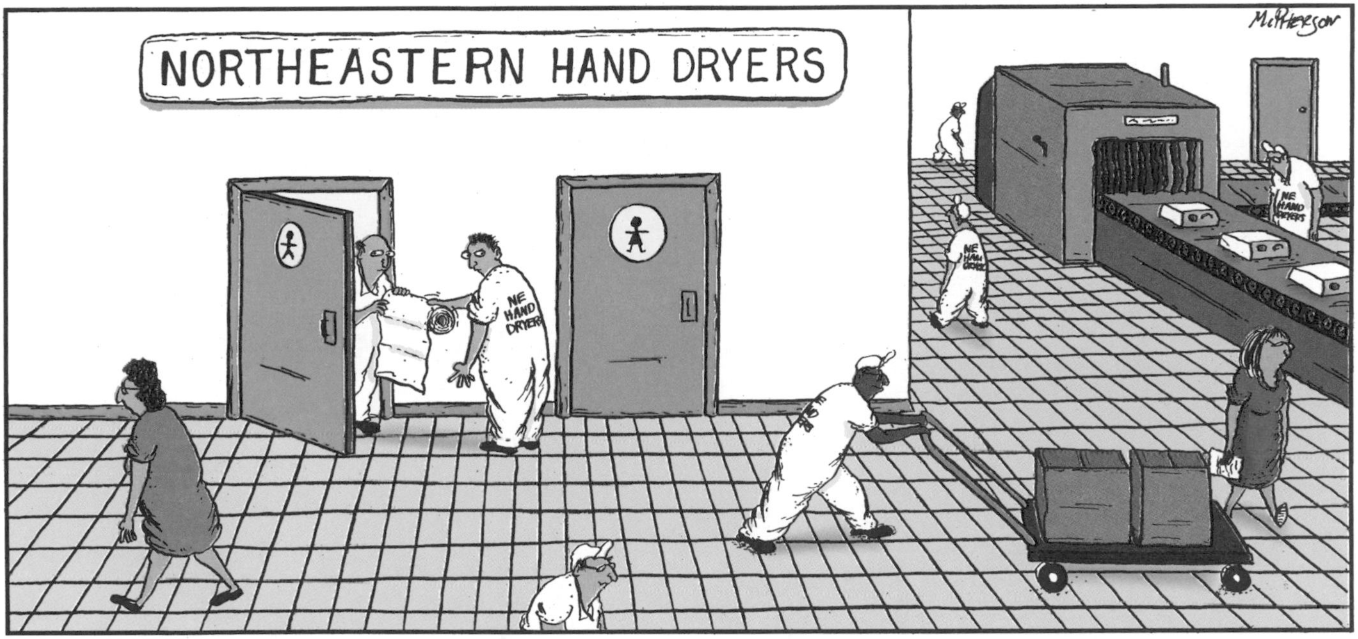
NORTHEASTERN HAND DRYERS
NE HAND DRYERS
NE HAND DRYERS
NE HAND DRYERS
McPherson

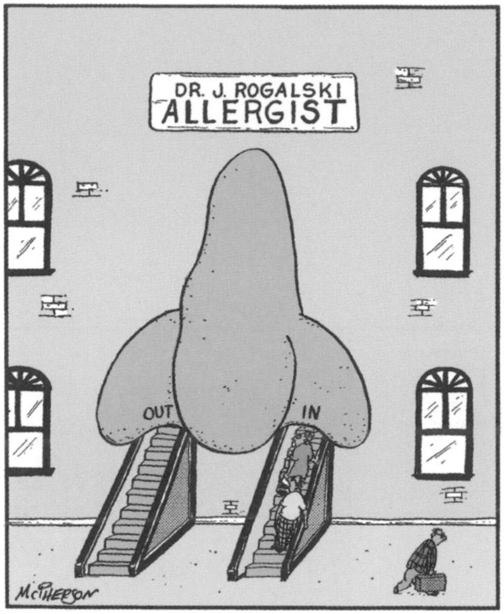
DR. J. ROGALSKI
ALLERGIST
OUT
IN

"You gotta admit it, it does make it easy to find the place."

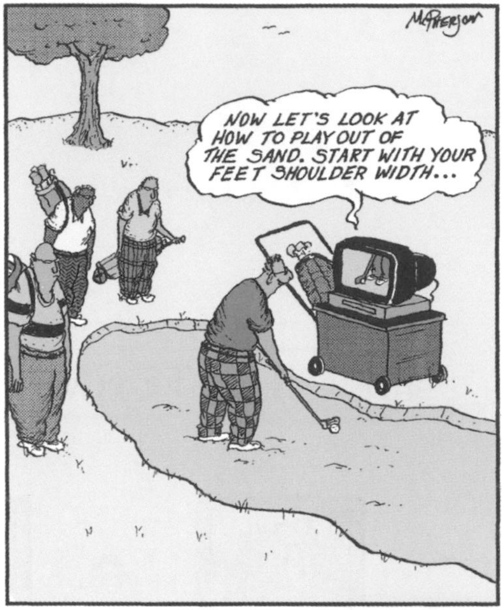
NOW LET'S LOOK AT HOW TO PLAY OUT OF THE SAND. START WITH YOUR FEET SHOULDER WIDTH...

Dwayne's playing partners quickly tired of his reliance on his new *Miracle Golf* video.

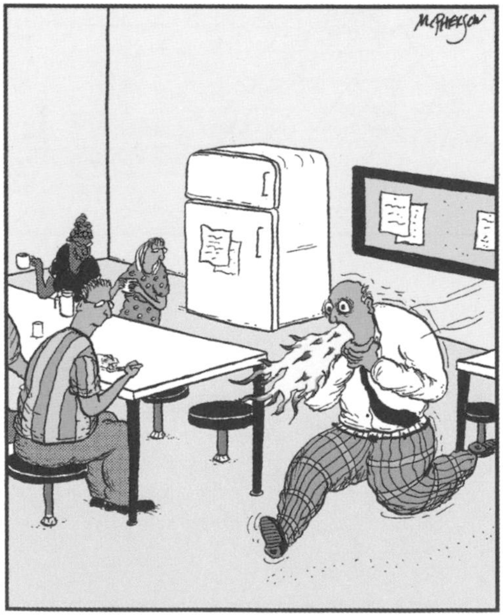

Tired of having her lunches stolen from the break-room refrigerator, Glenda spiked her sandwich with hot pepper sauce.

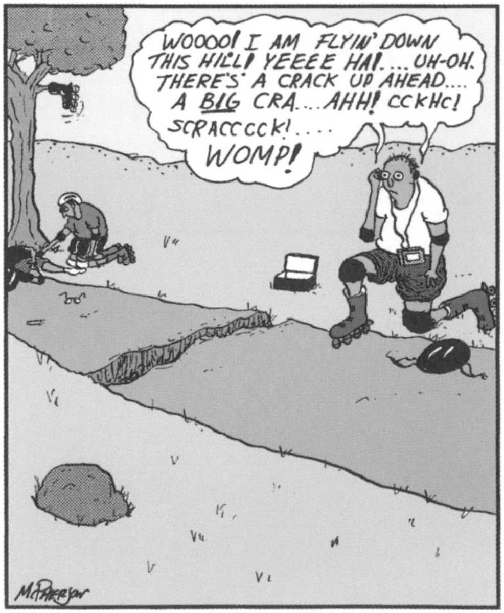
WOOOO! I AM FLYIN' DOWN THIS HILL! YEEEE HA!....UH-OH. THERE'S A CRACK UP AHEAD.... A BIG CRA....AHH! CCKHC!
SCRACCCCK!....
WOMP!

Arriving on the scene just moments after Brad's horrific wipeout, the others quickly located his black box.

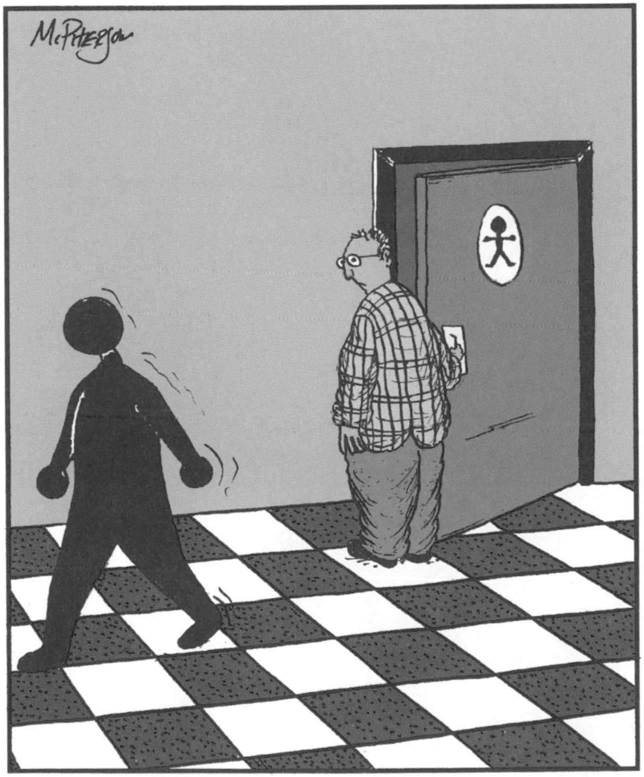
McPherson

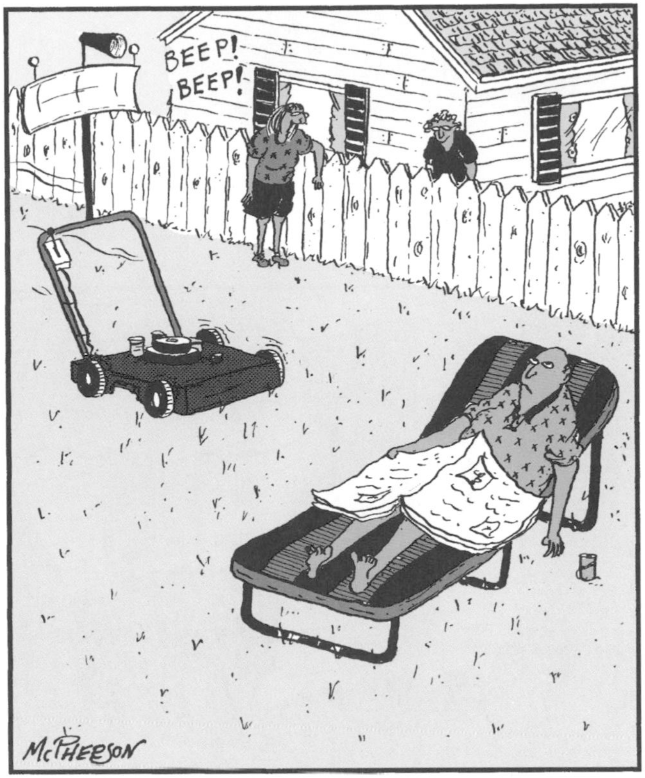
BEEP!
BEEP!
McPHERSON

"It's got a sensor on it that homes in on the smell of aftershave anytime the grass gets to be three inches high."

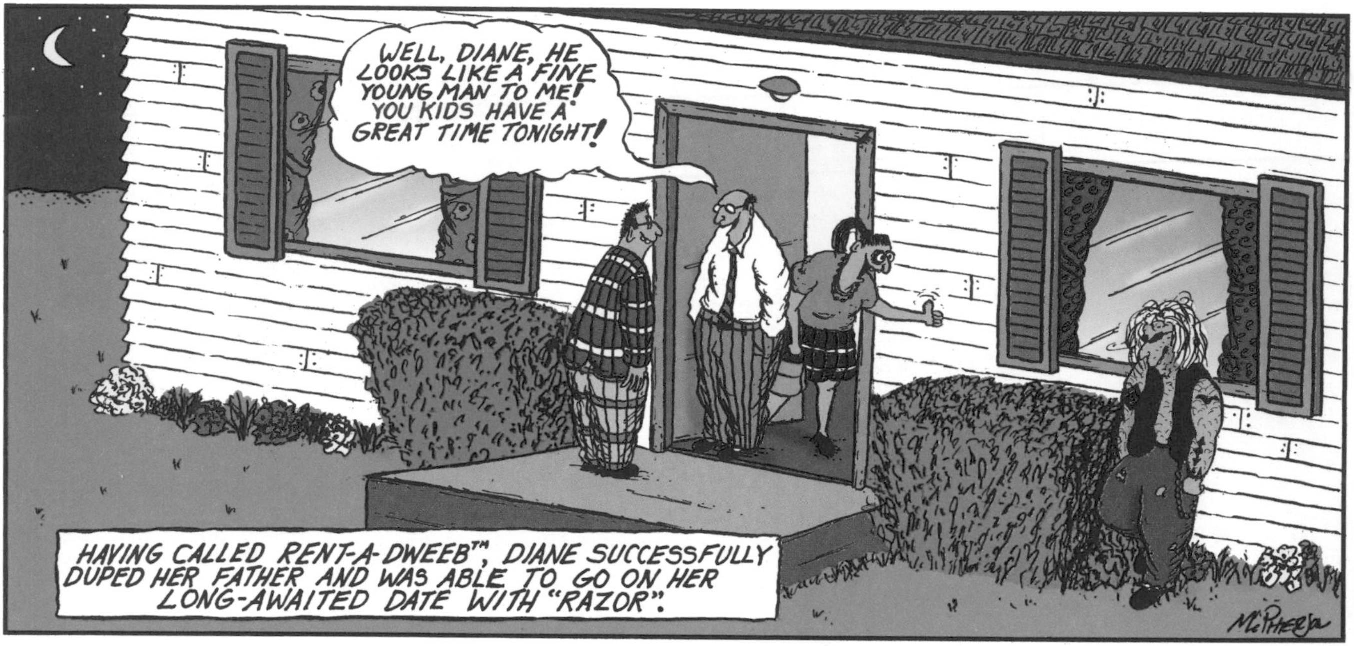
WELL, DIANE, HE LOOKS LIKE A FINE YOUNG MAN TO ME! YOU KIDS HAVE A GREAT TIME TONIGHT!
HAVING CALLED RENT-A-DWEEB™, DIANE SUCCESSFULLY DUPED HER FATHER AND WAS ABLE TO GO ON HER LONG-AWAITED DATE WITH "RAZOR".
McPHERSON

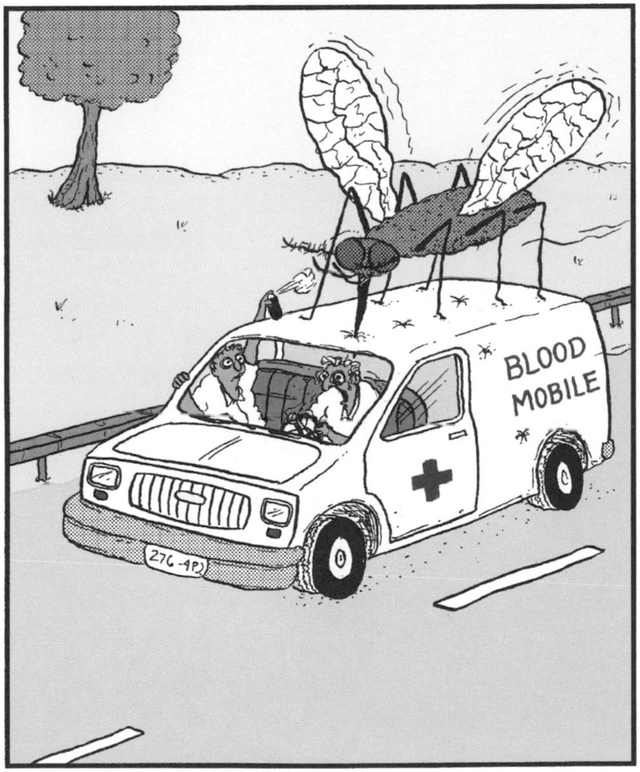
BLOOD MOBILE

"Is it still there?!"

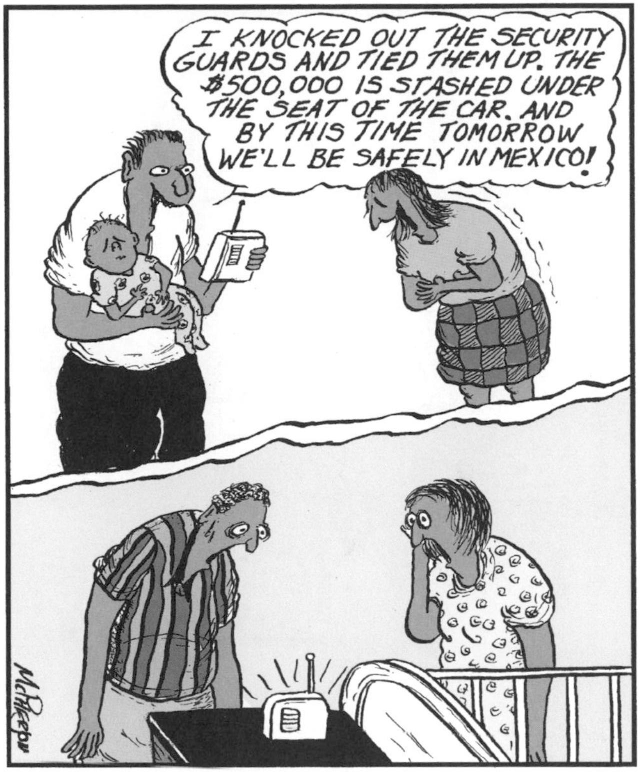
I KNOCKED OUT THE SECURITY GUARDS AND TIED THEM UP. THE $500,000 IS STASHED UNDER THE SEAT OF THE CAR. AND BY THIS TIME TOMORROW WE'LL BE SAFELY IN MEXICO!

Knowing that their neighbors routinely listened to their conversations via their baby monitor, the Morgans decided to have some fun.

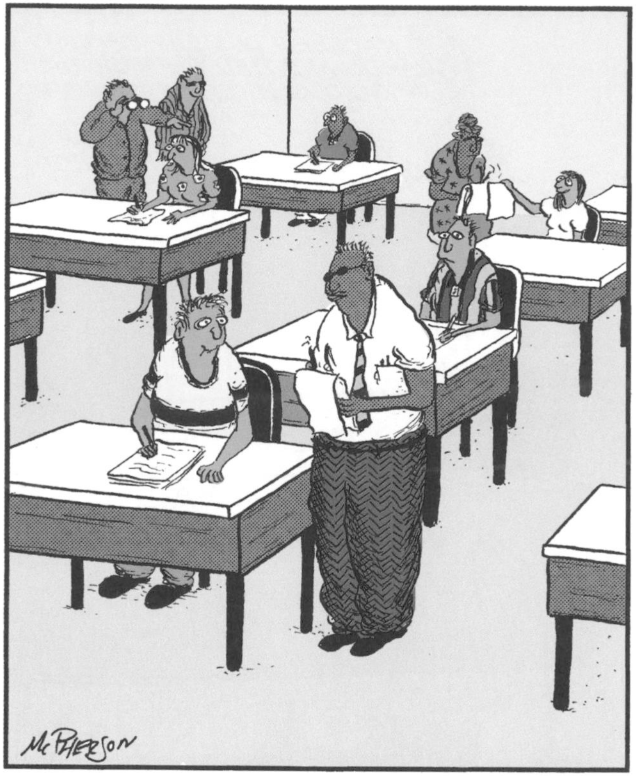
McPHERSON

Tensions during final exams rose even higher when it was learned that talent scouts from *Jeopardy!* would be watching.

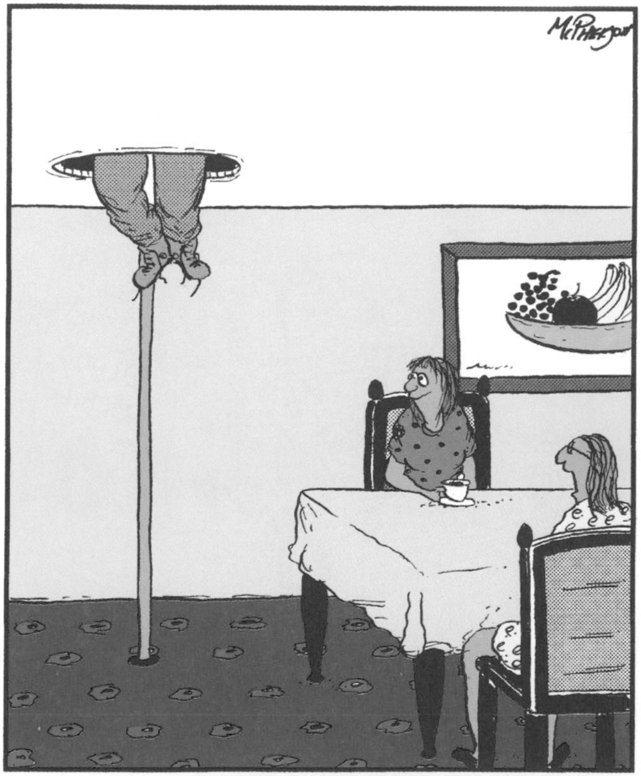
McPHERSON

"We just got tired of the kids being constantly late for school and dinner."

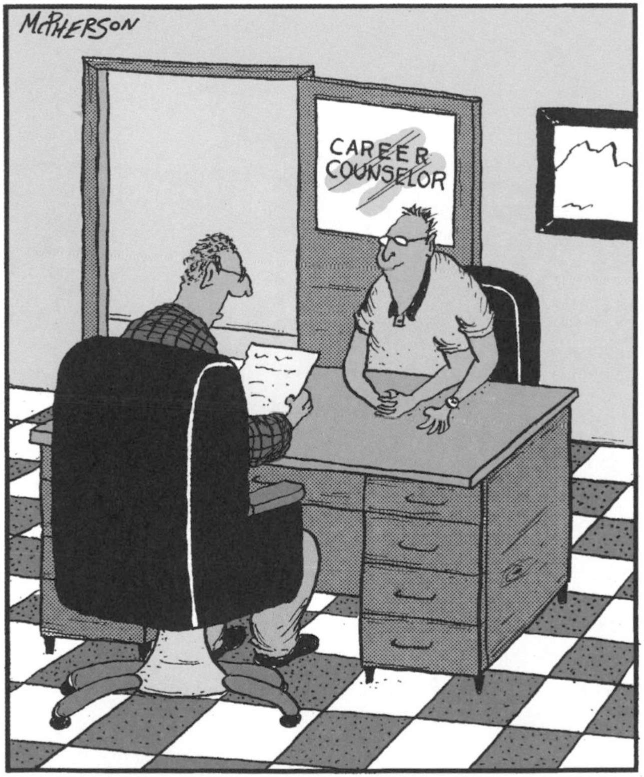
McPHERSON
CAREER COUNSELOR

"Well, Doug, according to your aptitude test, you'd do well as an apple picker, professional juggler, or concert pianist."

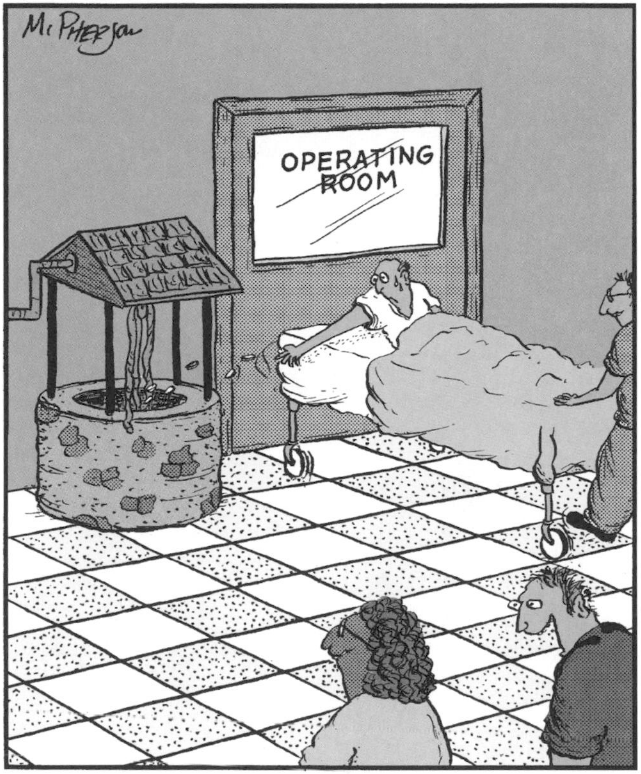
McPHERSON
OPERATING ROOM

"Man, we are making a *mint* off that thing!"

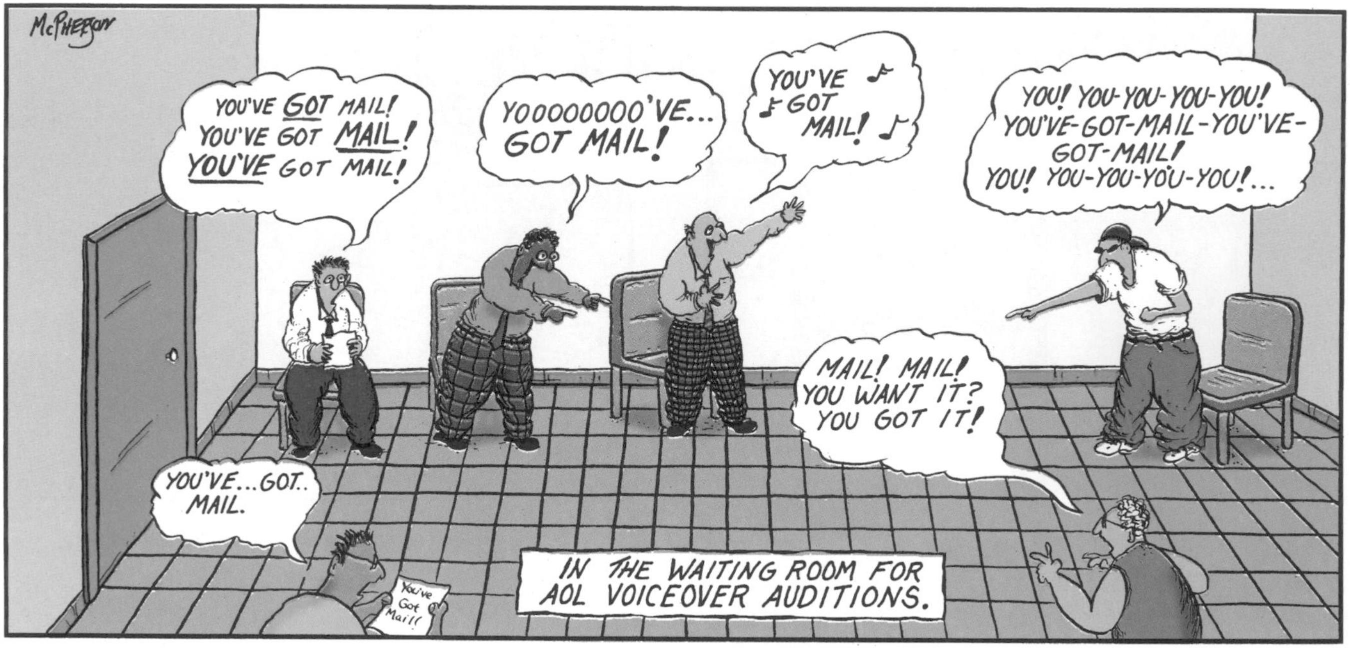
McPHERSON
YOU'VE GOT MAIL! YOU'VE GOT MAIL! YOU'VE GOT MAIL!
YOOOOOOOO'VE... GOT MAIL!
YOU'VE GOT MAIL!
YOU! YOU-YOU-YOU-YOU! YOU'VE-GOT-MAIL-YOU'VE-GOT-MAIL! YOU! YOU-YOU-YOU-YOU!...
MAIL! MAIL! YOU WANT IT? YOU GOT IT!
YOU'VE...GOT.. MAIL.
You've Got Mail!
IN THE WAITING ROOM FOR AOL VOICEOVER AUDITIONS.

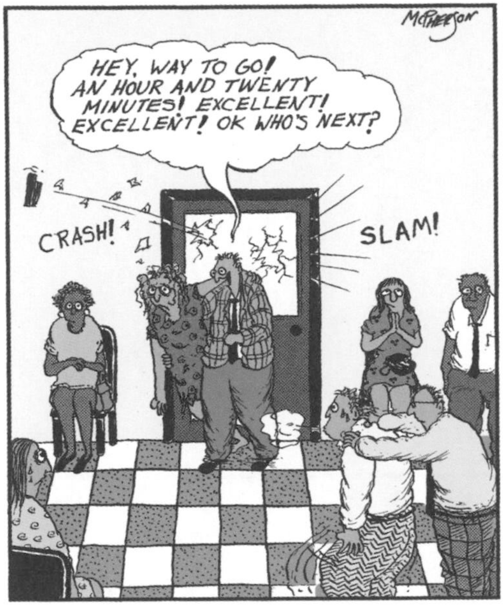
McPHERSON
HEY, WAY TO GO! AN HOUR AND TWENTY MINUTES! EXCELLENT! EXCELLENT! OK WHO'S NEXT?
CRASH!
SLAM!

Knowing that one substitute alone could not endure a full day in Mrs. Turbock's infamous fifth-grade class, Principal Eckley made sure to line up eight subs.

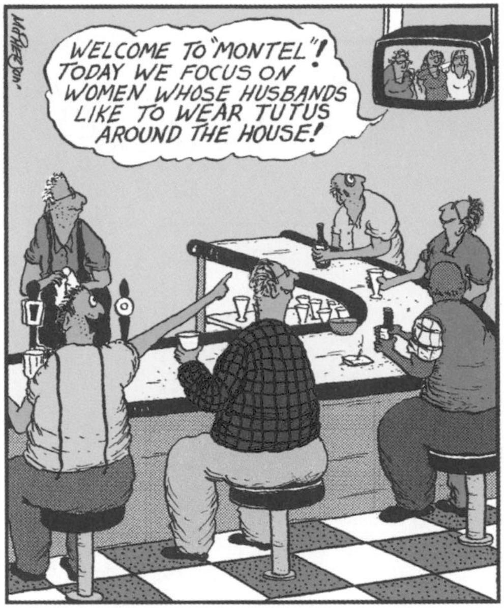
McPHERSON
WELCOME TO "MONTEL"! TODAY WE FOCUS ON WOMEN WHOSE HUSBANDS LIKE TO WEAR TUTUS AROUND THE HOUSE!

"Hey, Bert! Ain't that *your* wife?!"

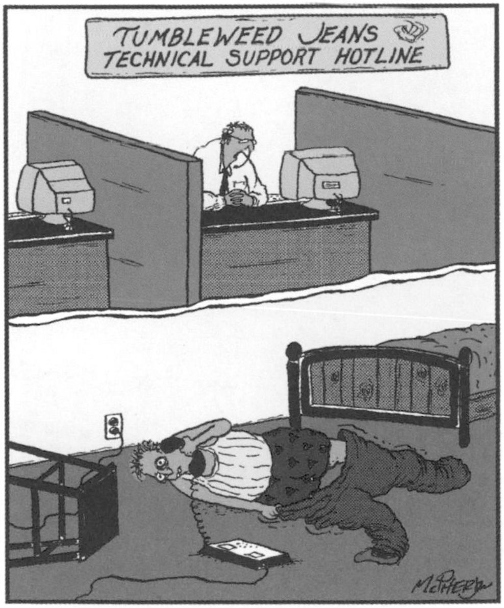
TUMBLEWEED JEANS
TECHNICAL SUPPORT HOTLINE
McPHERSON

"OK, sir. It sounds to me like you may have both legs in one pant leg. I want you to take the pants all the way off, and I'm going to walk you through a clean install."

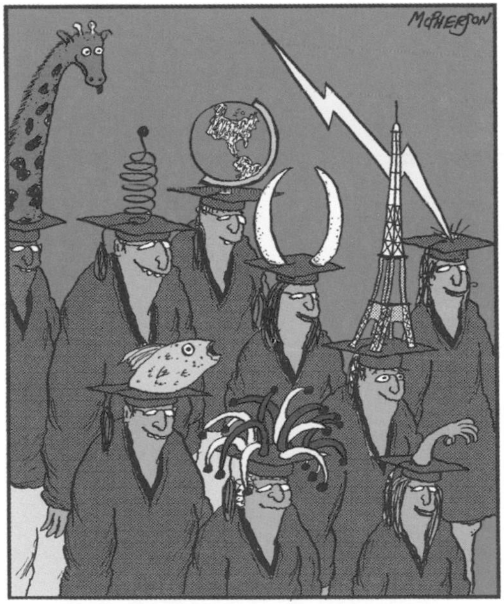
McPHERSON

New for 2007: designer graduation caps

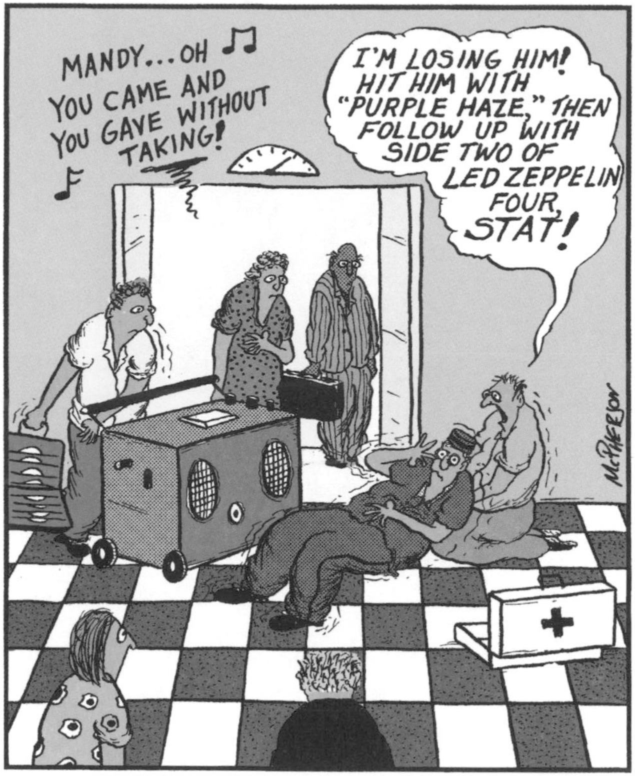
MANDY...OH
YOU CAME AND
YOU GAVE WITHOUT
TAKING!
I'M LOSING HIM! HIT HIM WITH "PURPLE HAZE," THEN FOLLOW UP WITH SIDE TWO OF LED ZEPPELIN FOUR, STAT!
McPHERSON

Eighteen years of elevator music finally push operator Bernie Huckleman over the edge.

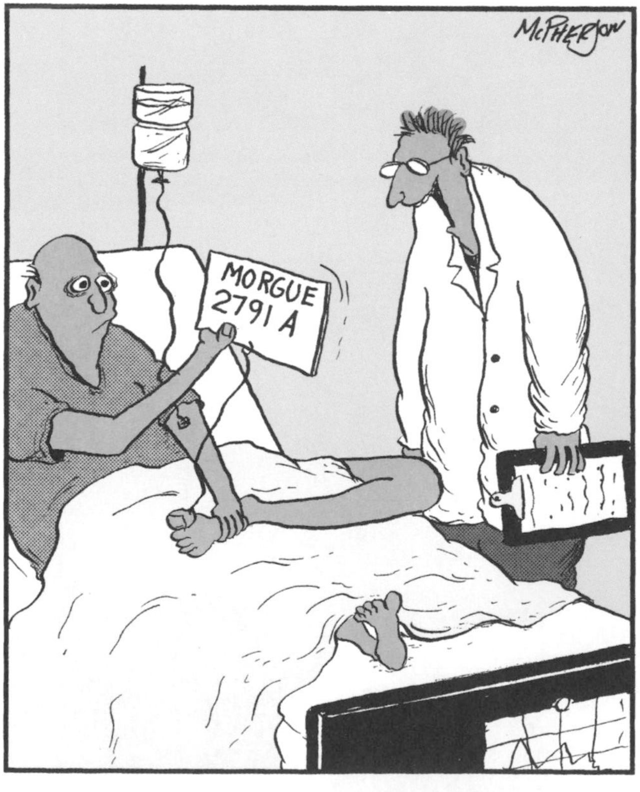
McPHERSON
MORGUE
2791 A

"Boy, have I got a story to tell you!"

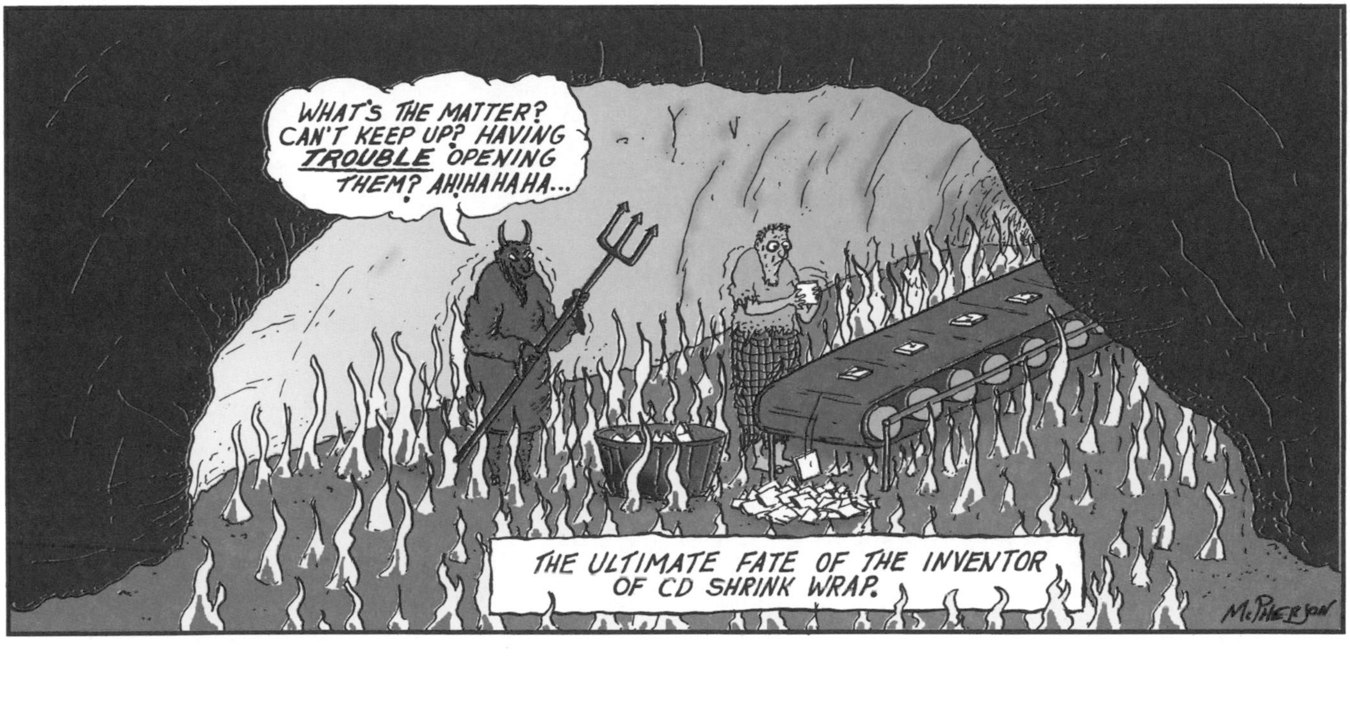
WHAT'S THE MATTER? CAN'T KEEP UP? HAVING TROUBLE OPENING THEM? AH!HAHAHAHA...
THE ULTIMATE FATE OF THE INVENTOR OF CD SHRINK WRAP.
McPHERSON

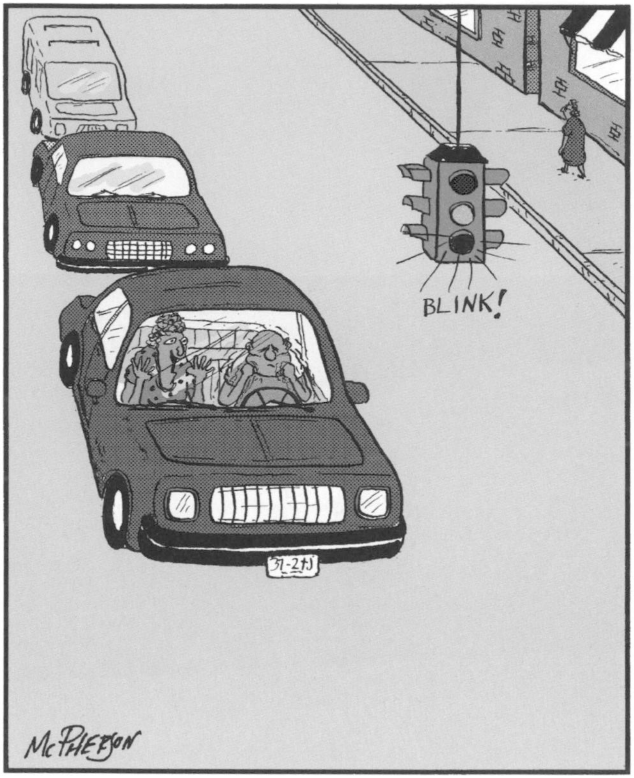
BLINK!
McPHERSON

Soon after his pacemaker was installed, Art made the amazing discovery that by holding his breath and clenching all his muscles, he could turn traffic lights green.

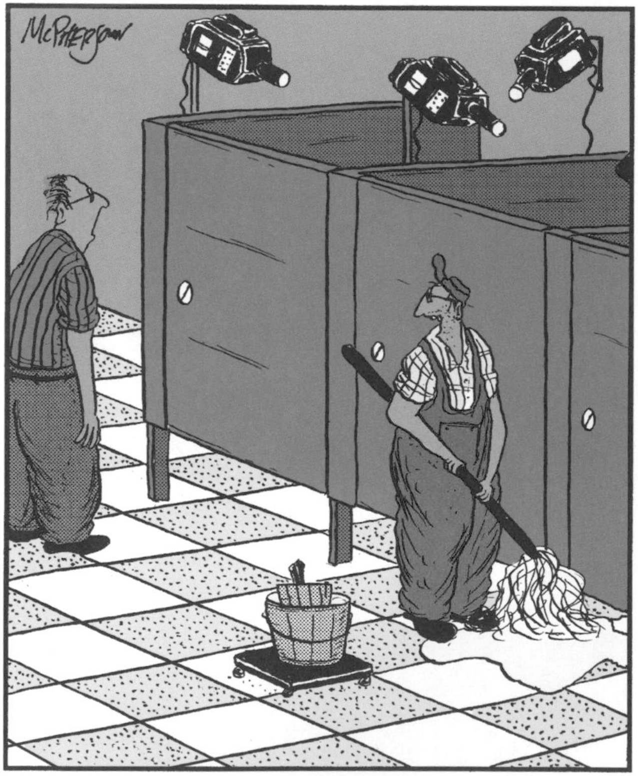
McPHERSON

"It's part of the company's big push to stamp out graffiti."

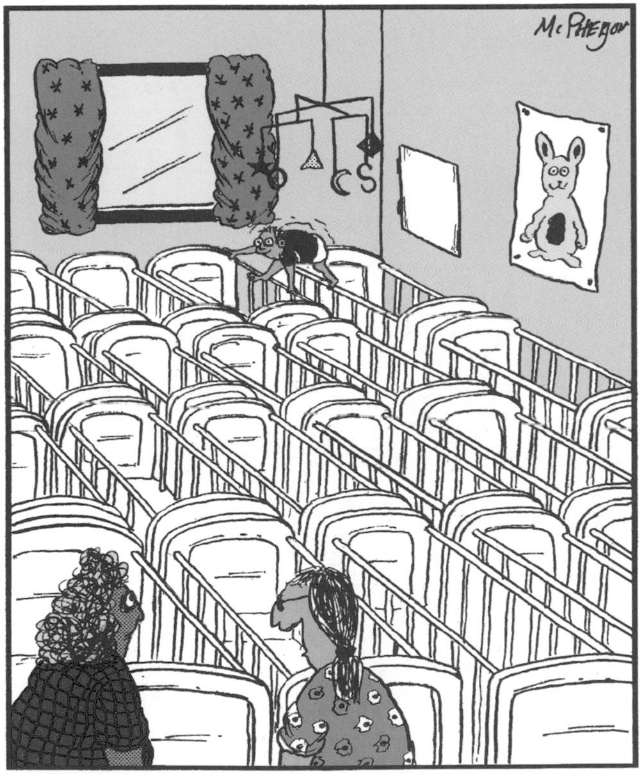
McPHERSON

"... and by the time he climbs into the third or fourth crib he's completely exhausted and finally falls asleep."

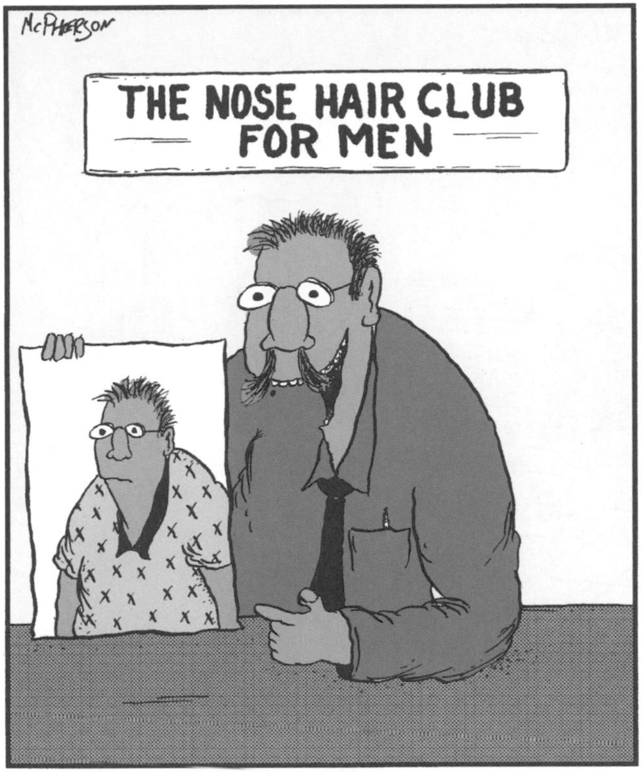
McPHERSON
THE NOSE HAIR CLUB
FOR MEN

"And remember, I'm not just the Nose Hair Club president, I'm also a client."

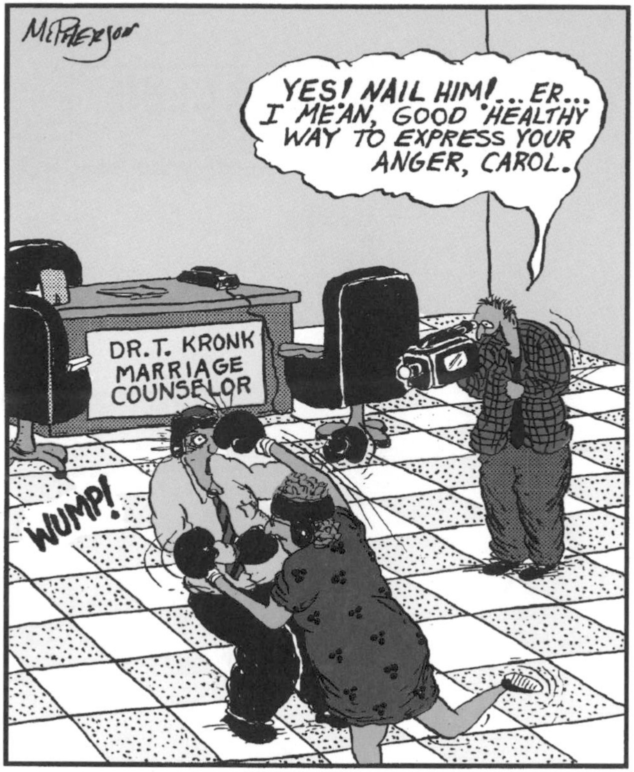
McPherson
YES! NAIL HIM!... ER... I MEAN, GOOD HEALTHY WAY TO EXPRESS YOUR ANGER, CAROL.
DR. T. KRONK MARRIAGE COUNSELOR
WUMP!

Unbeknownst to any of his clients, Dr. Kronk was making a fortune by posting Anger Resolution Bouts on his thriving "Amateur Fight Night" Web site.

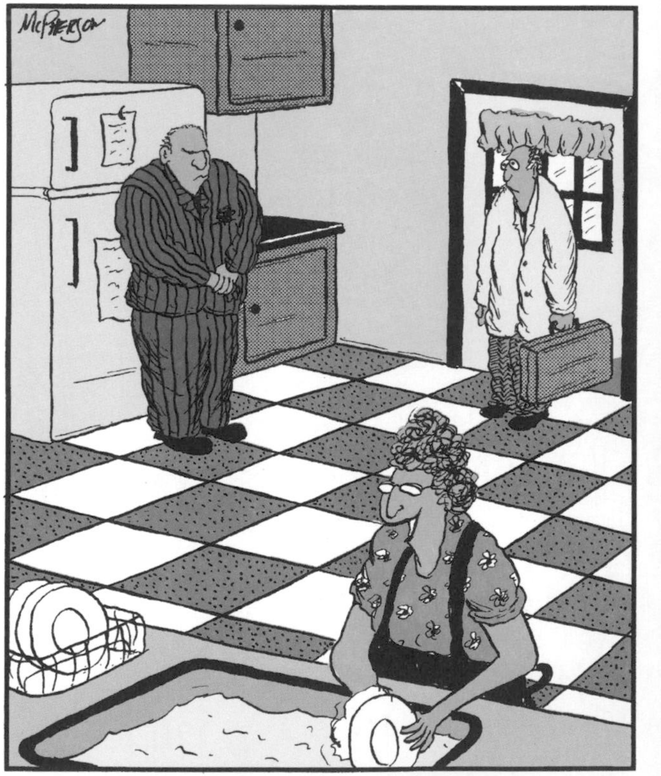
McPherson

"Oh, that's Mr. Cardazy. Our HMO has determined that we're in the high-risk group for heart disease, so Mr. Cardazy has been assigned to help us make smarter food choices."

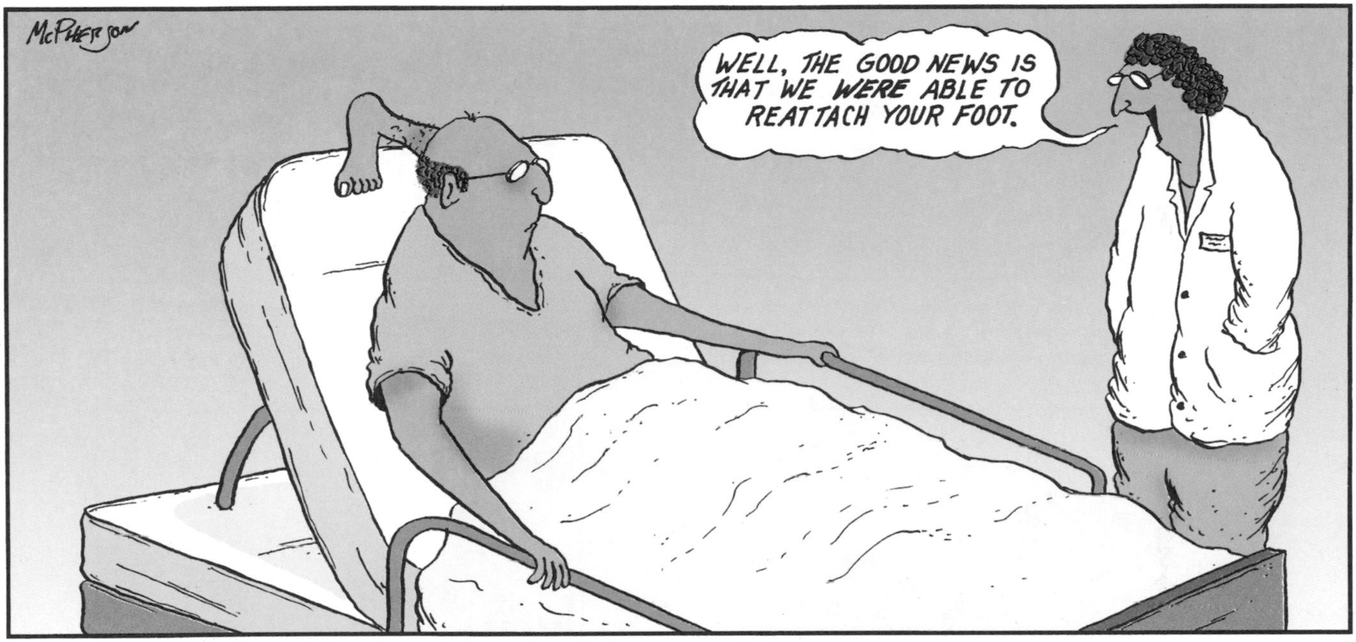
McPHERSON
WELL, THE GOOD NEWS IS THAT WE WERE ABLE TO REATTACH YOUR FOOT.

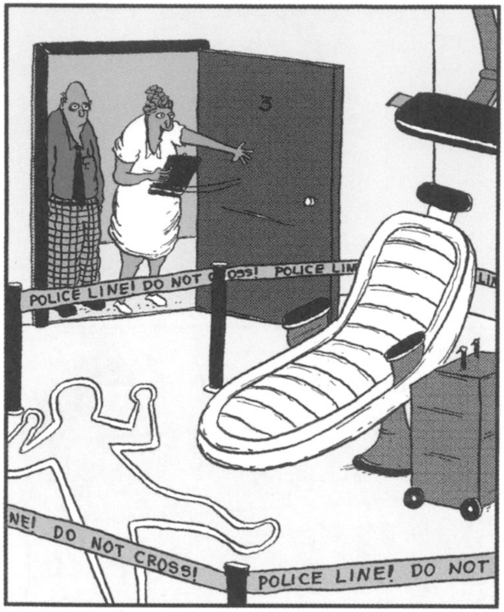
3
POLICE LINE! DO NOT CROSS! POLICE LINE!
NE! DO NOT CROSS! POLICE LINE! DO NOT

"OK, Mr. Dobner. Two fillings today. How about exam room three . . . whoops! I forgot! This room is out of commission for a while."

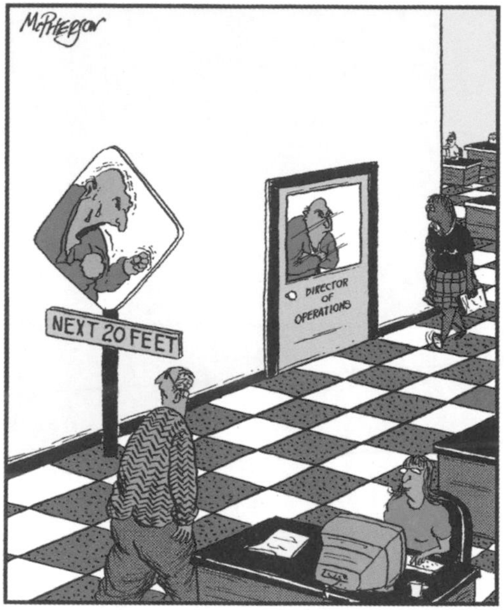
McPHERSON
NEXT 20 FEET
DIRECTOR OF OPERATIONS

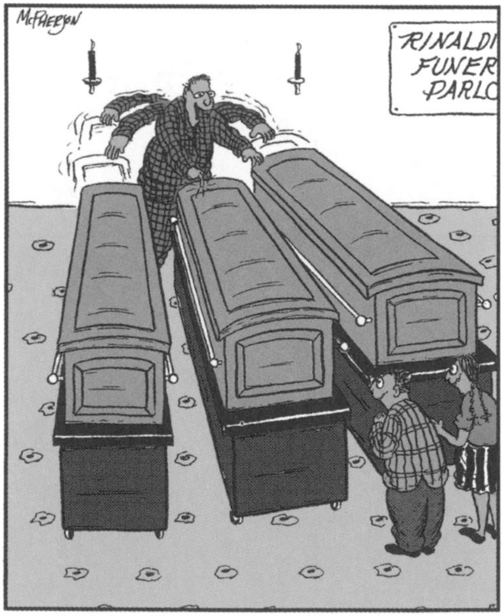
McPHERSON
RINALDI FUNER PARLO

"Ah, fooled you, didn't I? Let's try it again! Pay close attention. Your Uncle Frank is here . . . and I scramble them around and around . . ."

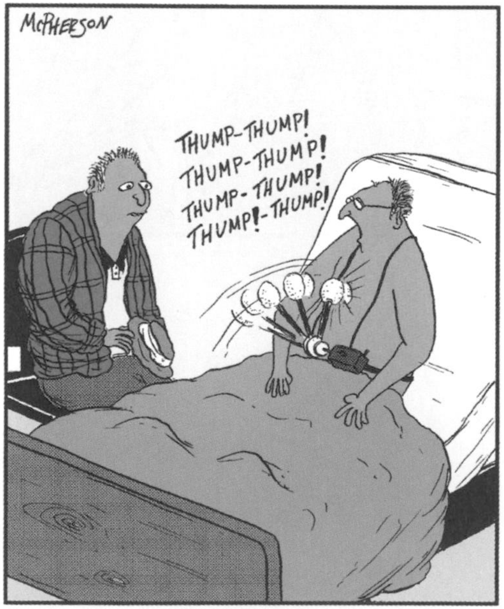
McPHERSON
THUMP-THUMP!
THUMP-THUMP!
THUMP-THUMP!
THUMP!-THUMP!

"They tell me it's the latest breakthrough—the nonsurgical pacemaker."

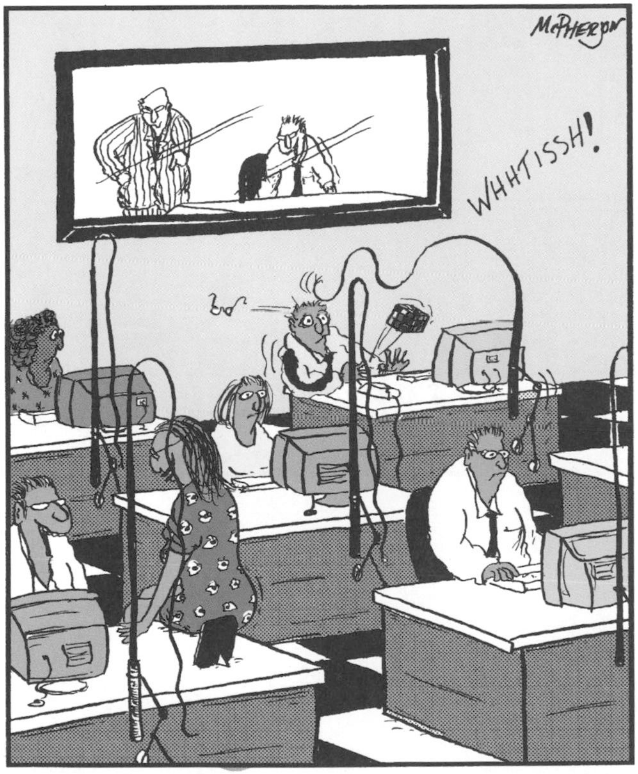
McPHERSON
WHHTISSH!

The company's new Whip-Matic Productivity System helped boost profits by 21 percent.

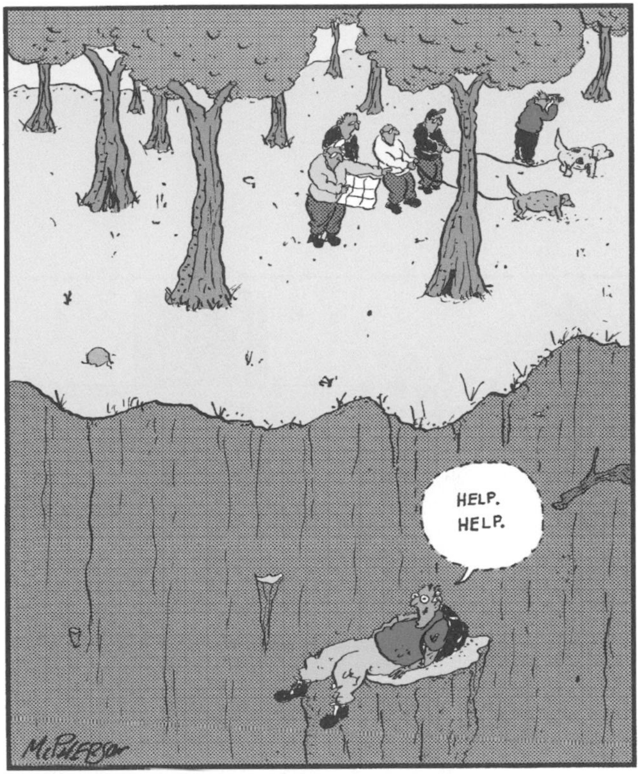
HELP.
HELP.
McPHERSON

Out hiking alone one day, professional golf announcer Fred Dornquist makes a grave misstep and is never heard from again.

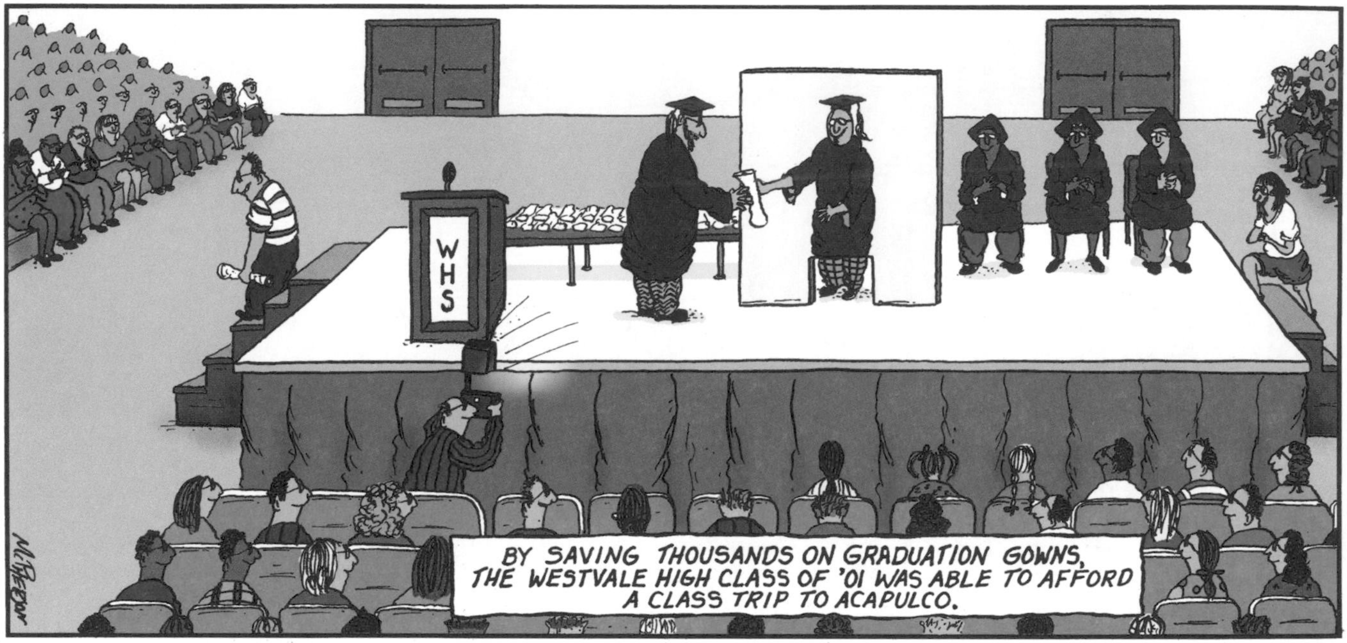
W
H
S
BY SAVING THOUSANDS ON GRADUATION GOWNS, THE WESTVALE HIGH CLASS OF '01 WAS ABLE TO AFFORD A CLASS TRIP TO ACAPULCO.

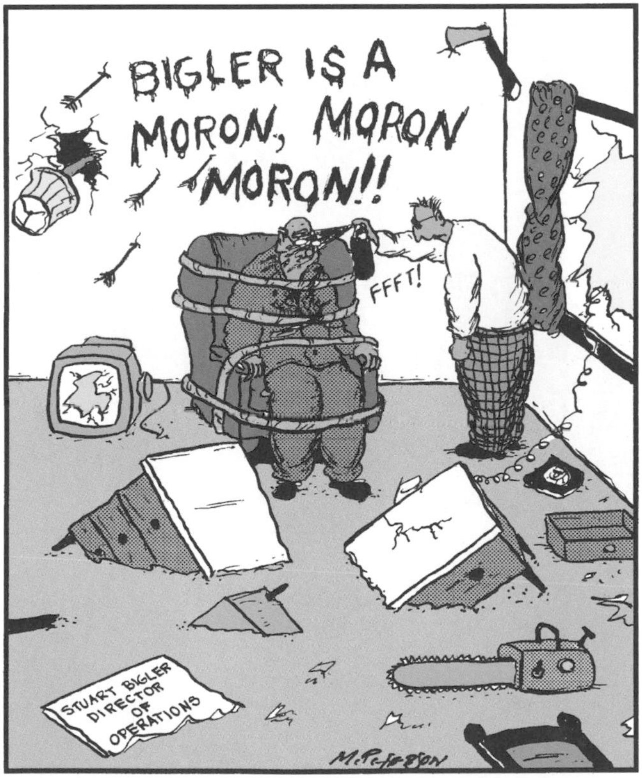
BIGLER IS A MORON, MORON MORON!!
FFFT!
STUART BIGLER DIRECTOR OF OPERATIONS
M.PETERSON

"Matthews, you've got three seconds to stop this nonsense, or you're going to have one sorry-looking second-quarter review."

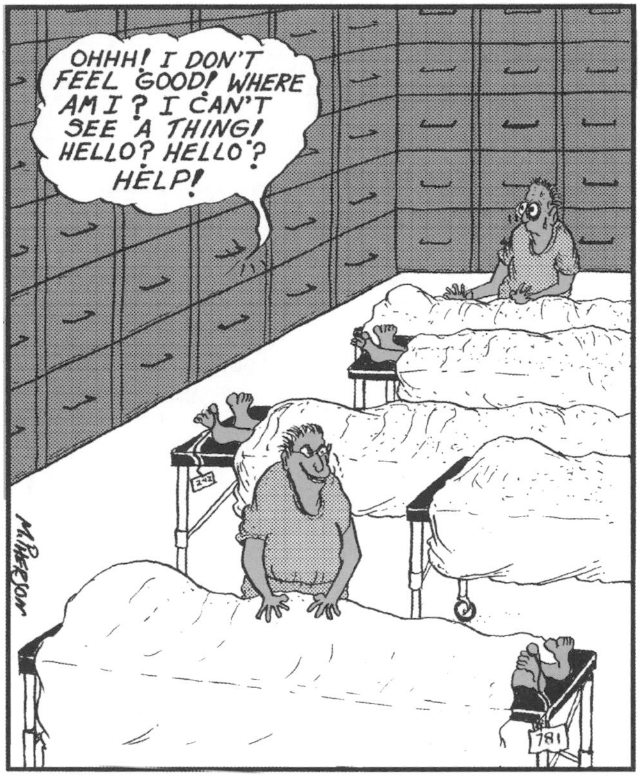
OHHH! I DON'T FEEL GOOD! WHERE AM I? I CAN'T SEE A THING! HELLO? HELLO? HELP!
781

A talented amateur ventriloquist, Ray loved it whenever a new guy was assigned to the morgue.

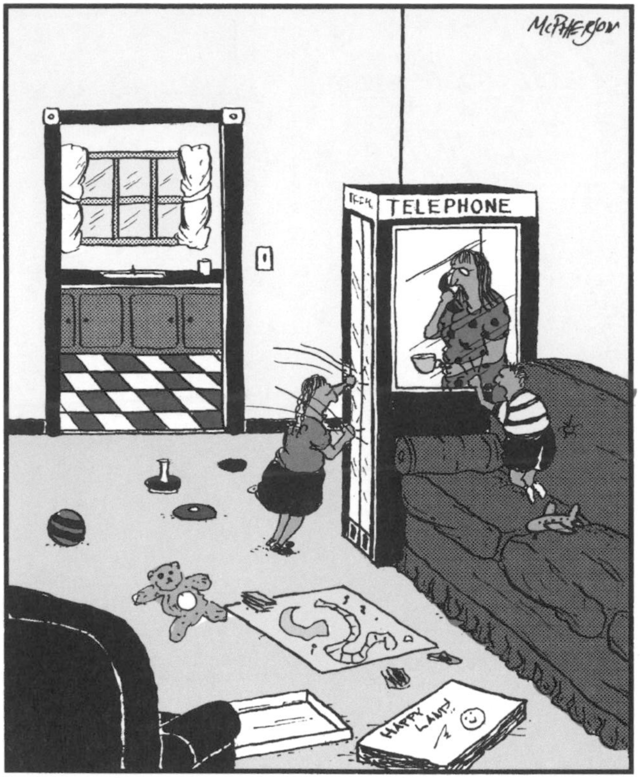
McPHERSON
TELEPHONE
HAPPY LAND

"Really, I'm serious. I'm talking to you from a phone booth in the living room. It's the only way I can talk on the phone without being harassed."

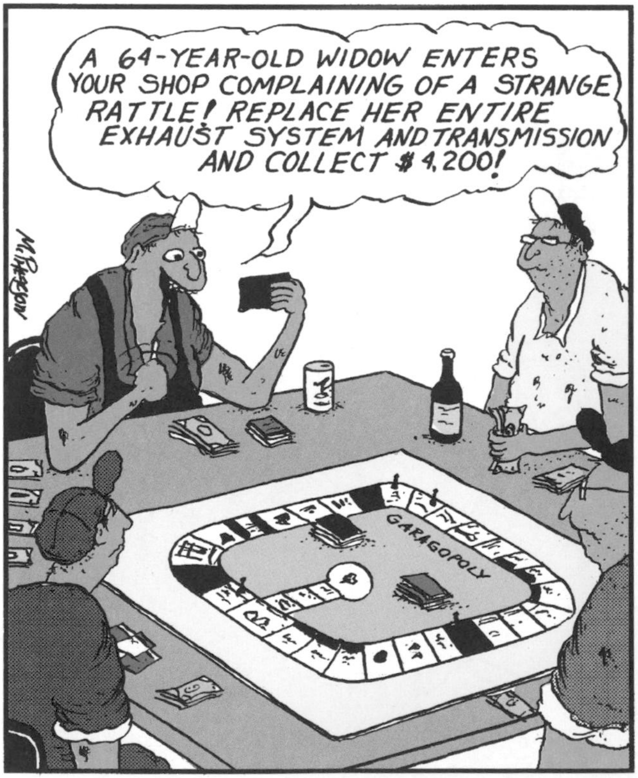
A 64-YEAR-OLD WIDOW ENTERS YOUR SHOP COMPLAINING OF A STRANGE RATTLE! REPLACE HER ENTIRE EXHAUST SYSTEM AND TRANSMISSION AND COLLECT $4,200!
McPHERSON
GARAGOPOLY

Board games for mechanics

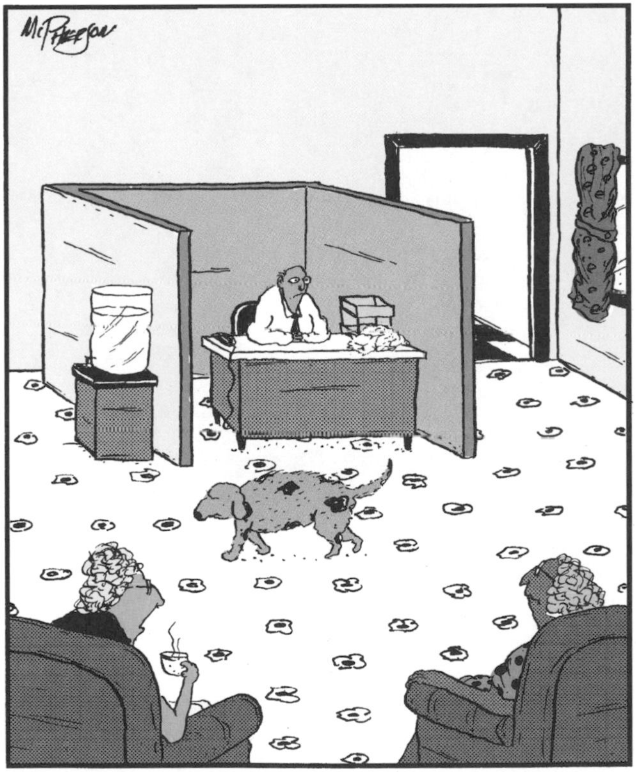

"Ed is having a tough time adjusting to retirement."

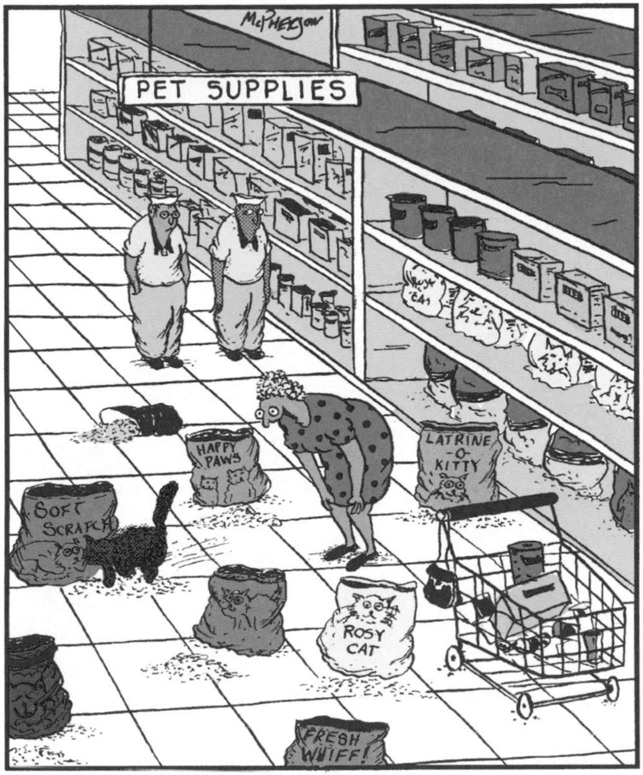
PET SUPPLIES
HAPPY PAWS
LATRINE-O-KITTY
SOFT SCRATCH
ROSY CAT
FRESH WHIFF!

"So is *that* your favorite, Toodles? Does that feel nicest on your paws? Mommy will get you whichever one you want!"

FIRST WEDDINGS

SECOND WEDDINGS

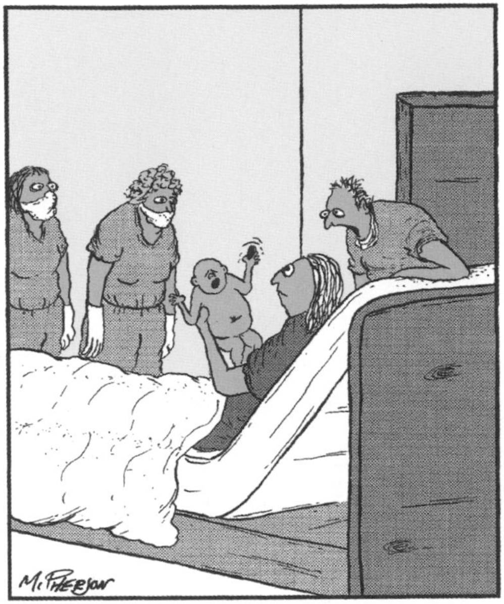

In an event that would go down in Litchfield Hospital history, infant Ryan Kledner is born holding the nickel that his mother swallowed when she was five.

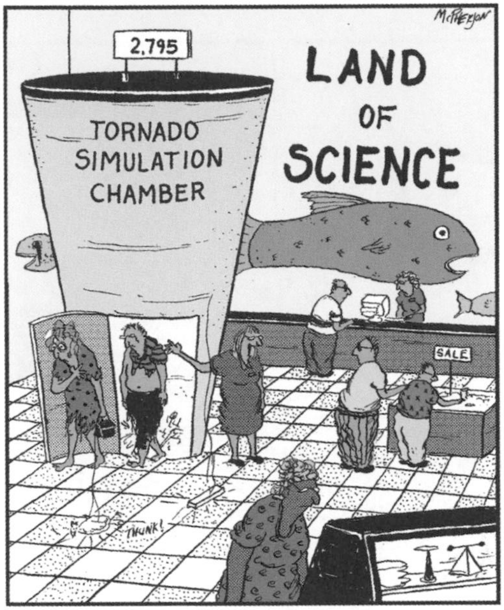
2,795
TORNADO
SIMULATION
CHAMBER
LAND
OF
SCIENCE
SALE
THUNK!

"How about you folks? Would you like to try our Tornado Simulation Chamber?"

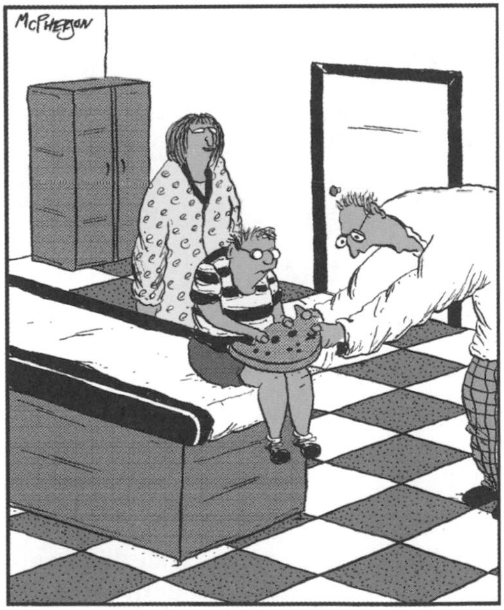

"For heaven's sake, you're right! His hands have actually grafted themselves onto the surface of the PlayStation controls!"

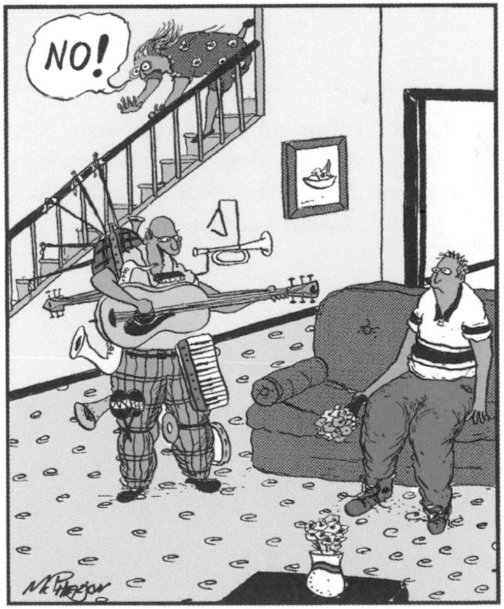
NO!

"Well, Tim, I thought that while you were waiting for Diane to get ready, you'd like to hear some of my hot new tunes."

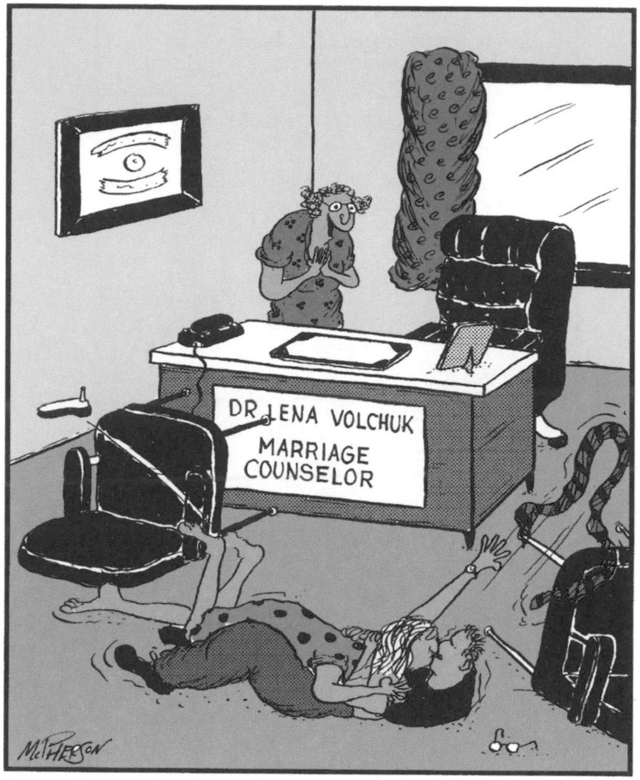
DR LENA VOLCHUK
MARRIAGE
COUNSELOR

"Gosh, folks, I think we've made some swell progress here today! You've made big strides in tempering your hostilities! Folks? . . . Hello? . . . Todd? Barb? . . . You-hoo?"

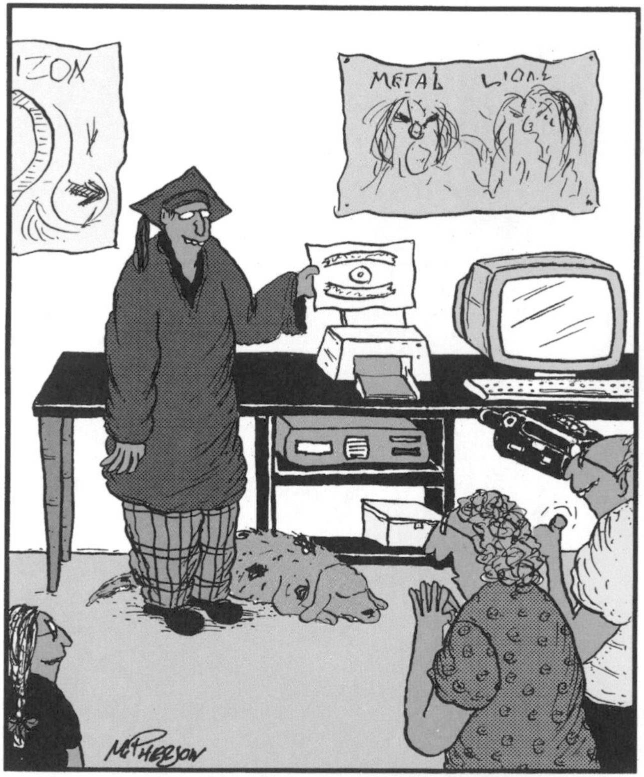

Rather than subject students, families, and faculty to another monotonous graduation ceremony, the administration at Permfeld High asked students to log onto its Web site and print out their diplomas.

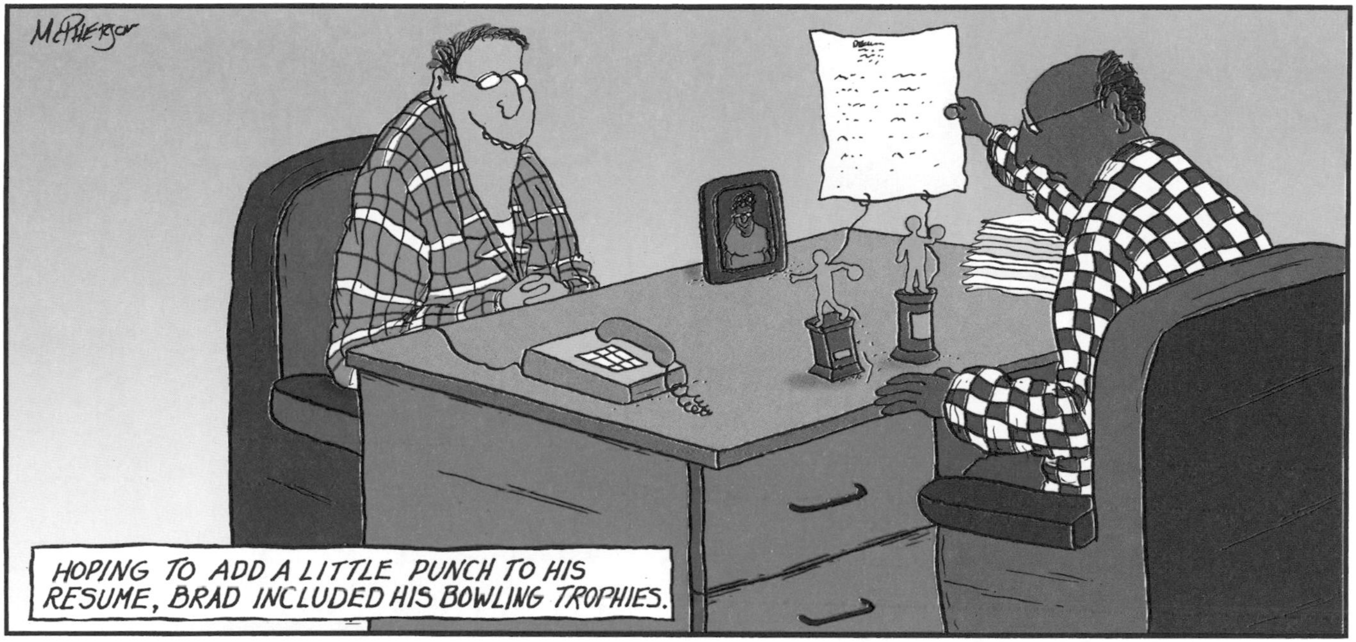
McPherson
HOPING TO ADD A LITTLE PUNCH TO HIS RESUME, BRAD INCLUDED HIS BOWLING TROPHIES.

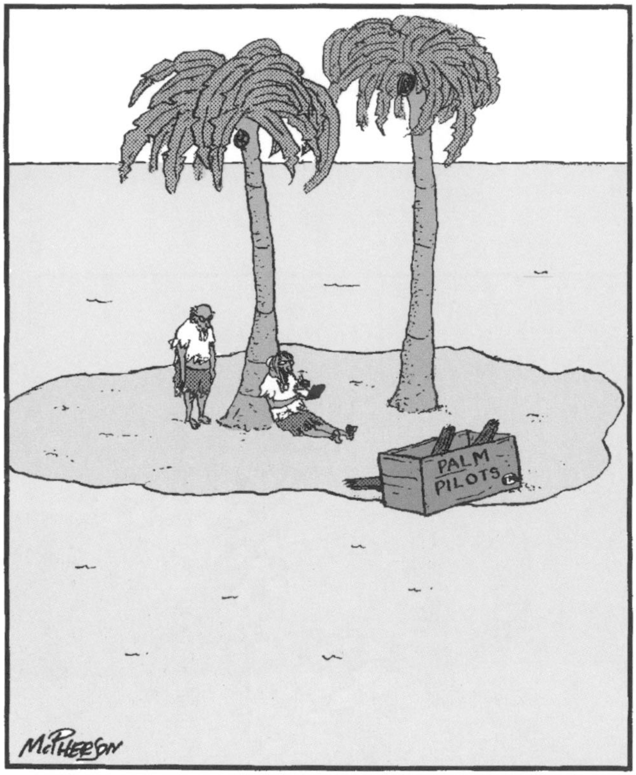
PALM PILOTS
McPHERSON

"Go fishing with you this afternoon? Let me see . . . Sorry, I can't. From 1 to 2 p.m., I'll be gathering coconuts, 2 to 3:30 I'm working on my shell jewelry, and from 3:30 to 5 is my yoga class."

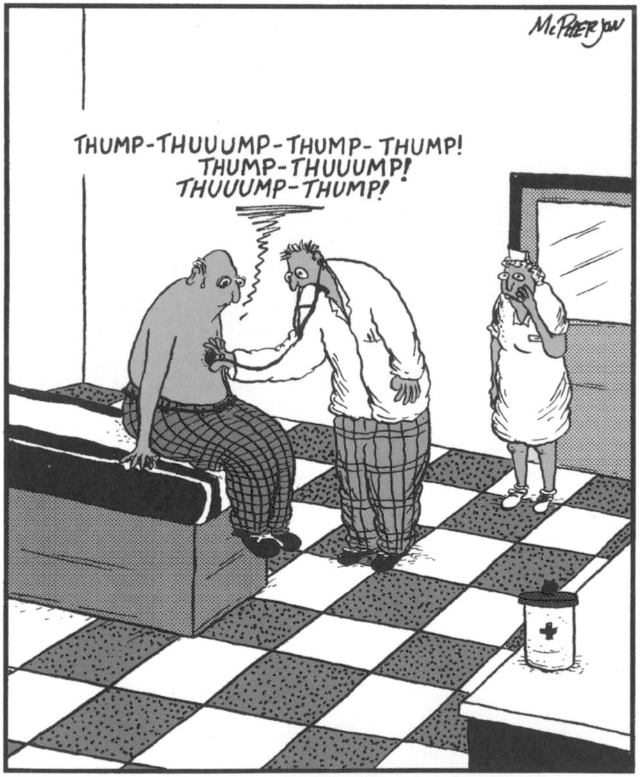
McPHERSON
THUMP-THUUUMP-THUMP-THUMP!
THUMP-THUUUMP!
THUUUMP-THUMP!

"I swear, it's beating something out in Morse Code! L-A-Y O-F-F T-H-E D-O-U-G-H-N-U-T-S A-N-D F-R-I-E-S!!!"

McPHERSON

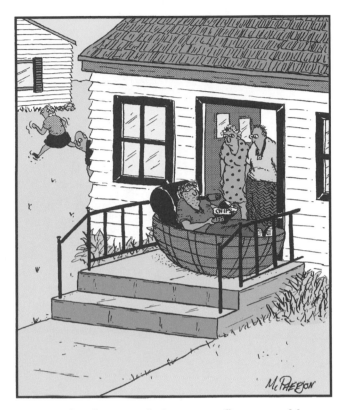

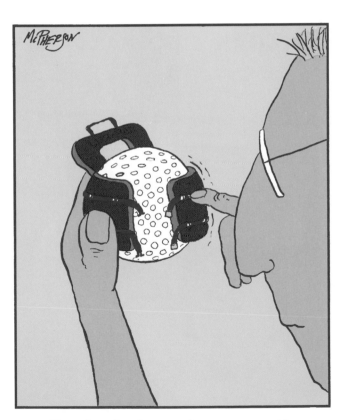

Knowing that it was a long way over the water hole, Rex took no chances with a four-dollar golf ball.

CHIPS
McPHERSON

Determined to get their twenty-five-year-old son, Lanny, out of the house, the Dermsleys make a desperate decision.

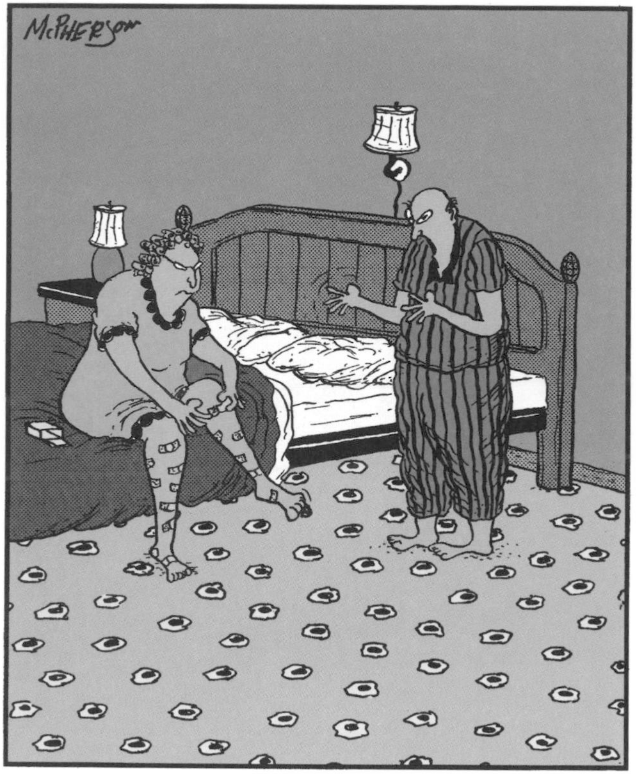
McPHERSON

"OK, I promise! I'll cut my toenails!"

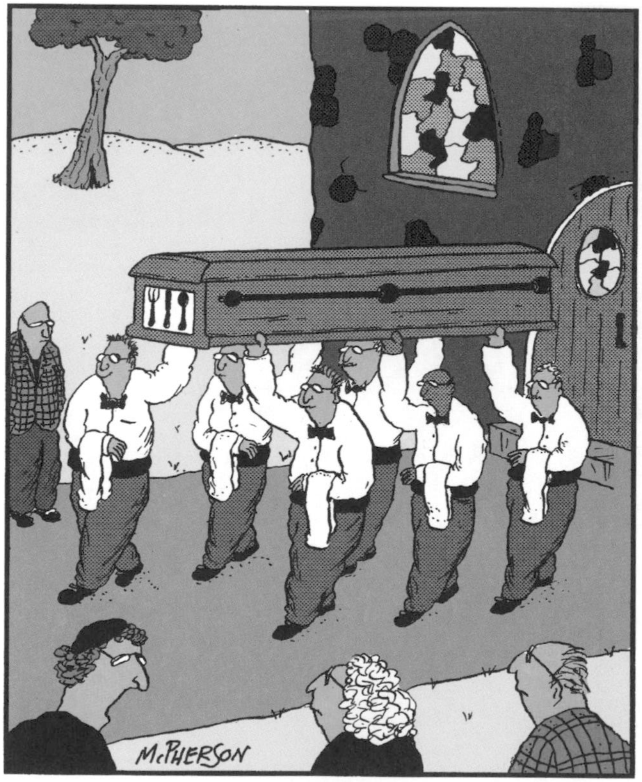
McPHERSON

"I'm so touched that the other waiters asked to be pallbearers."

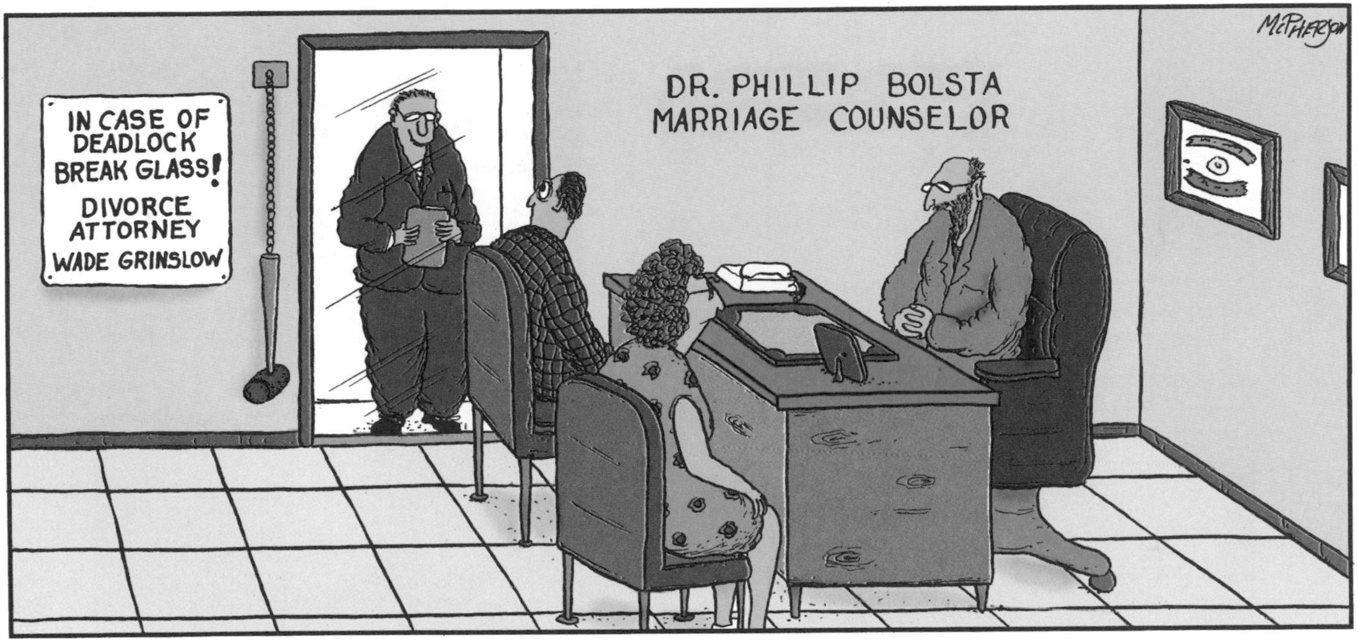
McPHERSON
DR. PHILLIP BOLSTA
MARRIAGE COUNSELOR
IN CASE OF
DEADLOCK
BREAK GLASS!
DIVORCE
ATTORNEY
WADE GRINSLOW

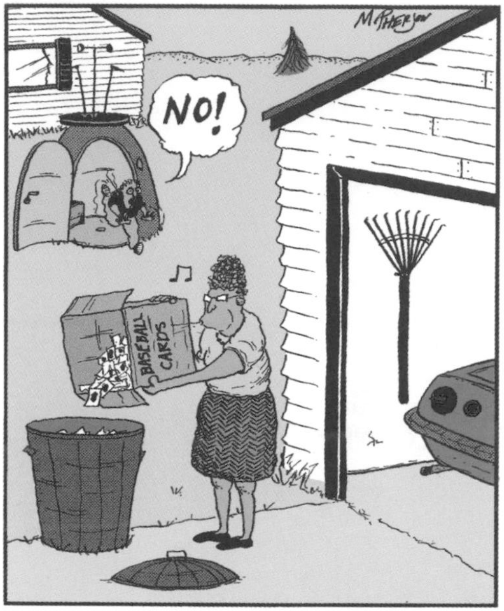
NO!
BASEBALL CARDS

Setting the time machine back for July 8, 1962, Greg returns to the most pivotal moment in his life.

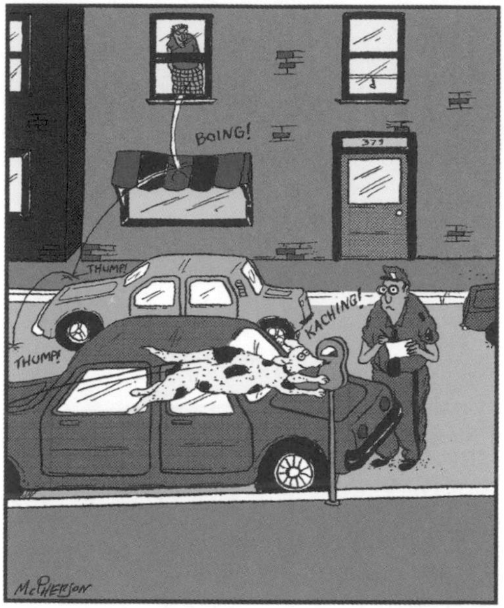
BOING!
THUMP!
THUMP!
KACHING!

Over the years, Darrel's Manhattan Meter Hound saved him hundreds in parking fines.

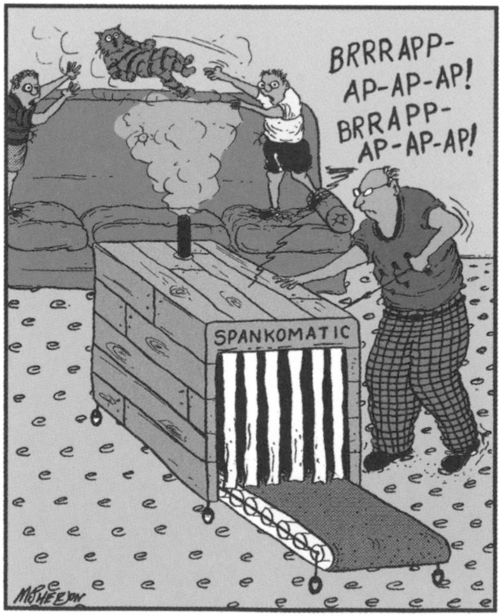
BRRRAPP-
AP-AP-AP!
BRRAPP-
AP-AP-AP!
SPANKOMATIC

Though made of simply a crate and a harmless old lawnmower engine, the mere sound of the Spankomatic assured that it never had to be used.

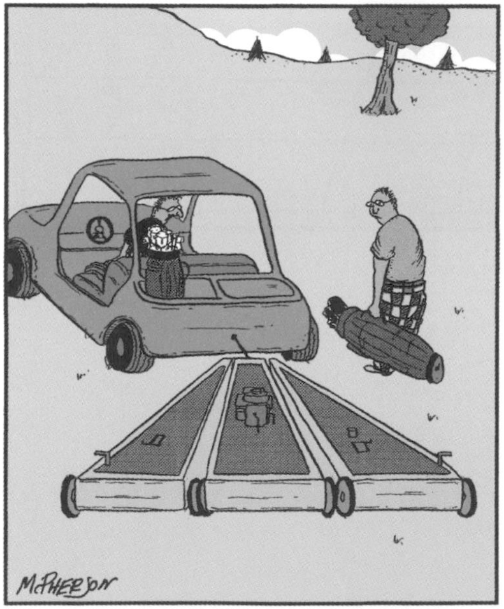

"The pro told me they just laid off nine greenskeepers. He wants us to swerve around as much as possible while we play."

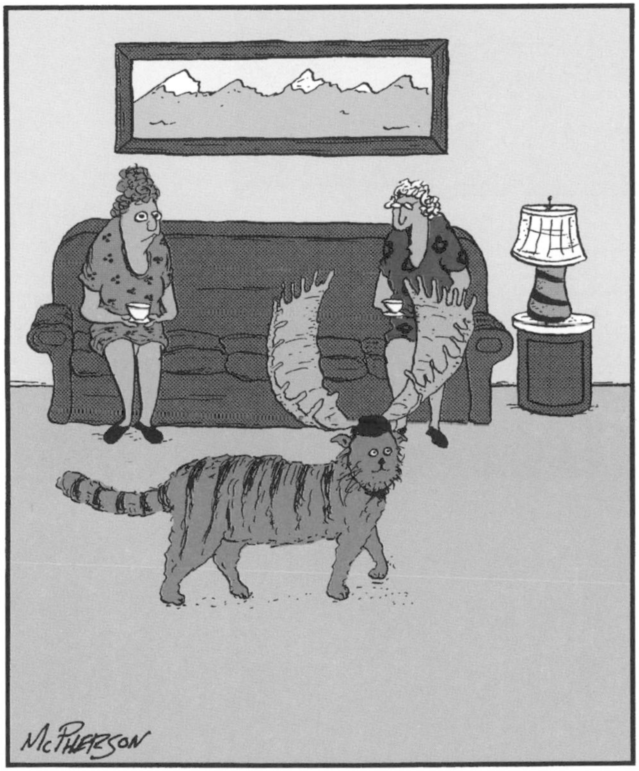
McPHERSON

"We had her declawed, but we wanted to make sure she could still defend herself against the other animals outdoors."

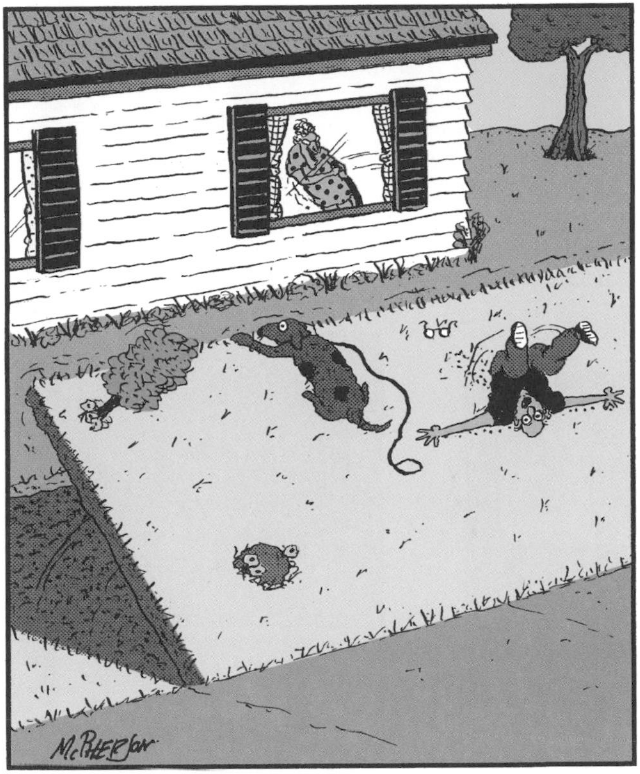
McPHERSON

Tired of people walking their dogs in her yard, Clarice shrewdly installed a hydraulically operated lawn section.

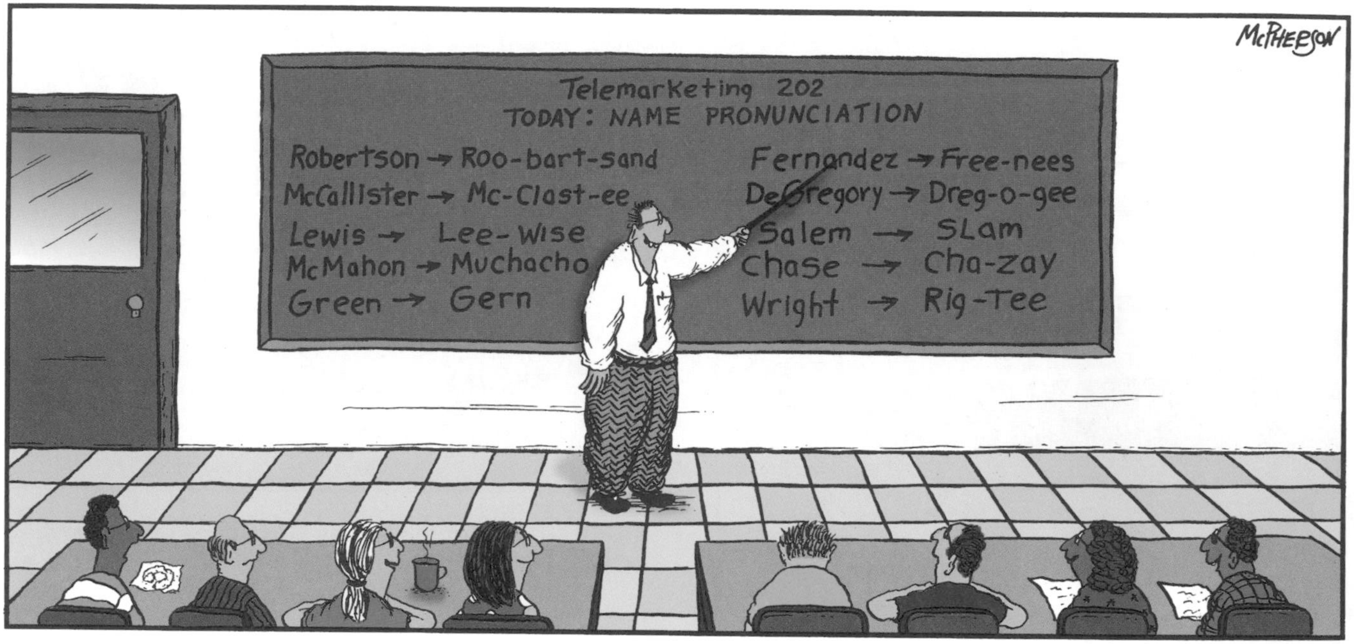
McPHERSON
Telemarketing 202
TODAY: NAME PRONUNCIATION
Robertson → Roo-bart-sand
McCallister → Mc-Clast-ee
Lewis → Lee-Wise
McMahon → Muchacho
Green → Gern
Fernandez → Free-nees
DeGregory → Dreg-o-gee
Salem → SLam
Chase → Cha-zay
Wright → Rig-Tee

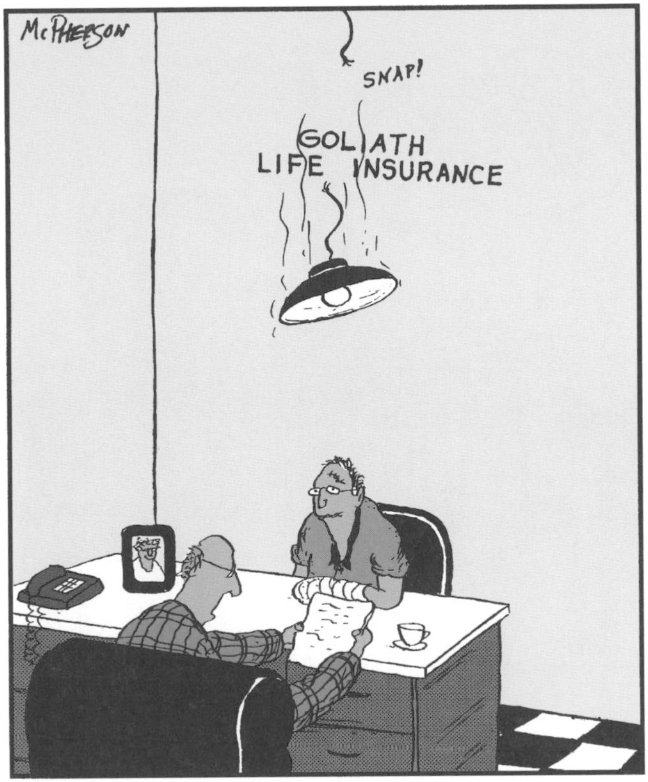
McPHERSON
SNAP!
GOLIATH
LIFE INSURANCE

"Fell down manhole, June '99; attacked by rabid chipmunk, April 2000; hit by pickle truck, October 2000. You seem to be quite accident-prone, Mr. Hibbard."

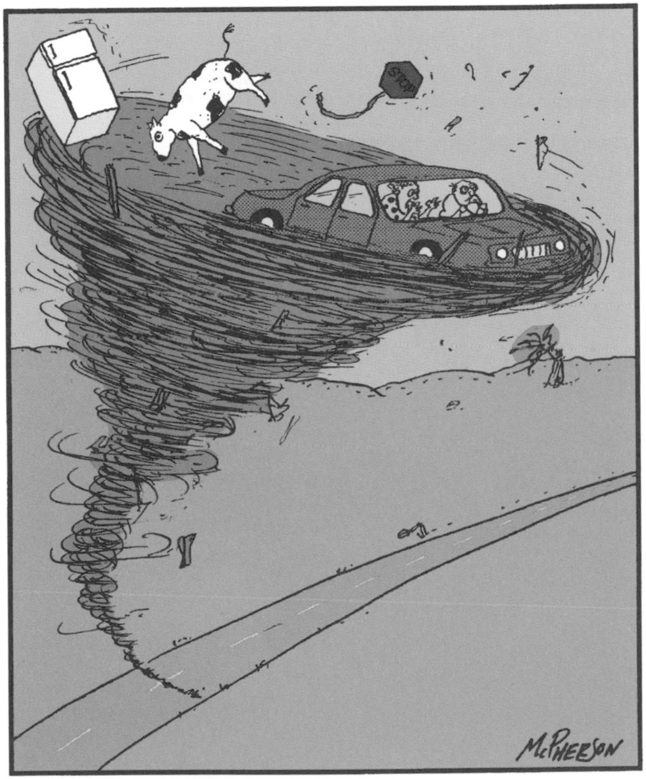
STOP
McPHERSON

"Try pumping the brakes!"

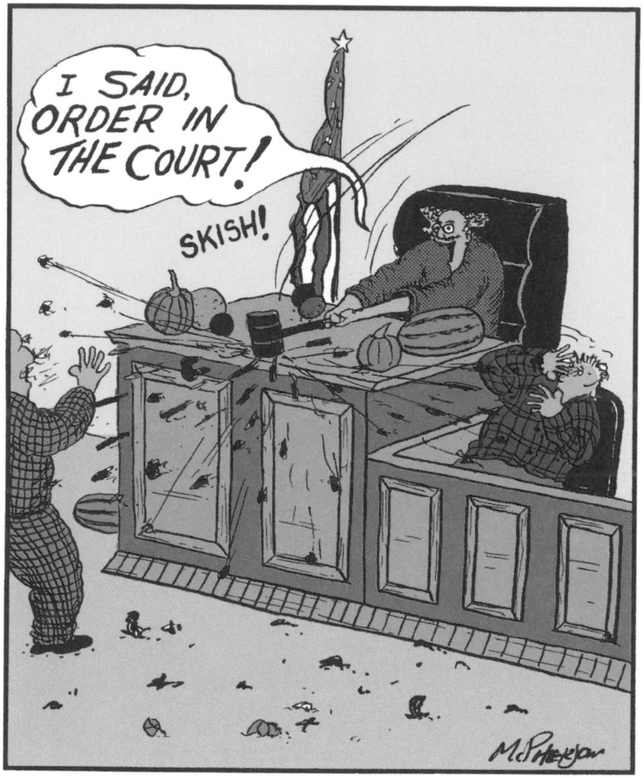
I SAID, ORDER IN THE COURT!
SKISH!

Tiring of the rigors of stand-up comedy, comedian Gallagher gets a law degree and eventually becomes a well-known judge.

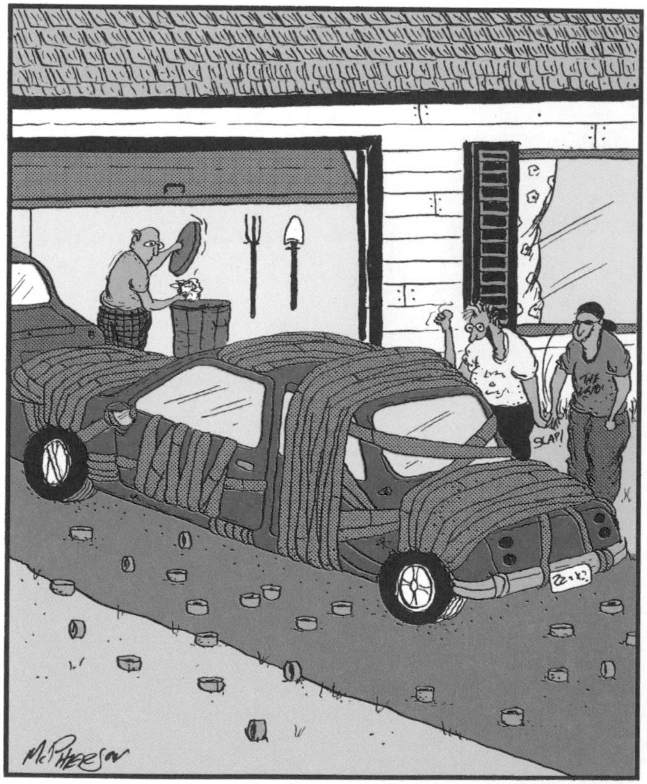
SLAP!

"Wooo! Awesome! One hundred and eighty-nine rolls of duct tape! Tell me this baby won't pass inspection *now*!"

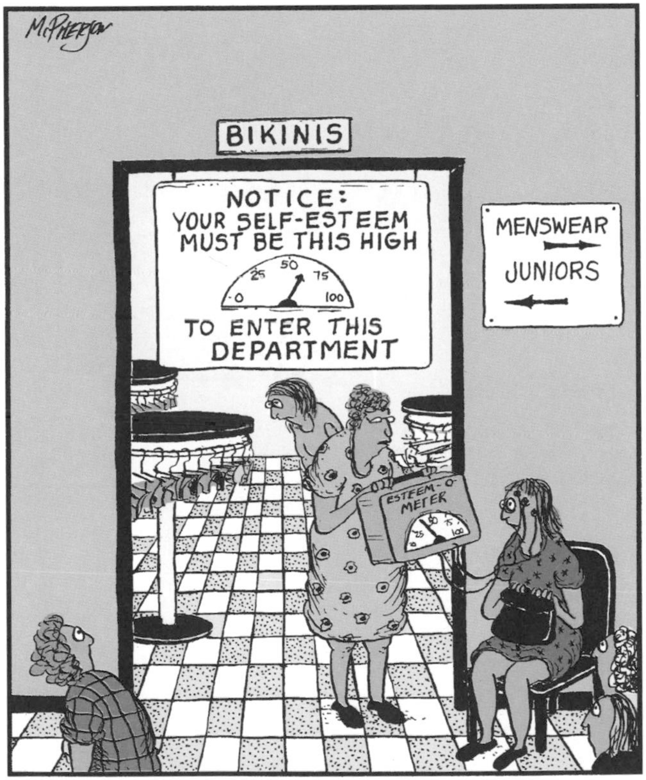
McPHERSON
BIKINIS
NOTICE:
YOUR SELF-ESTEEM
MUST BE THIS HIGH
0
25
50
75
100
TO ENTER THIS
DEPARTMENT
MENSWEAR
JUNIORS
ESTEEM-O-METER

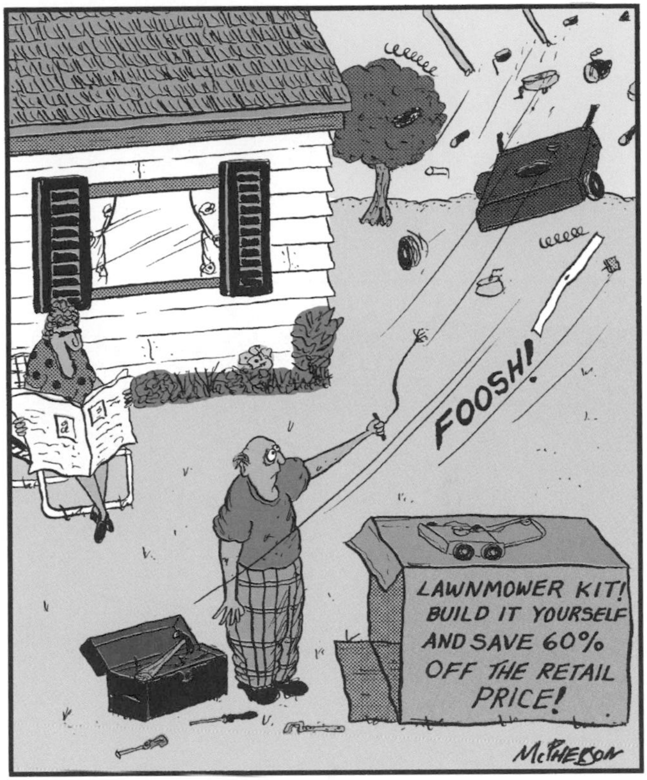
FOOSH!
LAWNMOWER KIT!
BUILD IT YOURSELF
AND SAVE 60%
OFF THE RETAIL
PRICE!
McPHERSON

"Say . . . I am *impressed*! You *do* know how to save us money!"

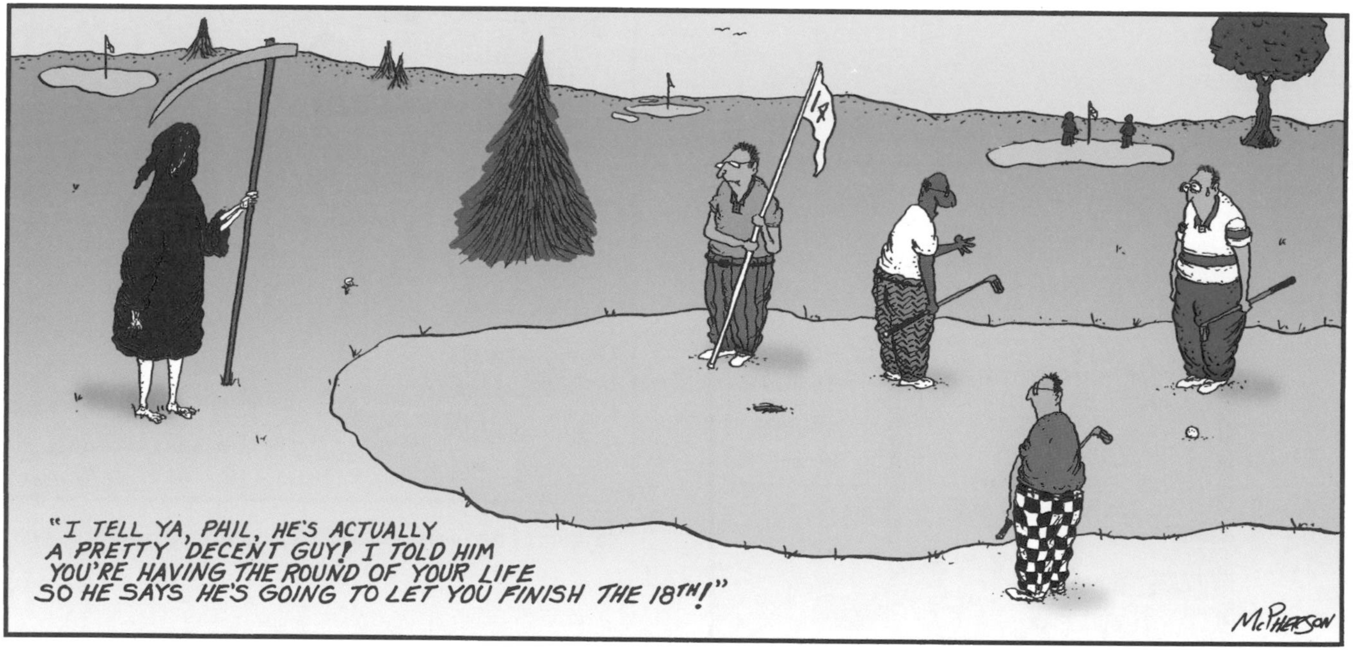
"I TELL YA, PHIL, HE'S ACTUALLY A PRETTY DECENT GUY! I TOLD HIM YOU'RE HAVING THE ROUND OF YOUR LIFE SO HE SAYS HE'S GOING TO LET YOU FINISH THE 18TH!"
McPHERSON

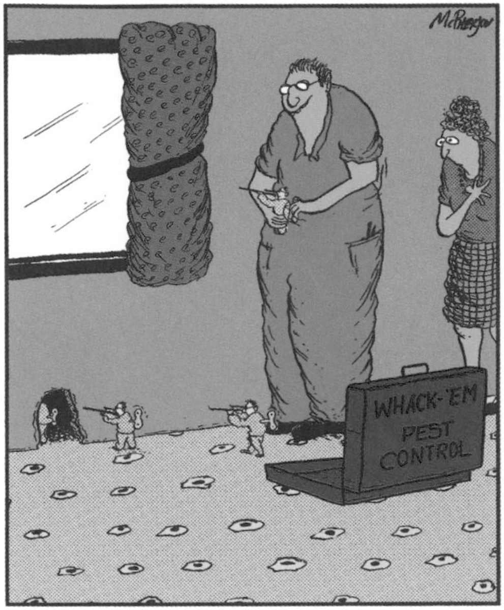
McPherson
WHACK-'EM PEST CONTROL

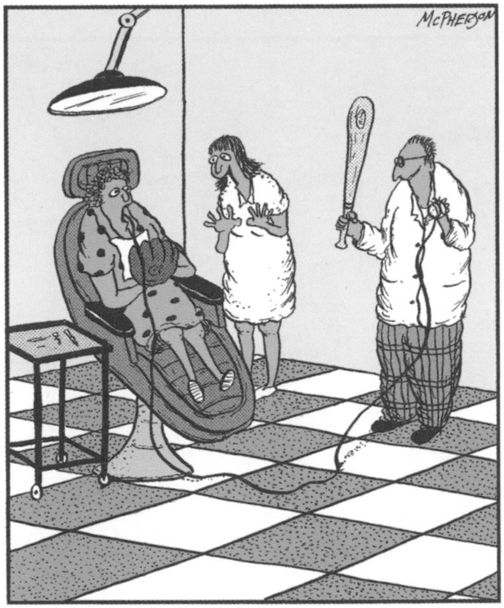
McPHERSON

"Now, remember how it works, Mrs. Cortlock? If Dr. Gundleson strikes out or if you catch a foul ball, your extraction is totally free!"

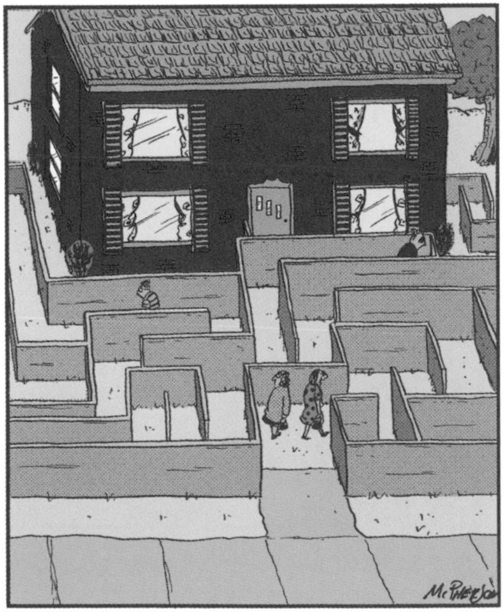
McPherson

"We teach the neighborhood kids we like how to get through the maze. Those who annoy us can get lost in here for hours until they just leave."

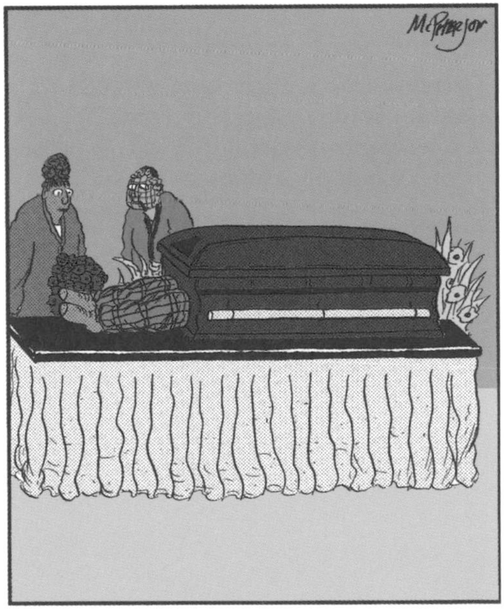
McPherson

"Reggie was always looking for ways to save a buck."

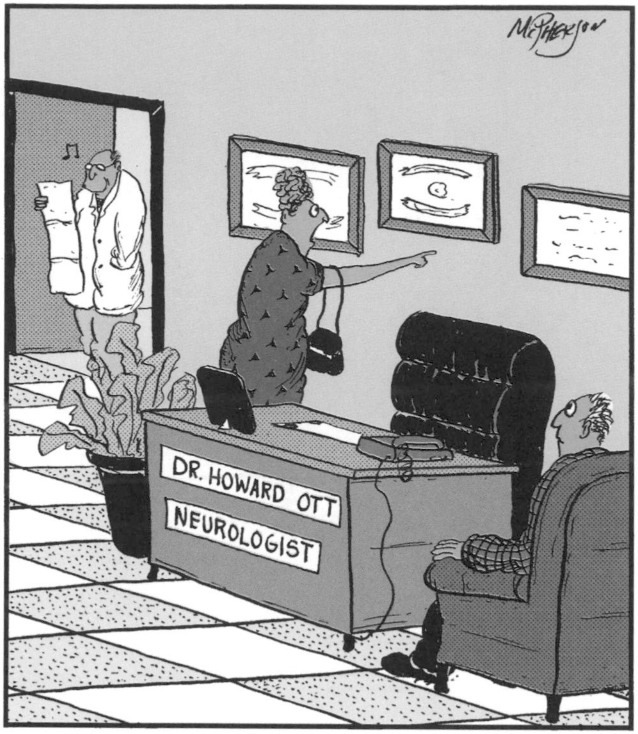
McPHERSON
DR. HOWARD OTT
NEUROLOGIST

"Dave? This diploma is from Uncle Willie's 21-Day College of Neurology, this is an award for second place in a bowling tournament, and this is for third prize in a pig-calling contest."

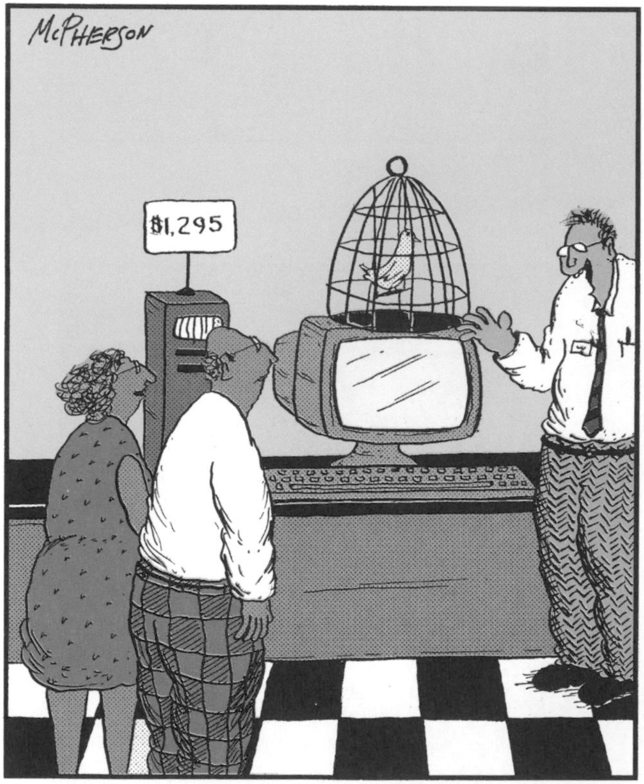
McPHERSON
$1,295

"And just in case your e-mail ever goes down, this system comes with a carrier pigeon."

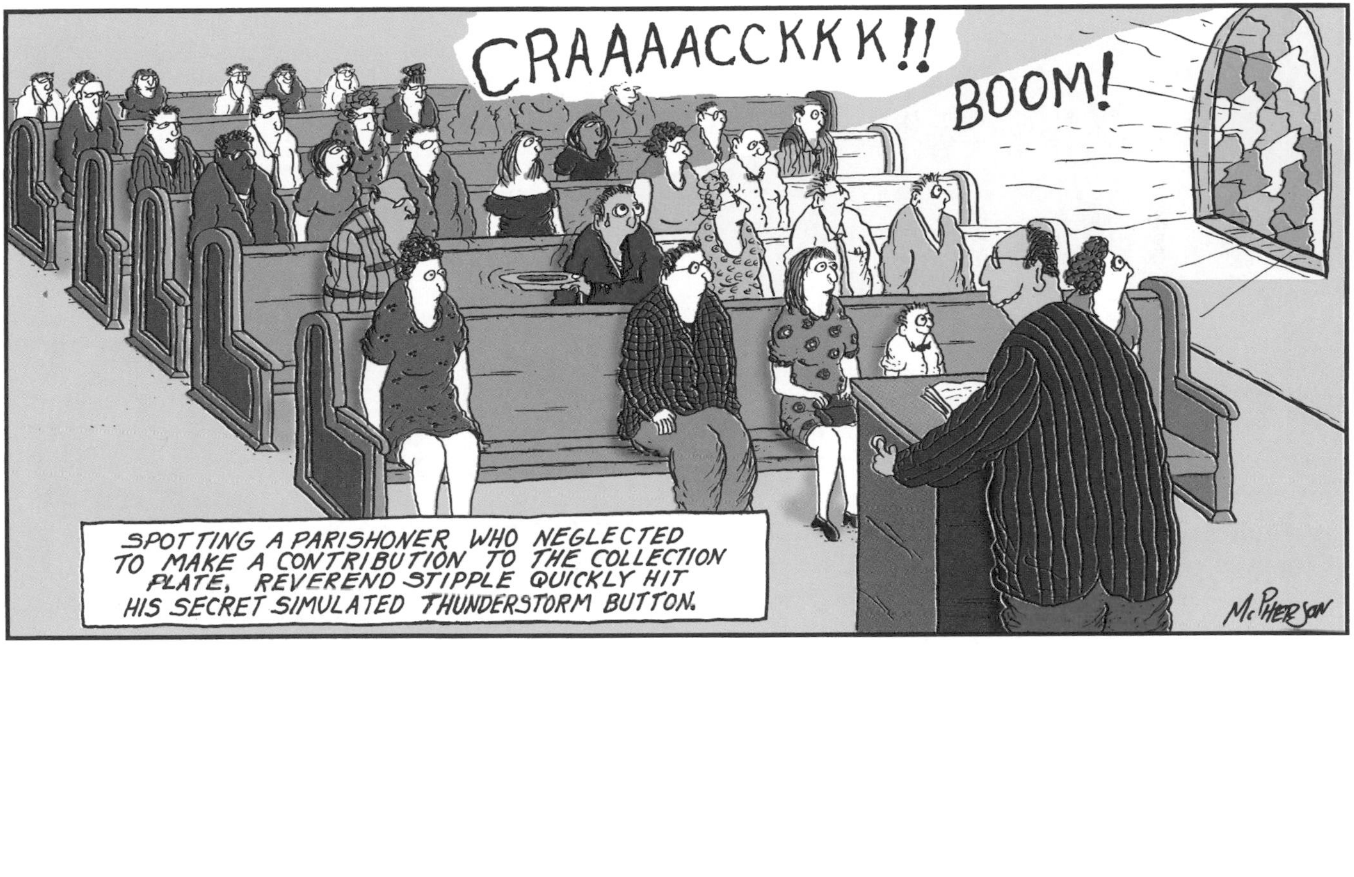
CRAAAACCKKK!!
BOOM!
SPOTTING A PARISHONER WHO NEGLECTED TO MAKE A CONTRIBUTION TO THE COLLECTION PLATE, REVEREND STIPPLE QUICKLY HIT HIS SECRET SIMULATED THUNDERSTORM BUTTON.
McPHERSON

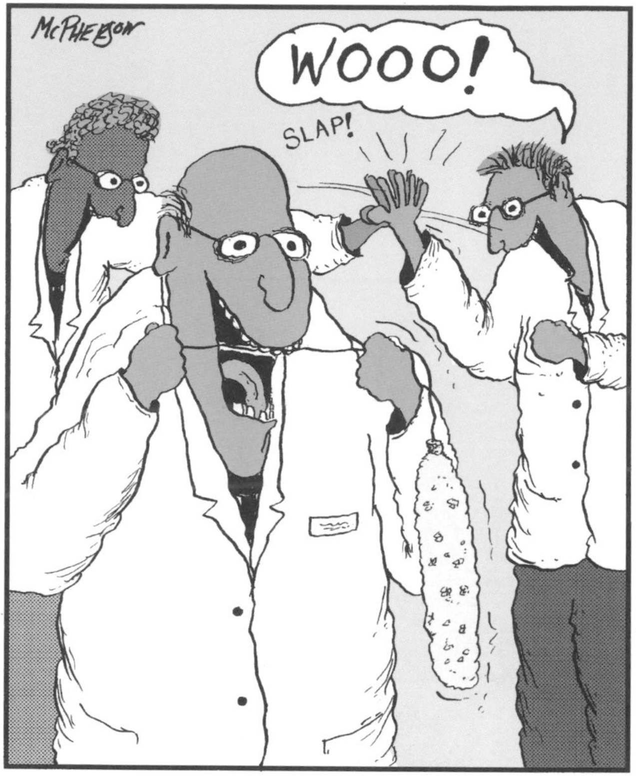
McPHERSON
WOOO!
SLAP!

Working tirelessly for more than seventeen years, a team of genetic engineers produces a variety of corn that has its own strand of dental floss.

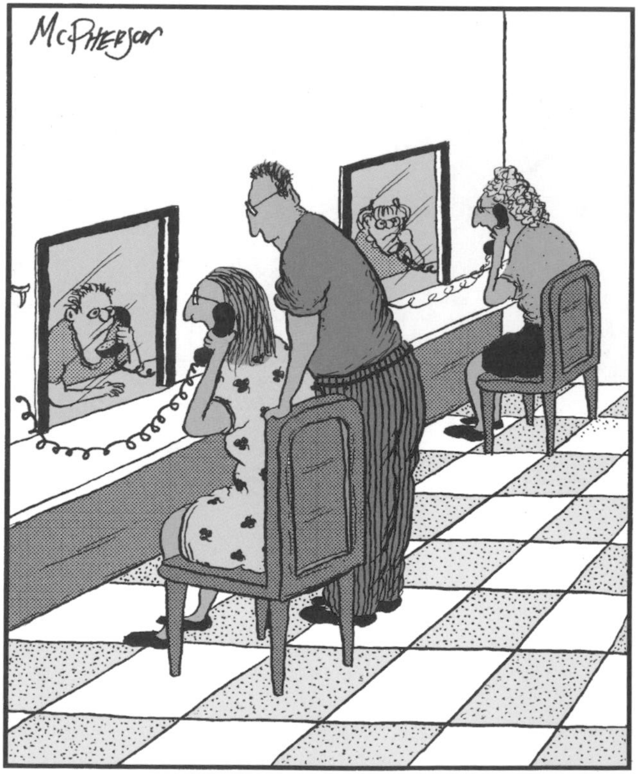
McPHERSON

"Kevin, we've been telling you for years, 'Eat your vegetables, or the Vegetable Police will get you!' You thought it was just a big joke, ha, ha, ha."

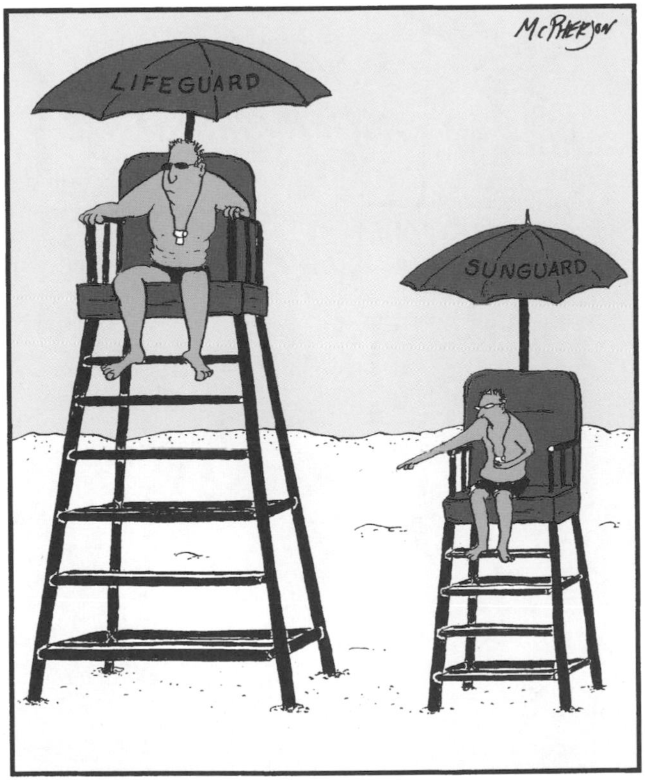
McPHERSON
LIFEGUARD
SUNGUARD

Tweet! **"You, in the red shorts! Your neck is starting to look like a slab of raw meet! Get some SPF 30 on there *now*!"**

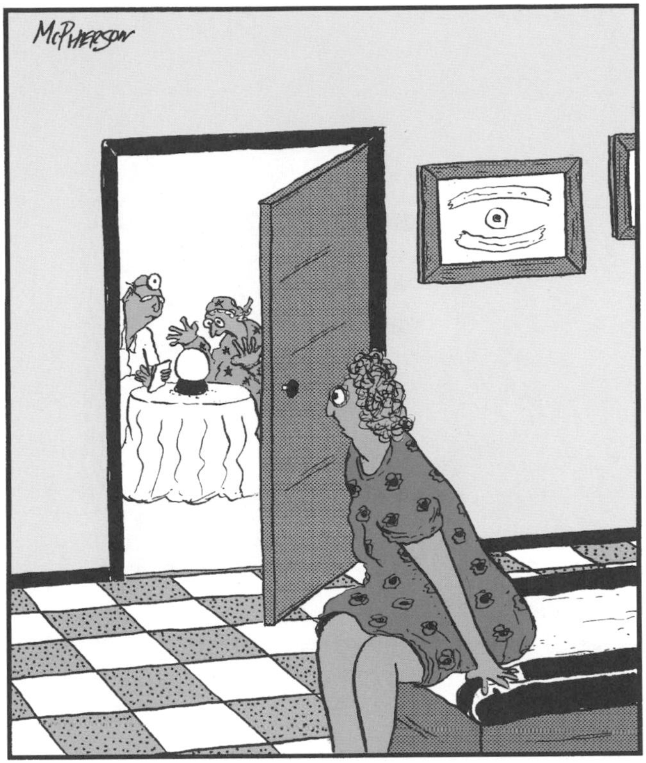
McPHERSON

"She has an inflamed gall bladder that must come out immediately! Aach! And that appendix! Remove it at once! I see a large polyp in a sinus cavity . . ."

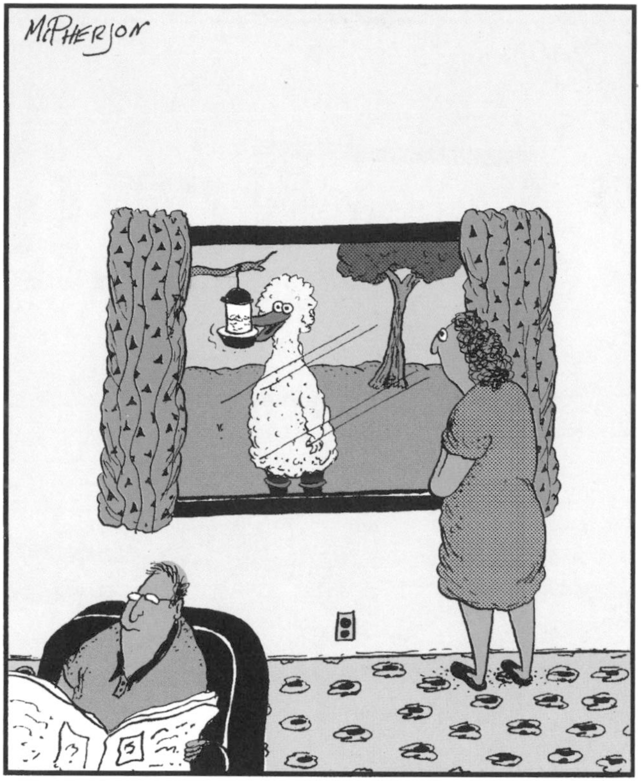
McPHERSON

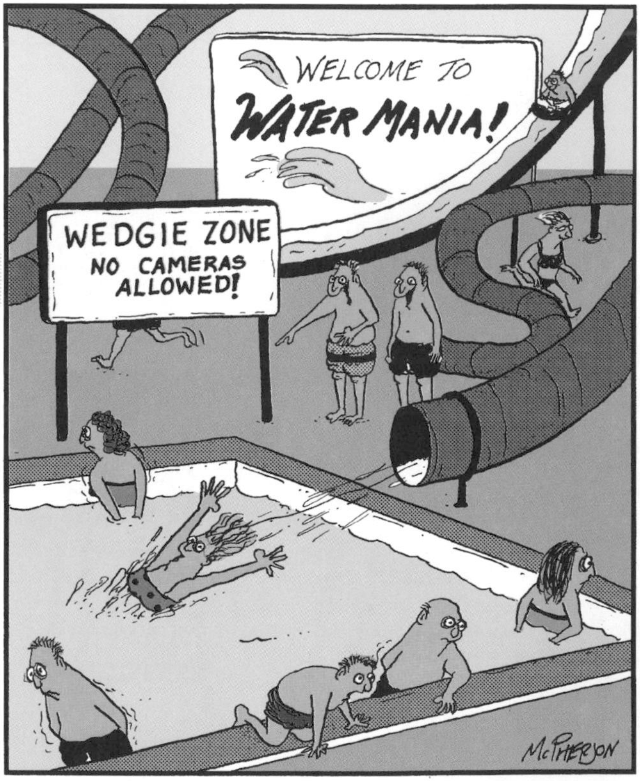
WELCOME TO
WATER MANIA!
WEDGIE ZONE
NO CAMERAS
ALLOWED!
McPHERSON